Zionism, Islam and the West

Kerry Bolton

BLACK
HOUSE
PUBLISHING

Zionism, Islam and the West

Kerry Bolton

Copyright © 2019 Black House Publishing Ltd

1st Edition - January. 2015
This Edition - February. 2019

ISBN-13: 978-1-912759-18-7

Black House Publishing Ltd
Kemp House
152 City Road
London
United Kingdom
EC1V 2NX

www.blackhousepublishing.com
Email: info@blackhousepublishing.com

Contents

Introduction

After every great cataclysm over the past one hundred plus years, there have been zealots assuring us that the world is on the brink of a new age of universal peace and plenty. The USA inherited a sense of messianic mission from both its Puritan and Masonic founders,[1] to remake the world in the USA's image. The Masonic Deists[2] put their motto on the reverse side of the U.S. Great Seal, declaring a coming *Novus Ordo Seclorum* ('Secular New Order'). The Puritans saw Godliness in the accumulation of money as a sign of God's blessings and a reward for hard work, to the exclusion of frivolous pursuits such as art, music, literature, and theatre. Both had Jewish roots: Masonry in Jewish Cabalistic mysticism; Puritanism in the Old Testament. These two streams of dogma at the founding of the USA converged in seeing America as having a messianic world mission and seeing the Jews as a special people inspiring that mission. That is why there was such enthusiasm for the creation of the State of Israel among both the Puritan and Masonic members of the ruling classes in the USA and Britain. That is how the Puritan, Lord Arthur Balfour, lent his name to the infamous 'Declaration' that committed British support for the creation of a Jewish state in Palestine. The Puritans, and their present-day heirs within Christian Fundamentalism, the so-called 'Christian-Zionists', constitute a significant pro-Zionist lobby.

Freemasonry, like Orthodox Judaism and Zionism, is based

---

1   For the Puritan-Masonic dichotomy in the founding of the USA see: Nicholas Hagger, *The Secret Founding of America: The Real Story of Freemasons, Puritans and the Battle for the New World* (London: Watkins Publishing, 2007).

2   Deism = the religion of Masons, French Jacobin revolutionaries and American Founding Fathers, who rejected traditional concepts of God for the 'worship of nature' or of the 'Grand Architect of the Universe'. In Jacobin France this supposedly 'rational' religion resulted in conflicts between the rival cult of Nature and the cult of the Grand Architect.

1

around the messianic aim of rebuilding the Temple of Solomon in Jerusalem (after demolishing the Al-Aqsa Mosque) as the centre of the world, claiming to have inherited this legacy from the Knights Templar. Hence there is a common mythos motivating at times seemingly disparate interests: Orthodox Judaism, Zionism, Masonry, Puritanism. Something of this was publicly celebrated in 1993 in Jerusalem, a newspaper report stating of a Masonic ceremony:

> The ceremony was attended by the Mayor of Jerusalem, Teddy Kollek, as well as by the Ashkenazi Chief Rabbi, Israel Meier Lau. Kollek told the gathered Masons, 'You do a great honour to Jerusalem. This is natural, considering that King Solomon was the great builder of the temple, which is at the roots of the Masonic idea, and that his workmen were the first Masons'.[3]

After the First World War, President Woodrow Wilson presented the world with his Fourteen Points as the ideological basis for an international order, based around the League of Nations.[4] Zionists and other Jewish messianists saw in the League of Nations the possibility of establishing a universal state inspired by Judaism. Nahum Sokolow declared at the 1922 Zionist Congress: 'The League of Nations is a Jewish idea. We created it after a fight of 25 years. Jerusalem will one day become the Capital of World

---

3   'Israel: There is a Pact Between Politicians and Masons', *La Republica*, Italy, October, 1993.

4   It is a well-documented but still little known fact that the Balfour Declaration was an offer of support by the British Government for a Jewish state *within* Palestine, in return for the mobilisation of Jewish influence in the USA to push the Americans into the war against Germany. According to Benjamin H. Freedman, a wealthy manufacturer, Jewish convert to Catholicism and committee member of Woodrow Wilson's Democratic Party, Wilson was blackmailed into the war by Supreme Court Justice Louis B. Brandeis, a Zionist. Freedman spent much of his long life and fortune trying to expose Zionist machinations, and was closely monitored by the FBI and Zionist agencies. Listen to his 1961 speech: http://www.youtube.com/watch?v=x8OmxI2AYV8

Peace'.[5] The celebrated Jewish author Israel Zangwill enthused with Messianic zealotry:

> With the arrival in France of President Wilson, the champion of the League of Nations, the most momentous episode in all human history begins, the true 'War for the World'.

> If mankind thus builds a brotherhood, the immeasurable slaughter and suffering of the war will be redeemed, and the prophetic gospel of ancient Judea will come to its own at last: 'They shall beat their swords into ploughshares and their spears into pruning-hooks: nation shall not lift up sword against nation, neither shall they learn war anymore.' But Judaism stands to gain also a minor traditional hope from the Peace Conference: the repossession of Palestine. And if this secondary consummation could be united with the setting up of Jerusalem as the seat of the League of Nations, instead of the bankrupt Hague, the two Hebraic dreams, the major and the minor, would be fused in one, and the Hebrew metropolis - that meeting-point of three world-religions - would become at once the centre and symbol of the new era.

> But the Jew is not content to record the crimes of Christendom. For him criticism is only the negative aspect of creation. He is out for victory. He will verify the legend of the Conquering Jew. With the sword of the spirit he will extirpate the heathen. He will overrun the planet. He will bring about a holy League of Nations, a Millennium of Peace. For the words of the Babylonian Isaiah still vibrate in his soul:

---

5   Nahum Sokolow, World Zionist Congress, Carlsbad, 1922. Sokolow was Secretary General of the World Zionist Organisation 1907-09; head of the WZO Political Department 1911; leader of the Zionist Delegation to the Paris Peace Conference 1919; Chairman, Zionist Executive 1921; President, WZO 1931-35; then Honorary President, and head of the WZO Cultural Department.

ZIONISM, ISLAM AND THE WEST

'I have put my spirit upon him, He shall make the right to go forth to the nations, He shall not fail or be crushed till he have set the right in the earth, And the isles shall wait for his teaching.'

The God whose spirit is thus interpreted, the God who uses a people to make the right to go forth to the nations, and who through faithful followers labours to establish His Kingdom on earth, may be only a national working hypothesis, a divine dynamic. But the conception at least makes the worship of any lesser or rival God impossible, and justifies that jealousy for His service which inspired the anonymous medieval poet whose verses are still sung in the synagogue: -

'All the world shall come to serve Thee And bless Thy glorious Name, And Thy righteousness triumphant The islands shall acclaim, And the peoples shall go seeking Who knew Thee not before, And the ends of earth shall praise Thee And tell Thy greatness o'er the uttermost peoples, hearing, Shall hail Thee crowned King.'[6]

Despite the platitudes about 'world brotherhood,' which is a façade that Zionists often operate behind to push sundry agendas in the name of 'human rights', albeit notably lacking in Zionist-occupied Palestine, Zangwill with his poetic bent waxes lyrical about the superiority of Judaism, which will displace the idolatry of the Gentiles. Indeed, while we fear Sharia Law taking over

---

6   Israel Zangwill, *Before the Peace Conference* (February 1919). Zangwill is quoted by ex-Israeli Prime Minister Benjamin Netanyahu in his book *A Place Among the Nations: Israel and the World* (New York: Bantam Books, 1993). Zangwill achieved fame as an Anglo-Jewish novelist. An early advocate of a Jewish State, Zangwill supported Herzl's call for a Jewish homeland in Uganda until Palestine could be secured. When this temporary measure was rejected by the 1905 Zionist Congress Zangwill formed his own Jewish Territorialist Organisation. When the Balfour Declaration eventuated the JTO was dissolved. Zangwill then advocated the expulsion of the Arabs from Palestine.

the West, Jewish messianists are committed to eliminating all forms of Gentile religion as 'idolatry' and replacing them with the 'Seven Noahide Laws'.

The reader might hopefully see that Zionism and the messianic Jewish teachings on which it is based, have far wider implications than setting up a Jewish state. The intent was to capture Jerusalem, rebuild the Temple of Solomon, and proclaim a Messianic Era. Prattling fears about the 'Caliph' and Sharia Law taking over Europe are distractions from a far more pervasive, immeasurably more powerful, plan for world conquest that emanates from Jerusalem and New York.

However, the League of Nations failed due to the intransigence of the newly formed Axis powers: Italy, Germany, Japan. For this they were punished with total war. During the Second World War President Franklin D. Roosevelt came forth to present to the world the Atlantic Charter as the basis of an international order, based around the United Nations Organisation. That ideal was stymied by the USSR despite the supposed friendship between Roosevelt and 'Uncle Joe' Stalin during the war. The outcome was a prolonged Cold War that served globalist interests in trying to scare sundry states into subordinating themselves to the USA as protection against the plans for world conquest supposedly being pursued by the Soviet Union. As I point out in my book Stalin: The Enduring Legacy, it is rather thanks to Stalin that we did not get lumbered with a World State seventy years ago.[7] After the Cold War, President George H. Bush declared that a 'new world order' could finally usher forth, with the opening shots being fired against Iraq, indicating that this 'new world order' of peace and justice would be imposed by force.

We stand today at a unique and extraordinary moment. The crisis in the Persian Gulf, as grave as it is, also offers a rare opportunity to move toward an historic period of

---

7   K. R. Bolton, *Stalin: The Enduring Legacy* (London: Black House Publishing, 2012), pp. 125-139.

cooperation. Out of these troubled times, our fifth objective - a new world order - can emerge. President George H. W. Bush, declaration of war against Iraq.[8]

Again Russia, with the rise of Putin, rejected the offer to play second fiddle to the USA, and so now we have what amounts to Cold War II.

NEOCONS

It was during the years of the Cold War that a most odd and bastardous phenomenon occurred, the rise of the so-called 'neo-conservative movement'. However, this is neither 'new' nor 'conservative'. It is largely the product of Jewish Trotskyite-communists and fellow-travellers who, after the expulsion of Trotsky, became so obsessively opposed to the USSR that they became the most avid Cold Warriors on behalf of the USA. Hence, the crypto-Trotskyite academic Professor Sidney Hook became the head of the CIA front, the Congress for Cultural Freedom and received from President Ronald Reagan the Congressional Medal of Freedom for his services to the USA during the Cold War.

A pack of Trotskyite intellectuals helped to found the neo-con house organ, *National Review*. A Trotskyite labour unionist, Tom Kahn, formed the National Endowment for Democracy, still run by Trotskyite veterans to promote revolutions worldwide for the USA reminiscent of the Comintern, but much worse.[9] Even Trotsky's widow, Sedova, supported the U.S. in the Korean War, rather than support anything associated with the USSR.[10] The USA in 'the war on terrorism', as it did during the Cold War, represents itself as the 'leader of the Western world,' and

---

8   George Bush, Address Before a Joint Session of the Congress on the Persian Gulf Crisis and the Federal Budget Deficit, 11 September, 1990, http://bushlibrary.tamu.edu/research/public_papers.php?id=2217&year=1990&month=9

9   K. R. Bolton, *Revolution from Above* (London: Arktos Media Ltd., 2011), pp. 218-221.

10   K. R. Bolton, *Stalin: The Enduring Legacy*, op. cit., pp. 114-119.

the defender of 'western values'. Rather, even by its founding principles of Deism, Masonry and Puritanism, it leads in the decay of all values that are truly traditional and Western. It is the enemy of all traditional societies in its messianic ideal of wanting to recreate the world in its own fetid image, and that is why it cannot tolerate traditional societies, whether they be Muslim or Christian, Hindu or Buddhist. That is also why U.S. messianism and Jewish messianism, converge with the same religious hatred.

While the predominantly Jewish Trotskyites jumped from Bolshevism to Americana, Israel also went from being a pro-Soviet state, to pro-U.S. during the Cold War. Soon Israel became much more than that as the body that wags the tail of the U.S. Stalin had not only stymied the plans of U.S. globalists to create a 'world order' after World War II; he eliminated Jewish influences from the USSR, and pursued a Russian nationalist and pan-Slavist ideology that purged Jewish-Bolshevik messianism. Hence, the worldwide phenomenon of Jews sliding from a pro-Soviet to an anti-Soviet position in short order.

With the USSR having imploded through a combination of inner treason, Zionist-backed subversion and the CIA-induced Islamic war against the Russians in Afghanistan, the old crypto-Trotskyite Cold Warriors promptly declared a war not only against Putin's Russia but against 'Islamic terrorism' to keep the world off-balance. The old crypto-Trotskyite 'neocons' adopted Israel as their *cause célèbre*, and have had a prominent role in U.S. foreign policy, and particularly as architects of the present 'war on terrorism,' which was hatched in their think tanks several decades ago.

WORLD EMPIRE

Now we have a very symbolic edifice representing the unholy trinity of Bank-Lodge-Synagogue, in the open for those who have eyes to see: the Supreme Court Building in Jerusalem, sponsored by the Rothschilds. Crowning its roof, overlooking the Holy City, is the Masonic symbol – the same as that on the U.S. Great Seal – a pyramid surmounted by an 'all-seeing eye.'[11] The interior of the building is replete with Masonic symbolism, representing the ages-old dream of Jerusalem as the seat of the 'Supreme Court of Mankind',[12] expressed among others, by David Ben Gurion, First Prime Minister of Israel:

> With the exception of the U.S.S.R. as a federated Eurasian State, all other continents will become united in a world alliance at whose disposal will be an international police force. All armies will be abolished and there will be no more wars. In Jerusalem, the United Nations will build a shrine of the prophets to serve the federated union of all continents; this will be the seat of the Supreme Court of Mankind, to settle all controversies among the federated continents, as prophesied by Isaiah.[13]

This messianic dream is still fostered and the Temple Mount Movement was created to bring it to fruition. They unequivocally declare their aims:

> The real 'United Nations Organization' will be the Kingdom of G-d which will soon be established in Jerusalem, based on the holy laws of G-d. The Temple will again be the heart, soul and focus of Israel and the nations. Mashiach ben David[14] will come and will be the king of Israel and the world. He will come to Jerusalem and rule from there and establish the Kingdom of G-d over all the world. Jerusalem instead of New York will be the center of the this godly 'United Nations Organization' and a new era of justice, spiritual holiness, a real law based on the word

---

11   U. S. Great Seal, http://www.greatseal.com/

12   Despite the lame attempt to ridicule conspiracy theories, see: See: 'Jerusalem Insider's Guide,' http://www.jerusalem-insiders-guide.com/israeli-supreme-court.html

13   David Ben Gurion, *Look Magazine*, 16 January 1962.

14   The Jewish Messiah, son of David.

of G-d in the Torah and a real peace will open and will be established in Jerusalem exactly as Isaiah prophesied... (Isaiah 2:1-5).[15]

And again, from a little known explanation of Zionist aims:

The people of Israel will conquer, spiritually, the nations of the earth, so that Israel will be made high above all nations in praise, in name and in glory. Only the Messianic flag... will remain, and all the nations will centre around that emblem... The Davidic ruler, to be recognised universally, will be the perfect ethical character... In general, the peoples of the world will be divided into two main groups, the Israelitic and the non-Israelitic. The former will be righteous... all the other peoples, on the other hand, will be known for their detestable practices, idolatry and similar acts of wickedness. They will be destroyed and will disappear from earth before the ushering of the ideal era... Thus, at the coming of the Messiah, when all righteous nations will pay homage to the ideal righteous leader, and offer gifts to him, the wicked and corrupt nations... will bring similar presents to the Messiah.... their gifts... will be bluntly rejected...[16]

As Ben Gurion et al indicated, the Zionist vision is much more than a homeland for the Jews. It has world-conquering ambitions predicated on religious teachings and prophecies of several thousand years duration. The Zionist programme consists of:

---

15 Temple Mount and Land of Israel Faithful Movement newsletter 13 Aug 2000. The Movement aims to rebuild the Temple of Solomon on the land presently occupied by the Dome of the Rock Mosque, the third holiest site of Islam. The messianists aim to destroy the mosque, which would ignite the whole of Islam. The messianists believe that the rebuilding of the Temple is a prerequisite for the return of the King-Messiah. They have increasing support in Israel among the ultra-Orthodox settlers movement.

16 Professor Martin Higger, *The Jewish Utopia* (Baltimore, Maryland: Lord Baltimore Press, 1932).

The creation of an Israeli Empire from the rivers Nile to the Euphrates (the 'deed of promise' in Genesis).

The rebuilding of the Temple of Solomon on the site where the Al-Aqsa Mosque, one of the holiest places of Islam, now stands. This, like the 'deed of promise', is non-negotiable, and is believed to be a prerequisite for the coming of the Jewish Messiah.

Divinely-ordained Jewish world rule, with Jerusalem as the world capitol, and the law 'coming forth from Zion', as promised by the Torah, the first five books of the Old Testament.

"CHRISTIAN ZIONISTS"

These are aims that Christian Fundamentalists, like their Puritan predecessors who were influential in U.S. and British governing circles, have been conned into thinking are part of a common 'Judaeo-Christian heritage', with Jews as the 'Chosen People', and their 'ingathering' to Israel an essential part of Biblical prophecy. Conversely, they have been misinformed by their pastors into believing that Islam is inherently anti-Christ. The truth has been stood on its head. Orthodox Judaism, whose religion is based on the Talmud, an encyclopaedic series of volumes, teaches that Jesus was the bastard son of a Roman soldier and a Jewish prostitute and is in hell. On the other hand, the Koran teaches that Jesus was a prophet of God, as were the Old Testament prophets, and Mary is honoured as his mother. If the Christian Fundamentalists, also called 'Christian-Zionists', whom the Zionist leaders have cynically cultivated for political support in recent decades, would look at a little history, they would find that Orthodox Judaism is directly descended from Pharisaism. The Jewish Encyclopaedia states of this:

> Henceforth Jewish life was regulated by the teachings of the Pharisees; the whole history of Judaism was reconstructed from the Pharisaic point of view, and a new aspect was given to the Sanhedrin of the past. A new chain of tradition supplanted the older, priestly tradition. Pharisaism shaped

the character of Judaism and the life and thought of the Jew for all the future.[17]

Should these Christians consult their Bibles they would readily see the conflict between the Pharisees and Jesus Christ.[18] They would see where the true conflict of the ages is delineated. They might be horrified to find that they have aligned themselves with those whom Jesus Christ damned as 'sons of the Devil', doing their father's bidding.[19] Whom do these Christian zealots for Zionism and the 'Chosen People' think the Pharisees were, and are? Or have they not stopped to ponder this?

Given that these aims are all supposed to have been promised by God Himself to the Jews as the 'Chosen People', and that Zionism considers itself the political expression of these promises and prophecies, there cannot be peace in the Middle East while an influential faction of Jewry, its allies and lackeys, have the power to inflict its psychotic schemes upon the world. That is why pro-Zionist American geopolitical strategist Ralph Peters wrote that the world will never know peace until all 'rejectionist' regimes are eliminated. As this is published world hysteria has reached new heights with the rise of 'The Islamic State' organisation, seemingly from nowhere, well armed and trained, that is scaring the 'world community' into ever-more mad-cap adventures in the Middle East, that has all the marks of yet another Mossad-CIA contrivance.

JIHAD?

Moreover, the much cited but seldom-defined buzzword Jihad is supposed to afflict the average Westerner with a Pavlovian-induced fear-response. Islamophobes wanting to subordinate Christian-Western interests to Judaism and Israel set up such propaganda outlets as 'Jihad Watch' to keep the war-hysteria in ferment. Jihad

---

17 'Pharisees', *The Jewish Encyclopedia* (1906), http://jewishencyclopedia.com/articles/12087-pharisees

18 See the 'Woes of the Pharisees' in Luke 11: 37-54; Matthew 23: 1-39.

19 John 8: 44.

means a spiritual quest; in particular the Muslim individual's overcoming of ignoble aspects of his own character. The Koran states for example: 'The true believers are those who believe in God and His messenger, then attain the status of having no doubt whatsoever, and strive (jahadu) with their money and their lives in the cause of God. These are the truthful ones.'[20] Jihad? It does not mean to kill or to wage war. While the Koran refers often to the 'cause of justice', which might be misinterpreted as killing non-Muslims, such wide interpretations can and have been applied in any and every religion, whether Christianity, Judaism, Hinduism, and even Buddhism has had its battles and warriors. However, Muslims are commanded to seek peace:

> 'You shall not kill - God has made life sacred - except in the course of justice. These are His commandments to you, that you may understand.'[21] 'If they leave you alone, refrain from fighting you, and offer you peace, then God gives you no excuse to fight them.'[22] 'There shall be no compulsion in religion ...'[23] 'You have your religion and I have mine.'[24] 'Had your Lord willed, all the people on earth would have believed. Do you want to force the people to become believers?'[25] 'Proclaim: "This is the truth from your Lord," then Whoever wills let him believe, and whoever wills let him disbelieve.'[26] 'You shall resort to pardon, advocate tolerance, and disregard the ignorant.'[27]

Yet the very words Jihad, and even Islam and Muslim, have been made synonymous with 'terrorism', like other propagandist

---

20   Koran, 49: 15.
21   Ibid., 6: 151.
22   Ibid., 4: 90.
23   Ibid., 2: 256.
24   Ibid., 109: 6.
25   Ibid., 10: 99.
26   Ibid., 18: 29.
27   Ibid., 7: 199.

buzzwords for mass consumption, such as 'Nazi' and 'anti-Semite'. The war-laws of the Torah, the first five books of the Old Testament, which form the basis of Judaism, but which Jesus Christ surpassed, are replete with commandments to exterminate Israel's enemies, and lay waste to their cities and towns. Is not this precisely what Israel has undertaken? Moreover ultra-Orthodox Judaism, which has a major influence in both Israeli and U.S. politics, does not even expect the worldwide conversion of the goyim[28] to Judaism. Rather, the messianic vision is for enforced submission to something called the Seven Noahide Laws, (עשׂ חנ ינב תווצמ Sheva mitzvot B'nei Noach).[29] These are the basis of a simplified religion for the subservient goyim, replacing Christianity, Islam, Hinduism, Buddhism; indeed every religion other than ultra-Orthodox Judaism and its adjunct black magic Cabalism.

The worldwide imposition of the Seven Noahide Laws far from being the crank ideal of a few obscure self-styled rabbis in a fringe sect, has already been decreed by U.S. Congress, in honour of the late New York Hasidic 'rebbe' Schneerson, believed by his followers to be the Jewish messiah who will return resurrected or reincarnated.

Rebbe Schneerson, proclaiming himself the 'King-Messiah' of the world, is revered by 1000 Hassidic rabbis throughout the world, was lauded by the former Chief Rabbi of Israel for his 'angelic holiness', and was awarded the Congressional Gold Medal by President George H. W. Bush. President Jimmy Carter inaugurated 'Education and Sharing Day' on 18 April 1978. The day in honour of Schneerson had been proclaimed by the president every year on the rebbe's birthday ever since. Bush proclaimed the Rebbe's birthday, March 26th, U.S. Education Day, the presidential proclamation, in the name of the Congress and Senate stating:

---

28   Derogatory word for non-Jews.

29   "Universal Morality," The Rebbe.org., http://www.chabad.org/therebbe/
      article_cdo/aid/62221/jewish/Universal-Morality.htm

Whereas the Lubavitch movement has fostered and promoted these ethical values and principles throughout the world;

Whereas Rabbi Menachem Mendel Schneerson, leader of the Lubavitch movement, is universally respected and revered and his eighty-ninth birthday falls on March 26, 1991;

Whereas in tribute to this great spiritual leader, 'the Rebbe', this, his ninetieth year will be seen as one of 'education and giving', the year in which we turn to education and charity to return the world to the moral and ethical values contained in the Seven Noahide Laws; and

Whereas this will be reflected in an international scroll of honour signed by the President of the United States and other heads of state: Now, therefore be it

Resolved by the Senate and House of Representatives of the United States of America in Congress assembled, That March 26, 1991, the start of the ninetieth year of Rabbi Menachem Schneerson, leader of the worldwide Lubavitch movement, is designated as 'Education Day. U.S.A.'. The President is requested to issue a proclamation calling upon the people of the United States to observe such day with appropriate ceremonies and activities.[30]

President Obama declared in 2009:

Few have better understood or more successfully promoted these ideas than Rabbi Menachem Mendel Schneerson, the Lubavitcher Rebbe, who emphasized the importance of education and good character. Through the establishment of educational and social service institutions across the country and the world, Rabbi Schneerson sought to empower young

---

30 Joint Resolution To designate March 26, 1991, as 'Education Day, U.S.A.', http://thomas.loc.gov/cgi-bin/query/z?c102:H.J.RES.104.ENR:

people and inspire individuals of all ages. On this day, we raise his call anew.

Hence, Senate and Congress decreed Rebbe Schneerson a 'holy man' to be revered by the whole nation and the U.S.A. officially declared its aim was to enact the Noahide Laws worldwide. … And the masses go into fearful hysteria or righteous indignation when some Muslims go through the streets of Europe with placards demanding 'Sharia law'. Rebbe Schneerson's teachings are revered in Jerusalem, Tel Aviv, New York and Washington, and they are apparently the ethical basis of the U.S.A. This is what Schneerson taught in Hebrew:

This is what needs to be said about the body: the body of a Jewish person is of a totally different quality from the body of [members] of all nations of the world … The difference in the inner quality between Jews and non-Jews is "so great that the bodies should be considered as completely different species."

"An even greater difference exists in regard to the soul. Two contrary types of soul exist, a non-Jewish soul comes from three satanic spheres, while the Jewish soul stems from holiness."

"As has been explained, an embryo is called a human being, because it has both body and soul. Thus, the difference between a Jewish and a non-Jewish embryo can be understood."

"…the general difference between Jews and non-Jews: A Jew was not created as a means for some [other] purpose; he himself is the purpose, since the substance of all [divine] emanations was created only to serve the Jews."

"The important things are the Jews, because they do not exist for any [other] aim; they themselves are [the divine] aim."

"The entire creation [of a non-Jew] exists only for the sake of the Jews."[31]

What the Noahide Laws mean for goyim is indicated in a campaign to abolish Christmas organised by rebbe Schneerson's Lubavitch Judaism, in an appeal to all Jews for assistance, citing religious sources:

> ...according to the known Jewish ruling that Christians are idol worshippers.(Likkutei Sichos 37:198). A gentile... is liable for the death penalty... if he has invented a religious holiday for himself... The general principle is we do not allow them to make new religious rituals and to make 'mitzvahs' for themselves by their own devices. Rather they may either become a Ger Tzeddek and accept all the Mitvahs; or he (the Noahide) should stand fast in his Torah (the seven Noahide Laws) without adding or diminishing...and if he does make some new 'mitzvah,' we lash him, punish him, and inform him that he is obligated with the death penalty for this..." (Rambam Mishne Torah—Hilchos Melachim 10:9). '...it is however obvious that if it will be perceived by them (the nations), also the matter of the negation of shituf, until they even have some recognition of the Unity of Hashem—that 'there is nothing else besides Him'; this will add both in their carefulness and meticulousness in fulfilling the seven Noahide Laws [with all of their ramifications!] and also in their aiding of Jewish people in all of their matters pertaining to Yiddishkeit and all of their needs in general...' (Likkutei Sichos 25: Yud Tes Kislev). 'Any person who has already worked successfully in this area should try to influence other Jews to do likewise. Resistance should not deter one when attempting to influence a further individual to accept upon himself the task of disseminating the Seven Noahide Laws amongst the nations.'[32]

---

31 The comments were translated by Dr. Shahak and Norton Mezvinsky from a Hebrew book by Schneerson published in 1965. See: Shahak and Mezvinsky, *Jewish Fundamentalism in Israel* (London: Pluto Press, 1999), pp. 59-61.

32 Jews and Hasidic Gentiles – United to Save America, 'Campaign to

The mystical Judaism of the Cabala explains in occult terms what Zionism applies in practical, political terms: the inferiority of the goyim, and the destiny of Israel:

It is axiomatic in Cabalistic writings that the higher souls of Jewish people are derived from the divine pleroma - the realm of Sefirot - whereas the souls of all other nations are derived from the 'shells.' Rabbi Hayim Vital does not exempt converts from this rule (Aitz Hayim 7, 10, 7) (Aitz Hadaat, Bemidbar). The 'Tanya' of Rav Sheneur Zalman was written for the general public. Its view of Gentile souls is in Chapter 6. The Zohar follows the same line, save that in the Midrash Haneelam; we note a certain effort to account for this difference. Before Adam sinned, he possessed the higher soul; after his sin, only his animal soul remained. Thereafter, the divine soul comes only to those who are preoccupied with Torah, entering the body of the Jewish male at age 13.[33]

Ultra-Orthodox Jews regard goyim as the empty 'shells' of the klippoth, the dark, 'satanic' sphere on the 'Tree of Life', which is the Cabalistic diagram of the cosmos, with spheres emanating from the godhead. The following passage from the Zohar, a primary book on Cabalistic mysticism, indicates the genocidal nature of certain aspects of Judaism influential in Israel and New York:

Happy will be the lot of Israel, whom the Holy One, blessed be He, has chosen from amongst the goyim of whom the Scriptures say: 'Their work is but vanity, it is an illusion at which we must laugh; they will all perish when God visits them in His wrath.' At the moment when the Holy One,

---

abolish X-mas celebration by gentiles', 'Why torah obligates all Jews in this campaign', http://www.noahide.com/infiltration/xmas.htm

33   Rabbi Jacob Agus, *Meta-Myth: The Diaspora and Israel*, Zohar Hodosh, Bereshit 18b-19a, Midrash Hane'elam. Etan Levine [ed.], *Diaspora: Exile and the Jewish Condition* (New York, Jason Aronson, 1983), p. 139.

blessed be He, will exterminate all the goyim of the world, Israel alone will subsist, even as it is written: 'The Lord alone will appear great on that day. [34]

A FOLLOWER OF THE REBBE PUTS HIS TEACHINGS INTO PRACTICE

The Israeli scholar, Shahak, explained that the basis of much Israeli policy and of the attitudes of many Zionists, particularly those in the Gush Emunim militant settler movement, the National Religious Party and kibbutzim, towards goyim, and in particular towards Arabs and Palestinians, is based on such teachings.[35] They are not long forgotten superstitions, but living realities, inflicted every day upon occupied Palestine, with consequences across the world.

Dr. Baruch Goldstein was a follower of both the Rebbe and of the late, assassinated Rabbi Meir Kahane, founder of the Jewish Defense League in the USA, and of the Kach Party in Israel.

Goldstein settled in Israel from the USA. As a medical officer in both the regular Israeli army and the reserves, he became problematic because of his refusal to treat not only wounded Arab prisoners, but also Gentiles serving in the Israeli Army, such as the Druze. He was following the Talmudic commandment that Jewish physicians should not render assistance to goyim unless failure to do so would bring discredit upon Jews. Nonetheless, because of the influence of ultra-Orthodox Judaism in Israel, Goldstein was protected, and in fact promoted to Major.

On the Feast of Purim[36], 25 February, 1994, Dr. Goldstein put the

---

34 *Zohar*, section Schemoth, folio 7 and 9b; section Beschalah, folio 58b.

35 Israel Shahak and Norton Mezvinsky, *Jewish Fundamentalism in Israel*, op. cit.

36 *Purim* is a Jewish annual celebration. It commemorates the killing of Haman, his ten sons and 75,000 Persians whose wealth was then appropriated by the Hebrews. Haman is a symbolic figure of the enemies of Israel. In recent times Saddam Hussein has been cursed as the present-day 'Haman'at Purim.

teachings of the Rebbe and Kahane into practice. Here is what the New Kach Movement[37] had to say about the Israeli 'saint':

> On the Feast of Purim Dr. Baruch Goldstein, dressed as an army officer, entered the Tomb of the Patriarchs, and shot to death 29 Arabs and wounded approximately a hundred more. It is our great misfortune that Dr. Baruch Goldstein may G-D avenge his blood, who was brutally murdered by the Arabs, is no longer with us.... Over the years [his] grave has become a site of pilgrimage. Numerous people, from all over the world come to pray in his honour.

Goldstein's tombstone reads: 'To the holy Baruch Goldstein, who gave his life for the Jewish people, the Torah, and the nation of Israel'.

In the following series of articles, written over several years, the historical, ideological, religious, geopolitical and political backgrounds of the so-called 'clash of civilisations' are brought into focus. The true causes and aims are exposed above the growing hysteria that has been contrived and directed in the interests of power-factions ensconced in New York, Washington, Tel Aviv and Jerusalem.

Haman, the Persian King's chief minister, was killed because he thwarted Hebrew influence. Esther, daughter of the King's Jewish adviser Mordechai, prevailed upon the King to kill his chief minister. The legend is related in the Old Testament in *The Book of Esther*

37 The New Kach Movement was one of several factions formed after the death of Kahane, who settled in Israel to become a Member of the Knesset, Israeli parliament. His call for the expulsion of all Palestinians from their own land resulted in his assassination.

ארגון צבאי לאומי

IRGUN ZWAÏ LÉUMI BE-EREZ JISRAEL

ORGANISATION MILITAIRE NATIONALE JUIVE D'EREZ JISRAEL

JEWISH NATIONAL MILITARY ORGANISATION OF EREZ JISRAEL

1931 Irgun poster – the map shows Israel defined in the borders of both Palestine and the Emirate of Transjordan, which the Irgun claimed in its entirety for a future Jewish state.

Symbiosis Between Anti-Semitism & Zionism

The *raison d'etre* for the establishment of the modern Zionist movement is that anti-Semitism is a pervasive and untreatable condition among Gentiles. When anti-Semitism is not overt and violent, it is latent and awaiting the right conditions to manifest as pogroms, according to Zionist dogma. Therefore the only ways Jews can escape this inherent anti-Semitism is by: (1) establishing a Jewish homeland, and (2) by total Jewish commitment to Zionism in whatever part of the world one resides. Zionist dogma further states that assimilation of Jews does not work; that ultimately even assimilated Jews will become victims of Gentile anti-Semitism.

ASSIMILATION

The doctrine arose during the latter part of the 19th Century in response to the widespread assimilation of Jews into Gentile society. It was feared by some that assimilation would destroy the Jewish identity. Whereas in past centuries, prior to the "emancipation" wrought by the French Revolution, Jews had been separated by the ghetto, modern society was breaking down the barriers. Jews were becoming "liberal" and "progressive." Yet even during the Middle Ages, "Jewish blood was intermingling with Christian blood. Cases of wholesale conversions were exceedingly numerous...," wrote the prominent French Jewish writer and onetime Zionist, Bernard Lazare.[1] He stated in this regard that "the entire history" of Jewry proves their assimilability; that "the Jew no longer lives apart, but shares in the common life..."[2] And there was the *real* problem.

---

1   Bernard Lazare, *Anti-Semitism: its history & causes*, Paris, 1894. (London, 1967), 178.
2   Ibid., 179.

THE DREYFUS AFFAIR

It so happens that Lazare wrote his book on anti-Semitism the very year of the "Dreyfus Affair". At the time, the Austrian journalist Theodor Herzl was in France observing the consequences of the allegation against the French-Jewish officer who was accused of spying for Germany, and which brought France to the verge of civil war. Herzl used the "Affair" as justification for his separatist ideology, claiming that if anti-Semitism could ignite so quickly in a nation as liberal and egalitarian as France, then assimilation was a myth, and anti-Semitism a constant that could not be eradicated. The only option was a return to Jewish separatism, the self-ghettoization of the pre-Emancipation era.

However, it is unlikely that Dreyfus was the real cause of Herzl's own separatism. If Dreyfus became a *cause célèbre* for French anti-Semites, so it was also for the multitudes of Frenchmen who came to the defense of the Jews, and Dreyfus was ultimately pardoned. The anti-Zionist rabbi Elmer Berger, who founded the American Council for Judaism, wrote of this:

> Where in all the world a century before would more than half a nation have come to the defence of a Jew? Had Herzl possessed a knowledge of history, he would have seen in the Dreyfus case a brilliant, heartening proof of the success of emancipation.[3]

Conversely, Herzl aligned himself with the anti-Semites, and found an ally in the leading French anti-Semite and campaigner against Dreyfus, M Drumont.

Herzl, while not the first Zionist, was the first to establish Zionism as an enduring and successful political movement. In response to the Dreyfus Affair he wrote the modern Zionist manifesto, *The Jewish State*.

---

3   Rabbi Elmer Berger, *The Jewish Dilemma* (New York: Devin-Adair, 1945), 207.

Emile Zola's open letter "J'Accuse!" published on the front page of L'Aurore

Many Jews, including the most influential, had assimilated and were suspicious of any movement that would again make Jews conspicuous as a separate people. The American statesman Henry Morgenthau Sr. for example said: "I refuse to allow myself to be a Zionist. I am an American." If this assimilationist attitude was to be replaced by a revival of Jewish separatism, anti-Semitism would have to be welcomed, even promoted, by Zionism as confirming its dogma and reversing the process of assimilation.

Zionists from the beginning welcomed anti-Semitism as a means of undermining what Zionists believed was the sense of false security of Jews in western, liberal societies, and as the means by which Jews would be kept in a permanent state of neurosis. Organizations such as the Anti-Defamation League of B'Nai B'rith exist mainly for the purpose of exaggerating the extent of anti-Semitism in order to keep Jews under the Zionist heel and keep the coffers for Israeli causes filled.

ZIONISM PROMOTES ANTI-SEMITISM

Many Jews – remarkably – have continued to resist the Zionist onslaught. Among these are the *Torah True Jews* who regard Zionism and the establishment of a Jewish state prior to the advent of a Jewish messiah as "blasphemy." The *Torah True Jews* explain the Zionist exploitation of anti-Semitism thus:

> Theodor Herzl (1860-1904), the founder of modern Zionism, recognised that anti-Semitism would further his cause, the creation of a separate state for Jews. To solve the Jewish Question, he maintained "we must, above all, make it an international political issue."

> Herzl wrote that Zionism offered the world a welcome "final solution of the Jewish question." In his *Diaries*, page 19, Herzl stated:

> "Anti-Semites will become our surest friends, anti-Semitic countries our allies."

Zionist reliance on Anti-Semitism to further their goals continues to this day. Studies of immigration records reflect increased immigration to the Zionist state during times of increased anti-Semitism. Without a continued inflow of Jewish immigrants to the state of "Israel," it is estimated that within a decade the Jewish population of the Zionist state will become the minority.

In order to maintain a Jewish majority in the state of "Israel," its leaders promote anti-Semitism throughout the world to "encourage" Jews to leave their homelands and seek "refuge."

Over the recent years there has been a dramatic rise in hate rhetoric and hate crimes targeted toward Jews…

On November 17, 2003 Zionist leader, Ariel Sharon, the Israeli prime minister, told Jews in Italy the best way to escape "a great wave of anti-Semitism" is to move and settle in the state of Israel.

This has been the Zionist ideology from the beginning to the present time. "The best solution to anti-Semitism is immigration to Israel. It is the only place on Earth where Jews can live as Jews," he said.

July 28, 2004: 200 French Jews emigrated to Israel following a wave of Anti-Semitism. They were personally greeted by Israeli Prime Minister Ariel Sharon, who recently urged French Jews to flee to Israel to escape rising anti-Semitism.

On July 18, 2004, Israeli Prime Minister Ariel Sharon urged all French Jews to move to Israel immediately to escape anti-Semitism. He told a meeting of the American Jewish Association in Jerusalem that Jews around the world should relocate to Israel as early as possible. But for those living in France, he added, moving was a "must" because of rising violence against Jews there.

THE ZIONIST/ANTI-SEMITIC AXIS

Benny Morris, professor of history at Israel's Ben-Gurion University, states of Herzl's attitude towards anti-Semitism:

> Herzl regarded Zionism's triumph as inevitable, not only because life in Europe was ever more untenable for Jews, but also because it was in Europe's interests to rid the Jews and be relieved of anti-Semitism: The European political establishment would eventually be persuaded to promote Zionism. Herzl recognized that anti-Semitism would be HARNESSED to his own–Zionist-purposes.[4]

Herzl's most fervent supporters were anti-Semites. Both Zionists and anti-Semites concur that the Jews are an unassimilable minority which needs to be removed from Gentile society. Hence, Zionists have historically aligned themselves with anti-Semites ranging from those in Czarist Russia to those in Nazi

---

4   Benny Morris, *Righteous Victims: A History of the Zionist-Arab Conflict, 1881-1999* (New York: Alfred A Knopf, 1999), 21.

Theodor Herzl (1860-1904), the founder of modern Zionism

Germany. Where the supposed latent anti-Semitism of Gentiles fails to manifest dramatically, and at times when Jews are in the process of assimilating into Gentile society (as they were in pre-Hitler Germany), Zionists provoke, encourage, and even directly create anti-Semitic movements and incidents.

In the wake of the 'Dreyfus Affair' Herzl used the opportunity as an opening for his separatism, writing his Zionist manifesto, *Der Judenstaat*, in 1895. Anti-Semites welcomed *The Jewish State* from the start. Of his publishers, Herzl noted in his *Diary*: "Was at the printing office and talked with the managers ... both are presumably anti-Semites. They greeted me with genuine cordiality. They liked my pamphlet."[5]

Jacob Klatzkin, leading Zionist ideologue, editor of the official

5   T Herzl, *The Diaries of Theodor Herzl* (New York, 1962), 91.

Zionist organ *Die Welt,* and co-editor of the *Encyclopaedia Judaica,* speaking of Russian anti-Semitism and the "Pale of Settlement," stated:

> The contribution of our enemies is in the continuance of Jewry in eastern Europe. One ought to appreciate the national service which the Pale of Settlement performed for us … we ought to be thankful to our oppressors that they closed the gates of assimilation to us and took care that our people were concentrated and not dispersed. Instead of establishing societies for defence against the anti-Semites who want to reduce our rights, we should establish societies for defence against our friends who desire to defend our rights.[6]

The same attitude by Zionists carries through to the present-day, as demonstrated by Jay Lefkowitz, who became US Deputy Assistant to the President for Domestic Policy: "Deep down, I believe that a little anti-Semitism is a good thing for the Jews – reminds us who we are."[7]

Herzl & Drumont

Herzl formed an early alliance with France's leading anti-Semite, Eduard Drumont, who had been the head of the anti-Dreyfus agitation. Drumont had written the influential anti-Semitic book *La France Juive* (1886) and was editor of *La Libre Parole.* Herzl wrote of Drumont: "But I owe to Drumont a great deal of the present freedom of my concepts, because he is an artist."[8] Herzl persuaded Drumont to review his manifesto in *La Libre Parole,* which he did favourably on January 15 1897, Herzl writing of this: [Drumont] "praises the Zionists of Herzl's persuasion for not seeing in us fanatics … but citizens who exercise the right of

---

6   J Klatzkin, *Krisis und Entscheidung in Judentum,* Berlin 1921, 118.

7   Jay Lefkowitz, *New York Times Magazine,* February 12, 1995, 65.

8   D. Stewart, *Theodor Herzl* (New York 1974), 25.

self-defence."[9] Writing of his experiences in Paris, Herzl stated:

> In Paris ... I achieved a freer attitude towards anti-Semitism, which I now began to understand historically and to pardon. Above all I recognize the emptiness and futility of trying to "combat" anti-Semitism.[10]

In his Austrian homeland it was among the anti-Semites that Herzl also found the most immediate support. Herzl's biographer Desmond Stewart, writes: "... Already in 1896 Austrian anti-Semites were finding ammunition in Herzl's arguments, as would the followers of Drumont ..."[11]

Max Nordau, Herzl's deputy, expressed the affinity between the Zionists and Drumont in an interview with Raphael Marchant, correspondent for Drumont's *La Libre Parole*, stating that Zionism, "is not a question of religion, but exclusively of race, and there is no one with whom I am in greater agreement on this position than M Drumont."[12]

HERZL & VON PLEHVE

In Russia, also, support among anti-Semites was effusive. Herzl's chief ally was the Russian Interior Minister Vyacheslav Konstantinovich von Plehve, whom Herzl met in August 1903. Just four months previously Von Plehve had been organizing pogroms at Kishinev. As Herzl was explaining his Zionist project, Von Plehve interrupted, according to Herzl's own account: "You don't have to justify the movement to me. 'Vous prêchez un converti' (You are preaching to a convert)."[13]

As in Nazi Germany from 1933, Zionism was given favourable

---

9   Ibid p. 251, fn

10   Ibid., 6.

11   Ibid., 25.

12   Ibid., 322.

13   R Patai (ed) *The complete diaries of Theodore Herzl* (London, 1960), Vol IV, 1525.

governmental recognition in Czarist Russia. Von Plehve wrote a letter pledging "moral and material assistance", which became "Herzl's most cherished asset."[14]

Due to Herzl's efforts in Russia, "there was no prohibition on Zionist activities and an official permit was even given for the holding of the second conference of Russian Zionists at Minsk (September 1902)."[15]

Zionists & Nazi Germany

Without Hitlerism, Zionism might not have succeeded beyond being a fringe movement. Germany was the most unlikely source for Zionist support among German Jews. Such was the assimilation of German Jewry and its full identification with the German nation that Herzl's original aim of having the First Zionist Congress held there had to be changed to Switzerland due to the opposition of German Jews.

Prior to Hitler, Zionism represented a minor faction within German Jewry. Whilst some Jews were conspicuous in their leadership of Marxism, communism and various anti-national movements, there was a more significant movement of German nationalism among Jews who regarded themselves as "Germans of Jewish descent."

If some Jews had been involved in revolutionary movements designed to undermine the war effort, many more gave a disproportionate sacrifice fighting for Germany during World War I. The prominent businessman and statesman Walther Rathenau, German Foreign Minister after World War I expressed the prevalent sentiment:

---

14 M Menhuin, *Decadence of Judaism in our time*, (New York, 1969), 46.

15 *Chaim Weizmann Letters and papers* (Oxford 1971), Vol. II, 284. Weizmann was instrumental in obtaining the *Balfour Declaration* in 1917, from Lord Balfour, another anti-Semite. As Home Secretary in 1905, Arthur Balfour had introduced the Aliens Act to keep Jewish refugees fleeing the pogroms out of Britain. The Zionist HQ in Britain was called *Balfour House* in the anti-Semite's honour.

I am a German of Jewish stock. My nation is the German nation, my fatherland is the German fatherland, and my faith is the German faith, which transcends the various confessions.

After World War I, these German-Jewish veterans formed the nucleus of a nationalist movement that was not only anti-Communist but also anti-Zionist. The League of German Nationalist Jews, formed in 1921, declared:

Our way is not the way of the Zionists... of people who clearly hesitate between Germany and Jewry... of internationalist fanatics... We reject a Jewish united front, the only united front we care for is a German one...

The National Association of Jewish Combat Veterans was also opposed to both Zionism and the Left. But it was the Zionists to which the Nazis looked as representatives of German Jewry, as both Nazism and Zionism shared a common aim: opposition to Jewish assimilation. Lenni Brenner writes of this commonality of interests:

...Believing that the ideological similarities between the two movements – their contempt for liberalism, their common volkish racism and, of course, their mutual conviction that Germany could never be the homeland of its Jews – could induce the Nazis to support them, the ZVfD[16] solicited the patronage of Adolf Hitler, not once but repeatedly, after 1933.[17]

Brenner cites Rabbi Joachim Prinz, a leading Zionist in Germany who was to become president of the American Jewish Congress, in regard to the German Zionist Federation welcoming the advent of Nazi Germany as a repudiation of German-Jewish assimilation:

---

16   German Zionist Federation.

17   Lenni Brenner, *Zionism in the Age of Dictators*, (Connecticut, 1983), 45.

In 1937, after leaving Berlin for America, Rabbi Joachim Prinz wrote of his experiences in Germany and alluded to a memorandum which, it is now known, was sent to the Nazi Party by the ZVfD on 21 June 1933. Prinz's article candidly describes the Zionist mood in the first months of 1933:

Everyone in Germany knew that only the Zionists could responsibly represent the Jews in dealings with the Nazi government. We all felt sure that one day the government would arrange a round table conference with the Jews, at which – after the riots and atrocities of the revolution had passed – the new status of German Jewry could be considered. The government announced very solemnly that there was no country in the world which tried to solve the Jewish problem as seriously as did Germany. Solution of the Jewish question? It was our Zionist dream! We never denied the existence of the Jewish question! Dissimilation? It was our own appeal! ... In a statement notable for its pride and dignity, we called for a conference.[18]

ZIONISTS OBSTRUCTED EFFORTS TO EVACUATE JEWS

Several efforts were made to evacuate Jews from Europe before the situation became dire as a consequence of war. The German Government was willing to assist in the facilitation of Jewish emigrants to the USA and European countries or colonies. The Zionists rejected all such efforts as detracting from the aim of herding the Jews to Palestine, even if it meant fewer Jews would be evacuated. Israeli author Tom Segev quotes Zionist leader David Ben Gurion as stating:

I was not well versed on matters of saving the Jews of Nazi-occupied Europe, even though I was chairman of

---

18 Joachim Prinz, "Zionism under the Nazi Government," *Young Zionist* (London, November 1937), 18. Rabbi Prinz was to return to Germany in 1960 to lecture the Germans about a revival of Nazism after Stasi-orchestrated anti-Semitic incidents.

the Jewish Agency. The heart of my activity was enlisting Jewry in the demand to establish a Jewish state.[19]

Ben Gurion's attitude towards Hitler was that: "We want Hitler to be destroyed, but as long as he exists, we are interested in exploiting that for the good of Palestine."[20]

When an international conference was convened in Evian, France, to discuss the problem of Jewish refugees, Ben Gurion warned that opening up other countries to Jewish refugees would weaken Zionist demands that they be evacuated to Palestine.[21] Citing Ben Gurion's *Memoirs*[22], Segev quotes him as stating:

> If I knew that it was possible to save all the [Jewish] children in Germany by transporting them to England, but only half of them by transporting them to Palestine, I would choose the second – because we face not only the reckoning of those children, but the historical reckoning of the Jewish people.[23]

This was in December 1938, just after the so-called "Crystal Night" anti-Jewish riots in Germany. Ben Gurion explained: "Like every Jew, I am interested in saving every Jew wherever possible, but nothing takes precedence over saving the Hebrew nation in its land."[24]

Segev states that the tendency of the Zionists was to see Jewish immigration as the means of establishing the Jewish state rather than as a means of rescuing Jews. Ben Gurion said that he would prefer young workers rather than old people or children;

---

19   Tom Segev, *One complete Palestine* (London: Abacus Books, 2002), 461.
20   Ibid., 393.
21   Ibid., 394.
22   Ibid., 398.
23   Ibid., 394.
24   Ibid., 402.

he wanted the children to be born in Palestine. Hence, during the 1930s most immigration permits were issued to young unmarried male "pioneers." While a small number of permits were allocated to children, the Jewish Agency stipulated that these should exclude retarded children.[25] In 1936, a special fund was established in Palestine for the RETURN of incurably ill Jews to Europe, because they had become a "burden" on the community and its social institutions.

However, Europe's Jews were not enthusiastic about going to Palestine to establish a Jewish state. Even in Poland there were few takers for permits from the Jewish Agency. Moshe Shertok of the Jewish Agency suggested creating a panic in Poland to encourage Jews to leave for Palestine.[26] Such an attitude would also explain why few Jews were accepted even into the USA even though Roosevelt was surrounded by advisers such as Henry Morgenthau Jnr.,[27] Bernard Baruch, and Felix Frankfurter.

Zionist Bombs in Iraq

Zionists have continued to foster and exaggerate anti-Semitism, and this has included the manufacturing of "false flag incidents." The following account by Zionist veteran Naeim Giladi should become widely known. It is a complete expose of the Zionist modus operandi in regards to anti-Semitism.

A particularly significant event was the creation of fake anti-Semitic incidents in Iraq to push Iraqi Jews into emigrating to Palestine. This was exposed by a former Israeli agent and Iraqi Jew Naeim Giladi, who had played a role in the operation, author of *Ben Gurion's Scandals: How the Haganah & the Mossad Eliminated Jews*.[28] Giladi's article "The Jews of Iraq" provides

---

25 Ibid., 395, citing "Report of the Immigration Dept. of the Jewish Agency 1937-39, Immigration of Unfit People."

26 Ibid., 395.

27 Not to be confused with his father, who was avidly anti-Zionist, as quoted above.

28 N Giladi, *Ben Gurion's Scandals: How the Haganah & the Mossad Eliminated*

a synopsis of the operations that the reader is urged to peruse in full online, from which I quote.[29]

Giladi, as an 18-year-old Zionist idealist in 1947, was caught by the Iraqi authorities smuggling Jews into Iran *en route* to Palestine. At the time, Giladi was not interested in the two and a half thousand years of Jewish history in Iraq, but his subsequent assessment indicates how completely Jews were a part of Iraqi society:

> Although Jews, like other minorities in what became Iraq, experienced periods of oppression and discrimination depending on the rulers of the period, their general trajectory over two and one-half millennia was upward. Under the late Ottoman rule, for example, Jewish social and religious institutions, schools, and medical facilities flourished without outside interference, and Jews were prominent in government and business.

Perhaps the scornful attitudes of Giladi's father when he found out his son was a member of the Zionist underground was indicative of the attitude of most Iraqi Jews towards Zionism, but the situation changed:

> About 125,000 Jews left Iraq for Israel in the late 1940s and into 1952, most because they had been lied to and put into a panic by what I came to learn were Zionist bombs.

With the declaration of the Zionist State in 1948, an Iraqi detachment were among the Arabs who fought against the Zionist interlopers.

In 1950, in a scenario reminiscent of the Lavon Affair in

Jews http://www.jewsagainstzionism.com/bookstore/productdetails. cfm?merchid=16

29 N Giladi, "The Jews of Iraq," http://www.bintjbeil.com/E/occupation/ ameu_iraqjews.html

Egypt just four years later on March 19, "a bomb went off at the American Cultural Center and Library in Baghdad, causing property damage and injuring a number of people. The center was a favourite meeting place for young Jews."

The first bomb thrown directly at Jews occurred on April 8, 1950, at 9:15 p.m. A car with three young passengers hurled the grenade at Baghdad's El-Dar El-Bida Café, where Jews were celebrating Passover. Four people were seriously injured. That night leaflets were distributed calling on Jews to leave Iraq immediately.

The next day, many Jews, most of them poor with nothing to lose, jammed emigration offices to renounce their citizenship and to apply for permission to leave for Israel. So many applied, in fact, that the police had to open registration offices in Jewish schools and synagogues.

On May 10, at 3 a.m., a grenade was tossed in the direction of the display window of the Jewish-owned Beit-Lawi Automobile Company, destroying part of the building. No casualties were reported.

On June 3, 1950, another grenade was tossed from a speeding car in the El-Batawin area of Baghdad where most rich Jews and middle class Iraqis lived. No one was hurt, but following the explosion Zionist activists sent telegrams to Israel requesting that the quota for immigration from Iraq be increased.

On June 5, at 2:30 a.m., a bomb exploded next to the Jewish-owned Stanley Shashua building on El-Rashid Street, resulting in property damage but no casualties.

On January 14, 1951, at 7 p.m., a grenade was thrown at a group of Jews outside the Masouda Shem-Tov Synagogue. The explosive struck a high-voltage cable, electrocuting three Jews, one a young boy, Itzhak Elmacher, and wounding over 30 others.

Following the attack, the exodus of Jews jumped to between 600-700 per day.

Zionist propagandists still maintain that the bombs in Iraq were set off by anti-Jewish Iraqis who wanted Jews out of their country. The terrible truth is that the grenades that killed and maimed Iraqi Jews and damaged their property were thrown by Zionist Jews. Wilbur Crane Eveland, a former senior officer with the CIA, states in his own book *Ropes of Sand*, whose publication the CIA opposed, of the incidents:

> In attempts to portray the Iraqis as anti-American and to terrorize the Jews, the Zionists planted bombs in the U.S. Information Service library and in synagogues. Soon leaflets began to appear urging Jews to flee to Israel. . . Although the Iraqi police later provided our embassy with evidence to show that the synagogue and library bombings, as well as the anti-Jewish and anti-American leaflet campaigns, had been the work of an underground Zionist organization, most of the world believed reports that Arab terrorism had motivated the flight of the Iraqi Jews whom the Zionists had "rescued" really just in order to increase Israel's Jewish population.[30]

Giladi continues:

> In 1955, for example, I organized in Israel a panel of Jewish attorneys of Iraqi origin to handle claims of Iraqi Jews who still had property in Iraq. One well known attorney, who asked that I not give his name, confided in me that the laboratory tests in Iraq had confirmed that the anti-American leaflets found at the American Cultural Center bombing were typed on the same typewriter and duplicated on the same stencilling machine as the leaflets distributed

---

30 Wilber C Eveland, *Ropes of Sand: America's Failure in the Middle East* (New York: W.W. Norton, 1980). Eveland worked as a Middle East specialist for the CIA, National Security Council and State Department.

by the Zionist movement just before the April 8th bombing.

Tests also showed that the type of explosive used in the Beit-Lawi attack matched traces of explosives found in the suitcase of an Iraqi Jew by the name of Yosef Basri. Basri, a lawyer, together with Shalom Salih, a shoemaker, would be put on trial for the attacks in December 1951 and executed the following month. Both men were members of Hashura, the military arm of the Zionist underground. Salih ultimately confessed that he, Basri and a third man, Yosef Habaza, carried out the attacks.

Neo-Nazis Receive Zionist Backing

Zionist backing of overtly neo-Nazi manifestations has been a means of generating feelings of insecurity within "Diaspora Jewry" in the all-too-peaceful Western world. Here are several dramatic examples.

THE NATIONAL RENAISSANCE PARTY

The National Renaissance Party (NRP) was one of the first "neo-Nazi" groups to emerge after World War II and one of the longest enduring (1949-1979). It ended only with the death of its leader, James H Madole.

In 1960, Joseph P Kamp wrote *Bigots Behind the Swastika Spree*[1] in response to the world-wide anti-Semitic activities that broke out in 1959, which even then detailed the Zionist contrivance and manipulation of neo-Nazi movements.[2] Kamp wrote his exposé in the midst of the world-wide uproar generated by the phony "anti-Semitic" vandalism that had been directed by the East German Stasi. Of course, the Zionists were making the most of the hysteria. Benjamin R Epstein, director of the Anti-Defamation League, went to Germany to discuss anti-Semitism with West German officials. He declared that the Germans need to be re-educated with a "long range education program..."[3]

"Coincidentally" whilst there was this flurry of international

---

1   Joseph P Kamp, *Bigots Behind the Swastika Spree* (New York: Headlines, 1960).

2   Investigations by West German authorities proved that the "anti-Semitic incidences" were instigated by the East German Stasi in order to discredit Bonn. *The Anti-Semitic and Nazi Incidents: White Paper* (Bonn: Government of the Federal Republic of Germany, 1960). A copy is available from this writer.

3   Kamp, op.cit., 16.

activity among journalists, communists and Zionists in response to the incidents in Germany, on January 26, 1960 three youths were jailed in New York after having allegedly shouted "Heil Hitler" at a rabbi, after the rabbi had approached the boys following a communist meeting protesting against the supposed resurgence of German anti-Semitism.[4] Ten days earlier three other youths had been arrested in New York for organizing a "neo-Nazi club." They were charged with disorderedly conduct, amidst demands by the prosecutor that they should be charged with "treason," with the possibility of a death penalty.[5]

The leader of the three "traitors" was a member of the National Renaissance Party, as were all three of those arrested on the 26th.

The NRP had its origins in a one-man effort by James Madole, which he called the Animist Party. Madole was contacted by Vladimir Stepankowsky, who offered to fund Madole. Stepankowsky put Madole in contact with others, and meetings were held in Stepankowsky's hotel in New York. Stepankowsky prepared Animist Party literature with an anti-Semitic emphasis. Stepankowsky then organized a conference between the Animist Party and other anti-Communists. Stepankowsky even gained contact with three anti-Communist Congressmen, who were duly implicated in a "fascist plot" when the convention was exposed by the Anti-Defamation League (ADL).[6]

Stepankowsky, the real founder of the NRP, America's first and longest running "neo-Nazi" group, was both a long-time communist agent and an agent for the Anti-Defamation League (ADL). Kamp reveals that Stepankowsky was a prominent veteran Marxist who had edited a communist newspaper in London in 1905. In 1917, he was jailed with communist revolutionary leader Trotsky in Russia. He was later deported from England for

4   Ibid., 24.

5   Ibid., 25-26.

6   Ibid., 27-28.

communist activities. In 1933 he was identified as a Soviet agent by the French Ministry of War and deported to Switzerland. There he became the head of what the Swiss secret service called the "Bolshevik Information Bureau" and was deported to Italy. He entered the USA illegally in 1936. In the USA, while writing for communist papers, he was employed by the ADL in 1937. In 1954, ex-Soviet spy Elizabeth Bentley exposed him as a Soviet agent. However, because he had influential friends via his association with the ADL, no action was taken.[7]

Working with Stepankowsky to set up Madole and the NRP were Gordon Hall, a.k.a. Walker and Charles R Allen Jr. Hall worked for the Friends of Democracy, at the time a division of the ADL.[8] Allen was an agent for both the Friends of Democracy and the ADL. He had written for Jewish Life, an organ of the US Communist Party.[9] Hence all three leading instigators of the USA's first and most enduring Nazi party were Left-wing agents for the ADL. Without these it is doubtful that the NRP would have ever existed.

When Madole broke with Stepankowsky in 1948, having discovered his communist background, the Animist Party became dormant. Madole renamed it the NRP in 1949. One of the earliest supporters of Madole's new NRP was Mana Truhill, who issued a crudely anti-Semitic bulletin without Madole's approval.[10] Truhill, a.k.a. Emanuel Trujillo, was an agent for the Anti-Nazi League (ANL), another division of the ADL. Rabbi Stephen S Wise, the president of the American Jewish Congress, had founded the ANL in 1933. Truhill had studied communist strategy at the Communist Party's Jefferson School of Social Science. He was funded by ADL functionary Sanford Griffith. By 1954, Truhill was de facto head of the NRP. He was chief liaison with "Nazis," "nationalists" and "anti-Semites"

---

7   Ibid., 28.

8   Ibid., 29.

9   Ibid., 29.

10   Ibid., 30.

throughout the world, and wrote the NRP's anti-Semitic literature, which was distributed via his world-wide contacts, and paid for by the ANL and ADL. He personally ensured that the NRP funds were replenished when short, with money supplied by the ADL.[11] Truhill became the first commander of the NRP's stormtroopers, which over the course of several decades were to become involved in frequent riots with Jews on the streets of New York City. It is interesting to note that the NRP never really extended beyond New York City, which has the USA's largest concentration of Jews. The NRP stormtroopers were equipped with Nazi type brownshirts paid for via funds provided by the ADL and the ANL. They were thus the most provocative and visible of America's neo-Nazis, in the midst of the USA's largest Jewish population center, until the formation of Rockwell's American Nazi Party in 1959. It was under Truhill's direction that the NRP used the swastika, whilst Madole's own preference was for the lightning bolt.

According to the late H Keith Thompson, whose activity within the American extreme Right spanned decades, writing in an autobiographical series on his life as an "American Fascist" in *Expose* tabloid, it was Truhill as NRP international liaison officer, who would write to nationalist, right-wing and "neo-Nazi" organizations throughout the world attempting to draw extreme responses on questions relating to Jews, and it was Truhill who would distribute anti-Semitic cartoons. Thompson relates also that when his own activities were quieting he would get a "pep talk" and suggestions from "ADL master spy" Sandy Griffith, Thompson relating that he had yet to learn that the ADL acted as "provocateurs and instigators" and were "the most dependable source of funds."[12] Thompson added: On other occasions, Sandy Griffith, who liked the role of a sort of "campaign manager," urged me into provocative anti-Semitism but I would not take the bait, even when accompanied by a few respectable bank-notes.[13]

---

11 Ibid.

12 Ibid., 32.

13 Ibid.

Other stalwart "Nazis" who swelled the ranks of the NRP included Ruth Ross, a member of the Labour Youth League, a registered communist front; and Lawrence Sestito and Louis Mostaccio, both members of the ANL. Sestito reported directly to Arnold Foster, director of the ADL, and to Sandy Griffith.[14]

These were the full-time workers for the NRP. There were other part-time helpers, including John Langord, who assisted at public meetings, an agent for the ADL and ANL. Langord had come from Poland on a diplomatic passport, being the son of a UN diplomat. Richard Hamel, an ADL agent, made anti-Semitic speeches for the NRP. Charley Smith, ADL agent, provided Madole with funds and advice. Even Sandy Griffith himself, under the alias of Al Scheffer, attended NRP strategy meetings to offer advice.[15]

The NRP remained on the verge of obliteration, however. This would mean there would be no highly dramatic neo-Nazi group by which the ADL could continue to scare Jews into providing funds for their "self-defence" against the imminent rise of anti-Semitism and to ensure their subservience to Zionism.

The ADL responded by prompting Sen. Velde of the House Committee on Un-American Activities (HCUA) into investigating supposed "hate groups". The focus was the NRP. Velde had not shown interest at first, but the power of the ADL and other Zionist organizations, acting through Edwin Lucas, chief counsel of the American Jewish Committee, was persuasive. The chief investigator for the HCUA and his staff dutifully showed up at the offices of the ADL where they were fed information on this supposed rise of neo-Nazism.[16] HCUA Chief Investigator Owens then set up his staff at the offices of the American Jewish Committee where Lucas supplied the congressional staffers

---

14   Ibid., 31.

15   Ibid., 32.

16   Ibid., 34.

with further phony evidence.[17] This typical smear-mongering information supplied by the ADL and AJC formed the basis of the Velde committee's *Preliminary Report on Neo-Fascist & Hate Groups*.[18]

The principal target of the report was the insignificant NRP. Congressman Francis Walter, who was due to take over the chairmanship of the HCUA, "denounced the whole procedure today. He charged that the committee had held no hearing relating to the report and had not discussed the subject in executive hearings." The NRP had virtually ceased to exist, yet the ADL/AJC-contrived congressional report farcically described the NRP as a "menace" whose "activities would destroy the very foundation of the American Republic."

On the day after the report, The *New York Times* stated that its reporters had failed to find any trace of the NRP, nor had the local police and FBI.[19] The NRP was thereby brought back to life by a Zionist-contrived publicity stunt using a Congressional committee. However, what scared the ADL and AJC was that the report called for investigation and prosecution of the NRP. Such an in-depth investigation would reveal the manner by which the ADL had birthed the NRP and sustained it. The ADL now urged the HCUA to ignore the NRP, and the American Jewish Committee dissociated itself from the House Committee's recommendation that the Justice Department indict the NRP under the Smith Act.[20] But the notoriety resuscitated the NRP, and it endured until Madole's death in 1979. In 1959, the NRP was superseded by Lincoln Rockwell's openly American Nazi Party, Rockwell being more charismatic and adept at generating publicity.

---

17 Ibid.

18 Committee on Un-American Activities, *Preliminary Report on Neo-Fascist & Hate Groups* (Washington: Government Printing Office, 1954). Online at: http://www.scribd.com/doc/24846175/Preliminary-Report-on-Neo-Fascism-and-Hate-Groups-1954

19 Kamp, op.cit., 35.

20 Ibid., 36.

CANADIAN NAZI PARTY

The Canadian Nazi Party (CNP), followed the same pattern as the NRP, and would not have existed without the support provided by the Canadian Jewish Congress. The CNP, like the NRP, existed virtually as the one-man band of John Beattie over the period 1965 to 1978. Beattie was a regular speaker at Allen Gardens, Toronto, accompanied by a handful of youthful bodyguards. None of these attracted any attention until May 30, 1965, when 5,000 demonstrators, agitated by Left-wing and Zionist organizations, converged on the park to hunt and beat any "Nazi" they could find. On this one crucial occasion when Beattie sorely needed his bodyguards he was alone. This is significant.

The day before the expected "Nazi rally," the *Toronto Globe and Mail* reported on May 31, that "more than 30 Zionist and other Jewish organizations had met to plan a protest at the announced Nazi rally." The result was a mob numbering 5,000, which converged on Allan Gardens. They included a faction estimated by the press at 500 who arrived at the park wielding bats.[21] Beattie, decked out as usual in swastika armband and uniform, was the only Nazi who was beaten, although a preacher and a few out of town visitors somehow got mistaken as "Nazis" by the mob and were also beaten. Beattie was jailed for 6 months for "public mischief."

Beattie had been set up. There was nothing different about this regular speaking excursion to Allen Gardens other than that he was not accompanied by his usual handful of bodyguards. These bodyguards, the few who actually comprised the Canadian Nazi Party, had in fact been working for the Canadian Jewish Congress. Three of Beattie's activists, Ronald Bottaro and John and Chris Dingle, appeared as guests on the CBC Radio network's "Don Simms Show" on October 20, and admitted to working for the Canadian Jewish Congress and the "N-3" "anti-racist" group. The total membership of Beattie's Nazi Party, they

---

21 Patrick Walsh, *The Unholy Alliance* (Ontario: Canadian Intelligence Publications, 1986), 9-12.

said, was ten; of whom perhaps three may have been genuine Nazis.[22]

The Rhodes Avenue home where the CNP's headquarters was located had been acquired with the help of the Canadian Jewish Congress and was chosen as the site because of its centrality where it could provoke maximum reaction[23], just as the NRP was centered in New York City. Henrick Van Der Windt, an agent for the Canadian Jewish Congress, had made the nominal down payment on the house. The *Toronto Telegram*[24] reported on Van Der Windt:

> A man claiming to be an undercover agent for the Canadian Jewish Congress has penetrated the ranks of the Canadian Nazi Party.
>
> Henrick Van Der Windt... was followed from a Nazi meeting.... by two *Telegram* reporters.
>
> Traced to his three story home.... Van Der Windt made no secret of his supposed connection with the Jewish Congress.
>
> "I was first involved with the Canadian Unity Party before the last war and worked for the Jewish Congress then too," he said.
>
> "...I don't get paid, they just pay my expenses," he said.
>
> "...The Congress had got lots of good information for their money, but I don't care if it all stops right now," he said.
>
> A top level official of the Congress, Sydney Harris, asked

---

22 Ibid., 13.

23 Presumably this means that it had a high concentration of Jewish residents.

24 June 25, 1965.

John Beattie leading members of the Canadian Nazi Party
in a march in Allen Gardens, Toronto.

to confirm or deny Van Der Windt's claim, would say only "no comment," last night.[25]

It was around this time, 1965, that the Canadian Government appointed a seven-man committee to investigate "hate literature" and to recommend action.

In the year 2000, Beattie was lined up to appear as a witness at a "human rights" hearing against German-Canadian "holocaust denier" Ernst Zündel. The Canadian Association for Free Expression, whose organizer, Paul Fromm, has acted for Zündel in legal matters, wrote of Beattie's impending appearance:

John Beattie to Expose the Nazi Party That Never Was

Monday at 2:00 p.m. William John Beattie, the former leader of the Canadian Nazi Party, will present shocking testimony to a Canadian Human Rights Tribunal inquiring into "hate" charges against Toronto publisher Ernst Zündel

25 Walsh, op.cit., 14.

for a site called the Zundelsite, located in California and owned and operated by a U.S. citizen. In the heady Spring of 1965, a 23-year old Torontonian John Beattie was on the front page of most Toronto newspapers, his every comment headline news.

Beattie will reveal that he was a dupe and a patsy, that everything from his group's name to its major activities was suggested or quarterbacked by persons acting as agents for or reporting to the Canadian Jewish Congress. Uncannily, at the very time that the Canadian Nazi Party was being built up and just as quickly destroyed a government committee was holding hearings to propose anti-hate legislation. The Cohen Committee made significant mention of the threat posed by John Beattie. The Canadian Jewish Congress, which largely created the short-lived Canadian Nazi Party, had, since the 1930s been lobbying for restrictions on freedom of speech.

Beattie will reveal how an agent for the Canadian Jewish Congress lured him into a technical breach of the law, which landed the now unemployed, penniless Nazi leader in prison for six months. Beattie will also expose the fact that the same agent proposed legal manoeuvres that were calculated to frighten and cause distress among Jews, thus heightening the "Nazi" menace, which was used as the argument for the 1971 "hate law" (Section 319 of the Criminal Code) and the subsequent section 13.1 (telephonic communication of hate) of the Canadian Human Rights Act, where truth is no defence. Beattie is one of a number of witnesses being called by the Canadian Association for Free Expression, Canada's foremost free speech group, in its role as an intervenor in these proceedings.[26]

For reasons unknown, Beattie failed to appear at the hearing.

---

26 Canadian Association For Free Expression, Press Release, November 26, 2000.

BOGUS ANTI-SEMITIC INCIDENTS

Given the history of Zionist machinations in regard to "false flag" operations, the Iraqi bombings, the very similar Lavon Affair, the propping up of neo-Nazi groups, and the historic associations between Zionists and anti-Semites since the days of Herzl, it should not be surprising that Zionists have also been involved in the direct perpetration of anti-Semitic incidents, often of a quite petty nature, which are nonetheless whipped up into epochal events and exploited to the hilt by Zionism.

Following are some incidents that have been contrived to serve some Zionist agenda.

The home of the Dreyfus Affair that encouraged Herzl to make his pitch for a Zionist State, has been the focus of allegations of resurgent "anti-Semitism" to try and drum up support for Israel and increased emigration. Ariel Sharon's remarks at a meeting of the American Jewish Association in Jerusalem that Jews should depart from France to Israel in the wake of "the spread of the wildest anti-Semitism" sparked a diplomatic row. In an article by Rannie Amiri on alleged anti-Semitism in France, an examination of some of the "anti-Semitic" incidences that prompted Sharon's warnings found the examples to be without substance.[27] Amiri writes:

> We can also glean additional insight into the claimed rampant anti-Semitism in France from Alex Moise. As head of the organization "French Friends of Israel's Likud Party," he filed a complaint in January [2004] after receiving numerous intimidating anti-Semitic calls and threats. In May, the Jewish Telegraph Agency reported Moise was fined and received a suspended jail sentence after confessing to staging the threats himself.

Another incident of "the spread of the wildest anti-Semitism"

---

27 Rannie Amiri, "Anti-Semitism in France, but which Semites?," *Studies in Islam & the Middle East*, http://www.majalla.org/news/2004/08/amiri-08.htm

in the year of Sharon's remark was also embarrassing. A Jewish community center in Paris was set alight, and anti-Semitic graffiti and swastikas scrawled in red marker, reading, "Without the Jews, the world is happy," and "Jews get out." An Islamic group was blamed, with a message claiming that the arson was to mark the 35th anniversary of a fire at Al-Aqsa Mosque in Jerusalem. A news dispatch observed:

> The assumption that the fire had been an anti-Semitic attack led French leaders to speak out strongly and declare war on racism. The visiting Israeli Foreign Minister, Silvan Shalom, toured the site a couple of days after the fire, condemning the attack but praising French efforts to curb a rise in anti-Semitism in the country.[28]

The culprit transpired to be a 50-year-old Jewish employee of the center. This writer recalls mentioning this good news to the *New Zealand Jewish Chronicle*, which had reported the incident as an example of "anti-Semitism," but which declined to print a correction for the peace of mind of its readers. An outcry had also been caused at around the time when a 23 year old woman claimed to have been attacked by Arabs who thought she was Jewish. She subsequently admitted she had contrived the story.

> The collapse of the "affair of the RER railway" embarrassed President Chirac as he prepared to give his annual Bastille Day pep talk to the nation today, with racism and hate crimes among the top subjects. ...The President no doubt regrets the way in which he seized on the reported attack last weekend as ministers and the media poured out a torrent of condemnation of mindless, anti-Semitic violence on suburban housing estates. M Chirac voiced horror at the reported actions of the youths who were said to have attacked the woman and her 13-month-old child as they

---

28 Verena Von Derschau, "French investigators sceptical about unknown group that claimed responsibility for the attack on Paris Jewish Center," Associated Press, August 23, 2004.

travelled on the RER Express Métro in the Sarcelles area. They were said to have cut off hair and sliced the clothes of the woman and daubed swastikas on her stomach with markers. The woman had told police that they had attacked her after wrongly identifying her as Jewish. They were also said to have thrown her child to the ground.....[29]

In Binghamton, New York, swastikas and slogans, including "Kill Kikes" and "Zionazi Racist," were found inside the door leading to the Jewish Student Union of the State University. The *New York Times*, November 15, 1989, reported that the perpetrator is the former president of the Jewish Student Union, James Oppenheimer, who led protests in condemning the vandalism.

Such bogus incidents are frequent but are usually undertaken by deranged individual Jews, rather than being Zionist organizational contrivances. However, what is notable is the manner by which Zionists will jump very quickly onto the bandwagon and exploit any such incident without evidence, to maintain the central Zionist myth of pervasive and inherent Gentile anti-Semitism, without which the Zionist enterprise would become quickly bankrupt.

---

29   Charles Brenner, "Woman's swastika ordeal exposed as fantasy," *The Times*, July 14, 2004.

Roots of Present World Conflict

This chapter contends that the present so-called "conflict of civilizations," or "war on terrorism," and the Arab-Israeli conflict have their origins in the covert machinations of the Great War that betrayed the Arabs, prolonged the war, and established a pestilential organism at the center of the Islamic world that will seemingly forever be a cause of conflict.

After the prior century of conflict between the European imperial powers and an agitated Arabia, World War I was an opportunity to forge a perhaps permanently cordial relationship between the West and the Arabs. The Arab leaders were given promises of independence in the fight against the Ottomans.

In October 1916 T.E.Lawrence, an Intelligence operative and one of the few who had a wide knowledge of the region, travelled with the diplomat Sir Ronald Storrs on a mission to Arabia where in June 1916 Husayn ibn 'Alī, *amīr* of Mecca, had proclaimed a revolt against the Turks. Storrs and Lawrence talked with two of the amīr's sons, Abdullah and Feisal, the latter then leading a revolt southwest of Medina. In Cairo, Lawrence urged the funding and equipping of those sheiks willing to revolt against the Turks, with the promise of independence. He was dispatched to Feisal's army as adviser and liaison officer.

However, a backroom deal had been reached between the Zionists and the British War Cabinet. The war was going badly for the Allies, and the only hope was to persuade the USA to enter. On the other had, the Zionists who had placed their hopes in the Kaiser and the Ottoman Sultan for securing Palestine, had been rebuffed. Sultan Abdul Hamid had responded to Zionist leader Theodor Herzl that a Jewish state in Palestine was not agreeable, as his people had "fought for this land and fertilized it with their blood... let the Jews keep their millions."[1] Zionist leaders approached the Kaiser, who was then trying to align with Turkey, the Zionists claiming that a Jewish state in Palestine would become an outpost of German culture.[2] The Kaiser did not acquiesce, and neither did the Czar.[3] The initial response from Britain to Herzl, by Colonial Secretary Joseph Chamberlain, was to support a Jewish state in Kenya.[4]

Despite the opposition of Jamal Pasha, Turkish Commander of Palestine, the Zionists continued to remind the Germans and the Turks of the benefits of a Zionist state in Palestine that could serve as a "counter-weight" to Arab demands for autonomy.[5] Other Zionists believed that Britain was the better option for securing Palestine, and Vladimir Jabotinsky, founder of the Revisionist Zionist movement, formed three Jewish battalions that served with the Royal Fusiliers in Palestine in 1918.[6] This however, does not diminish the Arab support for the Allied war effort, nor the promises that were made by the Allies to the Arabs. As will be seen, the Zionist belittling of Arab sacrifices in the war, under the leadership of T. E. Lawrence, was one of the original smears against the Arab people. Lord Kitchener, British Agent in Egypt and later Secretary of State for War, realized the potential for Arab support against the Turks. On October 31, 1914, Kitchener sent a message to Hussein, Sharif of Mecca and custodian of the Holy Places, pledging British support for Arab independence in return for support of the Allied war effort. The Sharif was cautious, as he did not wish to replace Turkish rule, which allowed a measure of self-government, with that of Western colonialism. At this time the Ottoman Sultan had declared a

---

1   Alfred M. Lilienthal, *The Zionist Connection What Price Peace?* (New York: Dodd, Mead & Co., 1978), 11.

2   One is reminded of the present Zionist claim that Israel is the outpost of "democracy" and of "Western values" in the region.

3   Lilienthal, op. cit., 11.

4   Ibid.

5   Ibid., 13.

6   Ibid.

jihad against the Allies to mobilise Arab support for the war, and while the Sharif feigned support, he sought out the views of Arab nationalist leaders. On May 23, 1915, the Damascus Protocol was formulated by the Arab leaders, calling for independence for all Arab lands other than Aden, and the elimination of foreign privileges, but with a pro-British orientation in terms of trade and defence. Correspondence between Sharif Hussein and Sir Henry McMahon, British Commissioner in Cairo, during 1915 and early 1916, culminated in McMahon's guarantee of British support for independence within the requested boundaries, so long as French interests were not undermined. [7]

With both sides satisfied as to the guarantees, which included a sovereign Palestine, the Arab revolt broke out in the Hejaz on June 5, 1916. With Arab aid, the British were able to repulse the German attempt to take Aden and blockade the Red Sea and the Indian Ocean. This was decisive.[8] The Arabs also diverted significant Turkish forces that had been intended for an attack on General Murray in his advance on Palestine. General Allenby referred to the Arab aid as "invaluable." Arabs suffered much from Turkish vengeance. Tens of thousands of Arabs died of starvation in Palestine and Lebanon because the Turks withheld food. Jamal Pasha, leader of the Turkish forces, recorded that he had to use Turkish forces against Ibn Saud in the Arabian Peninsula, when those troops should have been "defeating the British on the [Suez] Canal and capturing Cairo."[9]

Lawrence in *Seven Pillars of Wisdom* related the importance of the Arab contribution to the Allied war effort, stating that "without Arab help England could not pay the price of winning its Turkish sector. When Damascus fell, the eastern war - probably the whole war - drew to an end." [10] Lawrence stated

---

7   Sami Hadawi, *Bitter Harvest: Palestine 1914-79* (New York: Caravan Books, 1979), 11.

8   Lilienthal, op. cit., 17.

9   Quoted by Lilienthal, ibid., 17.

10   T. E. Lawrence, *Seven Pillars of Wisdom* (London: Black House Publishing,

T.E. Lawrence and Prince Faisal aboard a British warship 1918.

of the Arab revolt that "it was an Arab war waged and led by Arabs for an Arab aim in Arabia."[11] The Arab struggle owed little to British, or any other outside assistance. Lawrence relates in *Seven Pillars* with bitterness and shame the betrayal of the Arabs by his country's leaders after the war:

> For my work on the Arab front I had determined to accept nothing. The Cabinet raised the Arabs to fight for us by definite promises of self-government afterwards. Arabs believe in persons, not in institutions. They saw in me a free agent of the British Government, and demanded from me an endorsement of its written promises. So I had to join the conspiracy, and, for what my word was worth, assured the men of their reward. In our two years' partnership under fire they grew accustomed to believing me and to think my Government, like myself, sincere. In this hope

2013), 666.

11   Ibid., 29.

they performed some fine things, but, of course, instead of being proud of what we did together, I was bitterly ashamed.

It was evident from the beginning that if we won the war these promises would be dead paper, and had I been an honest adviser of the Arabs I would have advised them to go home and not risk their lives fighting for such stuff: but I salved myself with the hope that, by leading these Arabs madly in the final victory I would establish them, with arms in their hands, in a position so assured (if not dominant) that expediency would counsel to the Great Powers a fair settlement of their claims. In other words, I presumed (seeing no other leader with the will and power) that I would survive the campaigns, and be able to defeat not merely the Turks on the battlefield, but my own country and its allies in the council-chamber...[12]

The dismissal of Sir Henry McMahon, British Commissioner in Cairo, whose communications relaying British guarantees had set the stage for the Arab Revolt, confirmed Lawrence's belief in Britain's "essential insincerity" of their promises to the Arabs. This perfidy scarred Lawrence deeply for the rest of his life.

SYKES-PICOT AGREEMENT & BETRAYAL OF THE ARABS

In the Sykes-Picot Agreement of 1916 between Britain and France, "parts" of Palestine would be under international administration upon agreement among the Allies and with the Arabs represented by the Sharif of Mecca.[13] This Anglo-French agreement already had the seeds of duplicity as it gave the two powers control over Iraq, Syria, Lebanon, and Transjordan, reneging on the commitment that had already been given by the British to Sharif Hussein, and without his knowledge. Lord Curzon remarked

---

12 Ibid., 31-32.

13 Hadawi, op. cit., 12.

that the boundary lines drawn up by the Sykes-Picot agreement indicated "gross ignorance" and he assumed that it was never believed the agreement would be implemented. Prime Minister Lloyd George considered the Sykes-Picot Agreement foolish and dishonourable, but it was nonetheless implemented after the Allied victory.[14]

The Bolsheviks in the newly formed Soviet Union, eager to present themselves as the leaders of a world revolt against European colonialism, released the details of the Sykes-Picot Agreement, and the Turks took the matter to the Arabs in February 1918, stating that they were now willing to recognise Arab independence. Hussein sought clarification from Britain, and Lord Balfour replied that: "His Majesty's Government confirms previous pledges respecting the recognition of the independence of the Arab countries."[15] In 1918 Arab leaders in Cairo sought clarification from Britain and the British "Declaration to the Seven" on June 16 confirmed the previous pledge that had been made to Hussein.[16]

BALFOUR DECLARATION

Sir Mark Sykes, the individual responsible for the Sykes-Picot Agreement, approached the British War Cabinet with the suggestion that if Palestine was offered as a Jewish homeland, then Jewish sympathy could be mobilised for the Allied cause, and the USA might be induced to join the conflict. U.S. Supreme Court Justice Louis Brandeis used his influence to induce President Woodrow Wilson to adopt an interventionist policy.[17] In return for Zionist support the British reneged on their promises to the Arabs and secretly promised to support a Jewish homeland in Palestine; a guarantee that became known as the Balfour Declaration. This scheme prolonged the war, which

---

14   Ibid., 12-13.

15   Lilienthal, op. cit., 18.

16   Ibid.

17   Hadawi, op. cit., 13.

might have been settled in a more equitable manner towards Germany and Austro-Hungary and hence would surely have changed the whole course of history.

Samuel Landman, a leading Zionist in Britain, related that several attempts had been made to bring the USA into the World War by appealing to "influential Jewish opinion," but these had failed. James A. Malcolm, adviser to the British Government on Eastern Affairs, who knew that President Wilson was under the influence of Chief Justice Brandies, convinced Sykes, and then Picot and Goût of the French Embassy in London, that the only way to get the USA into the war was to secure the support of American Jewry with the promise of Allied support for a Jewish state in Palestine.[18]

Landman states that after reaching a "gentleman's agreement" with the Zionist leaders, cable facilities were given to these Zionist leaders through the War Office, Foreign Office, and British Embassies and Legations, to communicate the agreement to Zionists throughout the world. Landman comments that "the change of official and public opinion as reflected in the American press in favour of joining the Allies in the War, was as gratifying as it was surprisingly rapid."[19] Hence, the real power of the Zionists, even at that stage, over the press and politics, was evident, as noted by Landman. Of the subsequent Balfour Declaration, Landman states:

> The main consideration given by the Jewish people represented at the time by the leaders of the Zionist Organisation was their help in bringing President Wilson to the aid of the Allies... The prior Sykes-Picot Treaty

---

18 Samuel Landman, *Great Britain, the Jews and Palestine* (London: New Zionist Press, 1936), 2-3. Landman was Honorary Secretary of the Joint Zionist Council of the United Kingdom, 1912; Joint Editor of *The Zionist* 1913-1914; Solicitor and Secretary for the Zionist Organisation 1917-1922; and adviser to the New Zionist Organisation, ca. 1930s.

19 Landman, ibid., 3-4.

Foreign Office,
November 2nd, 1917.

Dear Lord Rothschild,

I have much pleasure in conveying to you, on behalf of His Majesty's Government, the following declaration of sympathy with Jewish Zionist aspirations which has been submitted to, and approved by, the Cabinet

"His Majesty's Government view with favour the establishment in Palestine of a national home for the Jewish people, and will use their best endeavours to facilitate the achievement of this object, it being clearly understood that nothing shall be done which may prejudice the civil and religious rights of existing non-Jewish communities in Palestine, or the rights and political status enjoyed by Jews in any other country"

I should be grateful if you would bring this declaration to the knowledge of the Zionist Federation.

Letter from Lord Arthur Balfour to Lord Walter Rothschild, the head of the Zionist Federation expressing British support for the establishment of a Zionist state in Palestine.

of 1916, according to which Northern Palestine was to be politically detached and included in Syria (French sphere) so that the Jewish National Home should comprise the whole of Palestine in accordance with the promise previously made to them for their services by the British, Allied and American Governments and to give full effect to the Balfour Declaration, the terms of which had been settled and known to all Allied and associated belligerents, including the Arabs, before they were made public.[20]

The contention of Landman and other Zionists that these dealings between the Zionists and the Allies to hand Palestine over to the Zionists were known to the Arabs, is nonsense, but has remained a basis of pro-Israeli propaganda. Even the Balfour Declaration refers only to British support for a Jewish homeland in Palestine, so long as it does not intrude upon the rights of the Palestinians. As shown, above, the Arab leaders would not countenance a Jewish homeland in Palestine, even to the limited extent deceptively stated by Balfour. Landman refers to promises of "the whole of Palestine" being made to the Zionists. The Declaration unequivocally states no more and no less that:

> His Majesty's Government view with favour the establishment in Palestine of a National Home for the Jewish People, and will use their best endeavours to facilitate the achievement of that object, it being clearly understood that nothing shall be done which may prejudice the civil and religious rights of existing non-Jewish communities in Palestine, or the rights and political status enjoyed by the Jews in any other country.[21]

The British Commander in Palestine, D. G. Hogarth, was instructed to assure Hussein that any settlement of Jews in Palestine would not be allowed to act in detriment to the Palestinians. Hussein for his part was willing to allow Jews to settle in Palestine and allow them ready access to the Holy Places, but would not accept a Jewish state. Hogarth was to relate that the promises being made to both Arabs and Jews simultaneously were not reconcilable.[22]

---

20   Ibid., 4.

21   Lord Balfour to Lord Rothschild, November 2, 1917.

22   Lilienthal, op. cit., 18-19.

These machinations were confirmed by Lloyd George to the Palestine Royal Commission in 1937, the report of which states that George told the commission that if the Allies supported a Jewish homeland in Palestine the Zionist leaders had promised to "rally Jewish sentiment and support throughout the world to the allied cause. They kept their word."[23] Even after the Bolsheviks revealed these secret agreements, the Arabs continued to fight, due to Allied assurances that neither Sykes-Picot nor the Balfour Declaration "would undermine the promises that had been made to them." Among the numerous reiterations of Allied support for the Arab cause, The Anglo-French Declaration of November 9, 1918 plainly stated that France and Britain would support setting up "indigenous governments and administrations in Syria (which included Palestine) and Mesopotamia (Iraq)."[24] With such assurances the Arab fight against the Turks was of crucial importance to the Allies.

JAMES A. MALCOLM

The memoir of James A. Malcolm, adviser to the British Government on Eastern Affairs, on the Balfour Declaration, confirms all of Landman's claims.[25] Malcolm states that his father was of Armenian stock, the family having settled centuries previously in Persia, where they were closely associated with the Sassoons, the opium trading dynasty that became a power in British politics. The Malcolm family also served as liaison between the local Jewish community and another Jewish luminary, Sir Moses Montefiore in England. When Malcolm arrived in London in 1881 for his education he was placed under the guardianship of Sir Albert Sassoon, and came into contact with Zionists at an early stage. Malcolm acted officially for Armenian interests in the Holy Land in liaising with the British and French Governments, and was in 'frequent' contact

---

23   Palestine Royal Commission Report cited by Hadawi, op. cit., 14.

24   Hadawi, ibid., 15.

25   James A. Malcolm, "Origins of the Balfour Declaration: Dr. Weizmann's Contribution" (London, 1944). The entire document can be read online at: http://www.mailstar.net/malcolm.html

with the British Cabinet Office, the Foreign Office and the War Office, the French and other allied Embassies in London, and met with French authorities in Paris.[26] These responsibilities brought Malcolm 'into close relation with Sir Mark Sykes, Under Secretary of the War Cabinet for the Near East, and with M. Gout, his opposite number at the Quai d'Orsay, and M. Georges Picot, Counsellor at the French Embassy in London'.[27]

It is here that Malcolm introduces one of the early Zionist slurs against the Arabs in justifying his proposition to Sir Mark Sykes that the USA could be brought into the war if the British promised Palestine to the Jews as a national homeland. Efforts to secure Jewish support in the USA had so far failed because of the "very pro-German tendency among the wealthy American Jewish bankers and bond issuing houses, nearly all of German origin, and among Jewish journalists who took their cue from them."[28] It was then that the whole Middle East imbroglio to the present was hatched by Malcolm with Sykes et al. Malcolm writes:

> I informed him [Sykes] that there was a way to make American Jewry thoroughly pro-Ally, and make them conscious that only an Allied victory could be of permanent benefit to Jewry all over the world. I said to him, "You are going the wrong way about it. The well-to-do English Jews you meet and the Jewish clergy are not the real leaders of the Jewish people. You have overlooked what the call of nationality means. Do you know of the Zionist Movement?" Sir Mark admitted ignorance of this movement and I told him something about it and concluded by saying, "You can win the sympathy of the Jews everywhere, in one way only, and that way is by offering to try and secure Palestine for them."[29]

---

26   James A. Malcolm, ibid., 2.

27   Ibid.

28   Ibid.

29   Ibid.

In a lengthy note Malcolm disparages the Arab Revolt and its contribution to the Allies, which contradicts the accounts by Lawrence in Seven Pillars, and the assessments of the British military leaders in that theatre of war. Malcolm writes:

> Early in the War the Arabs and their British friends represented that they were in a position to render very great assistance in the Middle East. It was on the strength of these representations and pretensions that the promise contained in the MacMahon letter to King Hussein was made. It was subsequently found that the Arabs were unable to "deliver the goods" and the so-called "Revolt in the Desert" was but a mirage. Their effort, at its maximum, never exceeded seven hundred tribesmen, but frequently less than 300, who careered about the desert some hundreds of miles behind the fighting line reporting for duty on "pay day." For this they received a remuneration of £200,000 per month in actual gold, which was delivered to them at Akabah. This sum represented a remuneration for every one of the tribesmen of more than the pay of a British Field Marshal. Lawrence himself made no secret of his profound disappointment with the Arab failure to carry out their engagements. That Hussein and Feisal were not in a position to give any effective help was afterwards made abundantly clear by the fact that Ibn Saud was easily able to drive Hussein out of his kingdom.[30]

It should be noted that Malcolm claims that Lawrence was "profoundly disappointed" with the Arabs. As Seven Pillars, and Lawrence's lifelong bitterness at the betrayal of the Arabs, shows, Malcolm is writing disinformation on the Arabs that has since become staple fare dished up by the Zionists and their Gentile apologists.

The acclaimed British military historian Captain Basil Liddell

---

30   Ibid., note on page 2.

Hart,[31] Chief Military Commentator with the Allied Forces during World War I, reiterates the effectiveness of the Arab Revolt and its contribution to the Allied war effort:

> In the crucial weeks while Allenby's stroke was being prepared and during its delivery, nearly half the Turkish forces south of Damascus were distracted by the Arab forces ... What the absence of these forces meant to the success of Allenby's stroke, it is easy to see. Nor did the Arab operation end when it had opened the way. For in the issue, it was the Arabs who almost entirely wiped out the Fourth Army, the still intact forces that might have barred the way to final victory. The wear and tear, the bodily and mental strain on men and material applied by the Arabs... prepared the way that produced their (the Turks) defeat.[32]

Clubb and Evans in their paper on Lawrence at the Paris Peace Conference sum up the importance of the Arab Revolt: "Thanks to Lawrence and the Arabs, the British not only successfully invaded Palestine in the autumn of 1917 but continued north into Jerusalem, reaching the city on 11 December. From there they advanced into Damascus in September 1918, right into the very heart of Syria."[33]

Feisal's small army adopted guerrilla methods that tied down the Turkish army, hitting bridges and trains. On July 6, 1917, after a two month march, Arab forces captured Aqaba, on the northern tip of the Red Sea. Thereafter, Lawrence sought to coordinate the Arab actions with General Allenby's advance towards Jerusalem. In November Lawrence was captured at Dar'ā by the Turks while reconnoitring the area dressed as a Bedouin. Recognized, he was brutalised by his captors before escaping.

---

31   Liddell Hart, *Lawrence of Arabia* (New York: Da Capo Press, 1989 [1935]).

32   Quoted by Hadawi, op. cit., 16.

33   Andrew Clubb and C. T. Evans, "T. E. Lawrence and the Arab Cause at the Paris Peace Conference," http://www.ctevans.net/Versailles/Diplomats/Lawrence/Background.html

In August Lawrence participated in the victory parade through Jerusalem, then returned to Feisal's forces who were pressing north. By now Lawrence had become Lieutenant Colonel and had been awarded the Distinguished Service Order.

The Arab army reached Damascus in October 1918. Lawrence had successfully established a government in Damascus, which was to serve as the centre of a unified Arab state under King Feisal. Having established order in Syria he handed rulership to Feisal. However, the Sykes-Picot Agreement between France and Britain had mandated Syria as part of the French domain. The Government that Lawrence had established for Feisal as the centre of a unified Arab state was deposed by French forces with much bloodshed. Feisal was given Iraq. A united Arab nation, thanks to Anglo-French perfidy and Zionist machinations, was not to be. History, as we know today, was shaped in the backrooms by lobbyists, politicians and diplomats in cynical disregard for the Arabs.

Lawrence returned to Britain shortly prior to the Armistice. At a royal audience on October 30 1918, he politely declined the Order of the Bath and the Distinguished Service Order that was to be awarded to him by the King, leaving George V, as the King was to state, "holding the box in my hand." Lawrence was demobilized as a Lieutenant Colonel in July 1919.

That year Lawrence, dressed in Bedouin garb, attended the Paris Peace Conference as a delegate in the entourage of Prince Feisal, with the approval of the British Government. He vainly lobbied for Arab independence, and against the French mandate that was imposed over Syria and Lebanon. Clubb and Evans:

> In the early days of the conference Lawrence and Feisal sought to present their case for Arab independence anywhere anytime, to anyone who would listen, delegates and pressmen alike, in private rooms and tea salons. They found willing audiences as people were curious about the

mysterious yet regal Arab and his English paladin. When not courting their audiences, Feisal and Lawrence busied themselves preparing the statement that would be delivered at the conference.[34]

However, the French attempted to waylay and thwart Feisal at every turn, and the British insisted that Palestine was not part of any arrangement that had been made with the Arabs during the war.[35] While the French were insistent on the primacy of the Sykes-Picot Agreement in their dealings with the Arabs, the British had made contrary promises to different interests, including contrary statements on the status of Palestine. The Anglo-India Office (which had never been in favour of British support for an Arab Revolt) regarded the presence of Lawrence at Paris as "malign," and that his views were not in accord with British policy. Lawrence was kept out of the British delegation that met again in Paris in 1919 to discuss the issue of Syria and France with Feisal. When Feisal returned to Damascus he declared Syria to be independent on March 7, 1920 and he was declared King of Syria, which included Palestine and Lebanon. The French forces attacked and Feisal was deposed on July 24, 1920, forced into exile in Italy,[36] but was installed as King of Mesopotamia in 1921 with the support of Britain.[37]

Arab support for the Allied cause during World War I, and the promises that were made to the Arabs, have been all but forgotten. As recent history indicates, the Arabs have had congenial relations with the West, and have been met with duplicity and betrayal. Now the West is reaping what its perfidious politicians had sown a century ago. There was nothing "inevitable" about this "clash of civilizations." Goodwill existed during World War

---

34 Ibid.

35 Ibid., "Politics gets in the way of a Settlement'."

36 Ibid., "A Death in the Family and a Parting of Ways," http://www.ctevans. net/Versailles/Diplomats/Lawrence/Paper.html

37 Ibid., "Postscript," http://www.ctevans.net/Versailles/Diplomats/Lawrence/ Postscript.html

I and was trashed for the sake of Zionism. Sycophancy towards Israel has assured ever since that accord between the Arabs and the West has been scuttled.

German Nationalist Jews

The presence of many Germans of Jewish descent in the German armed forces of the Third Reich came as a revelation to many. The recent book *Hitler's Jewish Soldiers: The Untold Story of Nazi Racial Laws and Men of Jewish Descent in the German Military*,[1] by Bryan Mark Rigg, shows that up to 150,000 part-Jews fought for the Third Reich, including those of high rank.

These part-Jews or Mischlinge were part of a graduated classification of those of Jewish descent under the Reich Citizenship Law, which determined to what extent Jewish heritage affected one's rights under the National Socialist regime. The designation of several types of Mischlinge was proclaimed in 1935. Half Jews who did not follow Judaism or who were not married to a Jewish person on September 15, 1935, were classified as Mischlinge of the first degree. One-quarter Jews were Mischlinge of the second degree. While the Yellow Star of David was required to be worn by Jews after September 14, 1941, Mischlinge were exempt.[2]

However, less recognised than the Mischlinge and Hitler's so-called "Jewish soldiers" were the Jews, including many World War I Jewish veterans, who were German nationalists.

MARXISTS AND ZIONISTS WERE
ABERRATIONS AMONG GERMAN JEWS

German Jews were the most assimilated of Europe's Jewish populations. Most identified themselves entirely with the German nation, people, and culture.[3] Jews who were Marxists

---

1   Bryan Mark Rigg, *The Untold Story of Nazi Racial Laws and Men of Jewish Descent in the German Military* (University Press of Kansas, 2002).

2   Raul Hilberg, *Documents of Destruction* (London: W H Allen, 1972), pp. 18-24.

3   Amos Elon, *The Pity of It All: A History of the Jews in Germany 1743-1933*

and subversives of other types, disparaging not only Germany, but also traditional morality, were among the most conspicuous and vocal of Germany's Jews. Hence, they were ready subjects for the anti-Semitic writers and agitators in Germany who could point to Jews as being in the forefront of a myriad of anti-German movements and ideologies that proliferated especially in the aftermath of World War I. Many Jews fought with distinction during World War I. Of the 96,000 Jews who fought with the Germany army, 10,000 were volunteers. 35,000 Jews were decorated, and 23,000 were promoted. Among the 168 Jews who volunteered as flyers, Lieutenant D R Frankl received the *Pour le mérite*. Twelve thousand Jewish soldiers died in combat.[4] It is from such Jews that a new seldom recognized German nationalist movement emerged.

The prominent Jewish businessman and foreign minister (1922), Walther Rathenau, urged German Jews to become German and "not to follow the flag of their philo-Semitic protectors any longer." There should be "the conscious self-education and adaptation of the Jews to the expectations of the gentiles." He further repudiated "mimicry" and sought rather "the shedding of tribal attitudes which, whether they be good or bad in themselves, are known to be odious to our countrymen, and the replacement of these attributes by more appropriate ones." The result should not be "Germans by imitation" but "Jews of German character and education." Furthermore, he advocated a willed change in the Jewish physiognomy and way of bearing, to physically renew the Jews over the course of several generations, away from the "unathletic build, narrow shoulders, clumsy feet, and sloppy roundish shape." In character the German Jews, noted Rathenau, rarely steered a middle course between "wheedling subservience and vile arrogance."[5]

(Allen Lane, 2003).

4   "Die Gangbarsten Antisemitischen Lügeneiniges zur Widerlegung," Abwhr-Blätter, XLII (October 1932), cited by Hilberg, op. cit., p. 11.

5   Walther Rathenau, "Hear, O Israel!", Zukunft, No, 18, March 16, 1897; in Paul R Mendes-Flohr and Jehuda Reinharz (editors), *The Jew in the Modern World: A*

Walther Rathenau was a German industrialist, writer, and statesman who served as Foreign Minister of Germany during the Weimar Republic.

Rathenau was also hostile to the influx of Jews from the East after World War I, a hostility that was widespread among the old established German Jewish population, and forcefully expressed by the German nationalist Jews. To them the Eastern Jews were the living stereotypes of anti-Semitic propaganda. Unlike the German-Jews they maintained their separatism, spoke Yiddish, the older Jews dressing in their conspicuous garb, while the younger ones were susceptible to Zionism and revolutionary movements. Their tendency to congregate in urban areas gave the impression of more numbers than there were, living a ghetto existence of their own making. These were the Ostjuden; beggars and peddlers. A Jewish exhibition on the Ostjuden states of the German-Jewish attitude that "most regarded the *Ostjuden* as a hindrance to German-Jewish integration, and many aid organizations therefore encouraged their settlement abroad.... Whether contemptuous or compassionate, responses to the

Documentary History (New York: Oxford University Press, 1980), p. 232.

plight of East European Jewry demonstrate the extent to which German Jews had dissolved Jewish national moorings."[6]

From conservative opinion, Oswald Spengler regarded Rathenau with esteem, a regard that Rathenau returned.[7] Rathenau's assassination by members of the Rightist paramilitary Freikorps in 1922 represents perhaps the first shot in the tragedy of German-Jews who regarded themselves above all as Germans during the Weimar and Third Reich eras. Jews being widely associated with Communism and the new Soviet Union, it was assumed that Rathenau's signing of the Treaty of Rapallo with the Soviet Union was a contrivance between Jewish capitalists (represented by Rathenau) and Jewish-Bolsheviks. Rather, this was a measure of realpolitik that was designed to make gains for Germany in bypassing the Versailles diktat, and was a formative move in what became a pro-Soviet orientation among much of the German Nationalist Right, especially with the rise of Stalin, a course that Spengler had himself suggested the possibility of an Eastern orientation for Germany.[8] As for the Treaty of Rapallo, Trotsky was so aggravated by what he saw as concessions to Germany that he resigned as commissar for foreign affairs, rather than continue negotiations with "German imperialists."

The Jews of anti-Semitic stereotype were conspicuous. They were guilty of playing into the hands of uncompromising anti-Semites, which also suited the agenda of the then insignificant Zionist movement in Germany. Indeed, from the birth of the

---

6   "The Ghetto comes to Germany: *Ostjuden* as Welfare Cause," *East European Jews in the German-Jewish Imagination*, Committee on Jewish Studies, University of Chicago Library, http://www.lib.uchicago.edu/e/webexhibits/ RosenbergerEastAndWest/TheGhettoComesToGermany.html

7   Spengler to Rathenau, May 11, 1918; Rathenau to Spengler, May 15, 1918, in *Spengler Letters 1913-1936* (London: George Allen and Unwin, 1966), pp. 62-63.

8   Oswald Spengler, "The Two Faces of Russia and Germany's Eastern Problems," *Politische Schriften*, Munich, February 14, 1922, cited in: K R Bolton, *Thoughts and Perspectives Volume Ten: Spengler*, Troy Southgate, editor (London: Black Front Press, 2012), p. 124.

Zionist movement, there has always been a symbiosis between anti-Semitism and Zionism to the point where Zionist agencies have provided the mainstay for neo-Nazi groups.[9] As will be seen here, briefly, the same symbiosis existed between the National Socialist party and the Zionists in Germany while both repudiated the German nationalists of Jewish descent. Until then, Zionism had received such opposition from Jews in Germany that Herzl's original plans to hold the First Zionist Congress in Munich had to be changed to Basel.[10]

WEIMAR JEWISH INFLUENCES

What then were the grievances of Germans against Jewish influences on the German political and cultural body? While the reaction of the "philo-Semites" mentioned by Rathenau, insisted then, as now, that Jews are eternally guiltless, the anti-Semitic movement that had been building in Germany, and was marked by a cultural basis that was most famously articulated by Richard Wagner,[11] objected to the Jewish over-representation in movements that were subversive to traditional morality, which also included the economic realm.[12] Weimar seemed to be the regime of the Jews.

A publication of the German League of Anti-Communist Associations, which appears to have been a National Socialist organisation, is instructive as to the period. According to this, Jewish doctors were in the forefront of campaigns and legal defenses in favour of abortion, heralded by the abortion case of two Jewish doctors, Friedrich Wolf and Kienle-Jakubowitz,

---

9   K R Bolton, "The Symbiosis Between Anti-Semitism and Zionism," *Foreign Policy Journal*, November 1, 2010, http://www.foreignpolicyjournal. com/2010/11/01/the-symbiosis-between-anti-semitism-zionism/

10   "The First Zionist Congress and the Basel Program," Jewish Virtual Library, http://www.jewishvirtuallibrary.org/jsource/Zionism/First_Cong_&_Basel_ Program.html

11   Richard Wagner, *Judaism in Music*, 1850, http://users.belgacom.net/ wagnerlibrary/prose/wagjuda.htm

12   Werner Sombart (1911), *The Jews and Modern Capitalism* (New Brunswick, New Jersey: Transaction Books, 1982).

which was backed by a support committee including many Jews, including Dr Mangus Hirschfeld, founder of the Institute for Sexual Science, and therefore one of the pioneers of sexology.[13] Much of what was deemed indecent then, behind the façade of "science", was also linked with Communist groups. Jews were prominent in all manner of Leftist parties,[14] and in the press, where they ridiculed the war veterans and any notion of patriotism.[15]

NATIONALIST GERMAN JEWS

Max Naumann, chairman of the League of German Nationalist Jews, said of the Jewish influence in the press in 1926:

> Anyone who is condemned to read every day a number of Jewish papers and periodicals, written by Jews for Jews, must on occasion feel an increased distaste, amounting to physical nausea, for this incredible amount of self-complacency, of slimy stuff about "honour", and exaggeration of the duty to "combat anti-Semitism" which is understood in these circles in the sense that, at the slightest reference, the sword should be drawn if any Jew whatever is meant.[16]

Disingenuously, the German League of Anti-Communist Associations, quoting Dr Naumann, states of his League of German Nationalist Jews that "unfortunately this association did not succeed in acquiring any influence." They then state, "It has not occurred at all to the majority of the Jews to adapt themselves to the forms of their German hosts..."[17]

Most German Jews were acculturated. What soon transpired

---

13 *Jewish Domination of Weimar Germany 1919-1932* (German League of Anti-Communist Associations (Berlin: Eckart-Verlag, 1933), p. 12.

14 Ibid., pp. 21-29.

15 Ibid., pp. 15-16.

16 Max Naumann, 1926, cited in *Jewish Domination of Weimar Germany*, ibid., p. 15.

17 Ibid.

is that the National Socialists were as avid as the hitherto inconsequential Zionists in Germany that German Jews should not become "good Germans." Dr Naumann's association of German Jewish nationalists was banned while the Zionist agencies in Germany were not only permitted to continue operating but enjoyed close relations with the new regime.

Naumann, a lawyer, had served as a Captain in the Bavarian Reserve during World War I,[18] and was awarded the Iron Cross First and Second Class. The League of German Nationalist Jews, Verband Nationaldeutscher Juden (VNJ) was founded in 1921. Naumann and his followers held that the Ostjuden migrants were responsible for anti-Semitism. It was a widely held opinion. Furthermore, he stated that when the authorities did not act against such Jewish agitators and subversives, loyal German Jews were duty-bound to do so, in their interests and in German interests, which were one.

In 1920 Naumann and three other colleagues called on Ludwig Holländer, head of the primary German-Jewish organization, Centralverein, of which Naumann was a member, to express concern that the organization encouraged Jews to make political decisions based on Jewish rather than German interests. Naumann was a member of the right-of-center German People's Party, and considered the Centralverein to be favoring other parties. It is notable that the Centralverein, like Naumann, was opposed to Zionism, and Holländer appealed to these common sentiments, however an invitation from Holländer for Naumann to write an article on his concerns fell through, as the article was regarded as too partisan in favor of the German People's Party.[19]

Naumann regarded this rebuff as proof that the Centralverein supported the Democratic Party, and he began to oppose the organization for what he considered its party political partisanship.

---

18   Donald L Niewyk, *The Jews in Weimar Germany* (New Brunswick: Transaction Publishers, 2001), p. 165.

19   Ibid.

An article written by Naumann for the People's Party Rhineland newspaper, Kölnische Zeitung, entitled "Concerning German Nationalist Jews," and reprinted as a pamphlet, late in 1920, laid out Naumann's doctrine. Here Naumann explained three types of German-Jews: (1) The Zionists, whose proselytising among the youth demoralised the German-Jewish community and whose international connections seemed to justify claims of an international Jewish conspiracy; (2) The great majority of German nationalist Jews whose standpoint in politics was always German and never Jewish; and (3) an amorphous group whose loyalties were divided between German and Jewish interests.[20]

Of the German nationalist Jews, the doctrine that Naumann claimed for them has its roots in the German romanticism of Fichte, Herder, et al, in defining a nation as a matter of common consciousness rather than common blood. In this respect the National Socialists were a nationalist departure from the origin of German nationalism, more akin to the racial theosophy that arose in Austro-Hungary prior to World War I, while Naumann's concept of nationalism seems to have been more in accord with that German national tradition.

The third group, which Naumann referred to as the "in-betweeners" (Zwischenschichtler) he regarded as being the real support base of the Centralverein, and the outlook included a hyper sensitivity to "anti-Semitism", including justifiable criticism of Jews.[21] The reaction of the Centralverein was dismissive and they claimed also to represent "German nationalist Jews." Naumann responded that the Centralverein after twenty-seven years had been a failure both in negating the causes of anti-Semitism and in forming a German identity among Jews. They had failed to respond to the challenge of the influx of Ostjuden, whom Naumann described as "the dangerous guest."[22]

---

20   Ibid., p. 166.

21   Ibid., p. 167.

22   Max Naumann, *Vom nationaldeuschten Juden* (1920), cited by Niewyk, ibid.

In responses to the failure of Naumann and the Centralverein to reach agreement, Naumann and eighty-eight others founded the League of German Nationalist Jews, Verband nationaldeutscher Juden (VNJ) on March 20, 1921.[23] The League was vehemently opposed to Marxists and other subversive, anti-patriotic and pacifistic tenancies among Jews, to Zionism and to extending support to the Ostjuden, whose presence fostered anti-Semitism. To the VNJ, the Eastern Jews gravitated to communism and Zionism and other organizations and doctrines that "stand in opposition to everything German." These foreign Jews were also involved in speculative capitalism.[24] Their actions had brought reaction against all Jews in Germany, and it was the duty of German nationalist Jews to fight these interlopers when the police would not or could not.[25]

The German Nationalist Jews actively opposed Zionist propaganda, and organized a boycott of a film on Palestine in 1924. In Breslau they persuaded the owner of the movie house to cancel the second screening of the film stating that the money it raised was destined for an English-held land, and was therefore unpatriotic. In 1926 the "Naumannites", as they were called, sponsored a lecture tour by an ex-Zionist, Robert Peiper, on the theme "The Truth About Palestine."[26] Naumann urged Zionists in Germany to reject German citizenship, and declare themselves a "national minority," as the claims of "anti-Semites" that Germany was being taken over by Jews would seem justified, and there might come a time when they would have that status forced upon them under less favourable circumstances.[27]

Naumann advocated that Jews support patriotic parties regardless of the anti-Semitism of those parties, and that the example

---

23 Niewykj, ibid.

24 Max Naumann, "Dennoch!", 1922, cited by Niewyk, ibid., p. 170.

25 Max Naumann, 1923, cited by Niewyk, ibid.

26 Niewyk, ibid., p. 171.

27 Max Naumann, *Von Zionisten und Jüdisch-nationalen* (Berlinm, 1921), pp. 26-48; cited by Niewyk, ibid.

of Jewish German patriotism was the best way of combating anti-Semitism: i.e. by countering the source within the Jews themselves, rather than defending Jews regardless of their actions. As seen previously, it is a view that seems akin to that advocated by Walther Rathenau. Therefore the VNJ, without endorsing any party, prompted Jews to vote on purely German interests.[28]

In 1925 the youth wing of the League's Munich branch came to the defense of General Ludendorff, implicated as a leader of the Munich putsch with Hitler, when the General had been criticized by the Centralverein, although the League leadership was not supportive of Ludendorff.[29] The League also combated "anti-Semitism" within the German People's Party, but the crucial differences between these German Nationalist Jews and other Jewish organizations was that it recognized that Jews were not invariably guiltless of the charges levelled against them for disloyalty and subversion, and advocated working with these "anti-Semitic" parties, rather than confronting them. Although at least two League members remained members of the Centralverein committee, the Centralverein and the VNJ were increasingly antagonistic towards each other, and "the liberal Jewish press in Germany was virtually unanimous in concluding that the Naumannites were 'Jewish anti-Semites'", states Niewyk, who remarks that the Jewish leadership were fearful of alienating the socialist movement. The Centralverein went on the offensive in opposing Naumann, who responded by libel suites against leaders of the organization.[30] The Centralverein was largely successful in preventing Naumann from advocating among German Jews. In 1930 the VNJ's "German List" of candidates for the Berlin Jewish community's representative assembly drew less that 2% of the vote. The circulation of the VNJ's newspaper never exceeded 6,000 according to Niewyk.[31]

---

28 Ibid., p. 172.

29 Ibid.

30 Ibid., p. 173.

31 Ibid., p. 175.

From 1932 the Naumannites gained renewed attention by focusing on the anti-Semitism of the National Socialist party, and the legitimacy of the National Socialists as German patriots. The Naumannites saw an "idealistic essence" in National Socialism, which was obscured by racism, and considered that Hitler would outgrow Judaeophobia. The Naumannites advocated that Jews should join non-Nazi nationalist organizations, which could nonetheless aid the Nazis, and perhaps diminish the influence of the more vitriolic of the anti-Semites. Naumann supported the "German socialism" that had been a feature of the Right, and not only among the National Socialists. Oswald Spengler for example had advocated as a type of "ethical socialism" that would place the German state above class and other factional divisions.[32] Like Spengler, Naumann opposed German Social Democracy and Marxism, and was concerned at the number of Jews involved with the Left.[33]

In 1933 Naumann endorsed the German National People's Party, now allied with the National Socialists, hoping that such an alliance would moderate some of the National Socialist views.[34]

It is here relevant to note that in the 1932 presidential election the National People's Party candidate, standing against Hitler, was Lieutenant Colonel Theodor Duesterberg, second in command of the monarchist-nationalist veterans' organization, the Stahlhelm. Duesterberg was attacked by Goebbels' newspaper *Der Angriff* because of his Jewish background. Officers of the Stahlhelm responded that "if Duesterberg is of Jewish origin the absurdity of racial discrimination is proved inasmuch as Duesterberg was an outstanding officer on the war front and was delegated by true Germans as their candidate for president of the German republic."[35]

---

32 Oswald Spengler, *Prussianism and Socialism*, 1920, http://archive.org/details/PrussianismAndSocialism

33 Niewyk, op. cit., p. 175.

34 Ibid., p. 176.

35 "Duesterberg, Stahlhelm Leader, Candidate for President, says he is of Jewish

While Duesterberg claims he was unaware of his Jewish background it is the supportive reaction of his fellow veterans that is of interest, while Ludendorff, like the Nazis, denounced him, which resulted in his withdrawal from the second run-off of the presidential race. While Duesterberg resigned from his position in the Stahlhelm following his defeat in the presidential elections, and the revelations as to his Jewish background, his resignation was rejected. The Jewish Telegraphic Agency reported at the time:

> Leaders of the Stahlhelm have labelled as absurd that racial descent should be regarded as in any way inimical to Duesterberg's continuation in office and have not hesitated to denounce the Nazi campaign against him on this score as deliberate provocation. For this reason, the praesidium of the Stahlhelm did not accept the proffered resignation of Duesterberg and prevailed upon him to remain in office. Leaders of the Steel Helmet are not desirous of acknowledging that the Nazi campaign against Duesterberg has had any repercussions in the Steel Helmet camp. This is said to explain the silence which is being maintained on what transpired at the meeting of the praesidium.[36]

The Stahlhelm further stated of Duesterberg:

> We are aware that Duesterberg's father in 1813 volunteered as a soldier for the liberation of Germany and was awarded the iron cross. Duesterberg himself was wounded in the Expedition to China.[37] Subsequently he fought in the world war in the most dangerous places.[38]

Origin," Jewish Telegraphic Agency, September 7, 1932.

36 "Confirm Proffer of Duesterberg Resignation; Stahlhelm Prevails on him to remain," Jewish Telegraphic Agency, September 9, 1932.

37 Boxer Rebellion.

38 "Stahlhlem Headquarters reveal Duesterberg Became Ill when Jewish Origin Revealed," Jewish Telegraphic Agency, September 14, 1932. (Duesterberg had a nervous breakdown as a result of the vitriolic Nazi campaign against him).

Although being offered, and refusing, a position in Hitler's first Cabinet, Duesterberg was arrested during the Night of the Long Knives in 1934 and interned at Dachau, but was released, dying in 1950.

GERMAN JEWISH NATIONALIST YOUTH ORGANIZATIONS

In 1932 a three-way split between Leftist and Rightist factions in the German Jewish youth organization Kameraden resulted in the formation of the Black Squad (Schwarzes Fähnlein) by 400 conservative-nationalist members. The Black Squad sought to revive the medieval Teutonic martial ethos.

In 1933 a young Jewish theologian, Dr Hans-Joachim Schoeps, established a 150 member "German Vanguard – German Jewish Followers" also devoted to martial values. In April 1933 the Black Squad and the German Vanguard aligned with the VNJ and the National League of Jewish Frontline Veterans into an Action Committee of Jewish Germans that hoped to negotiate with the National Socialist regime on a new dispensation for German Jews. This organisation, like the VNJ and the other German Jewish nationalist groups, was outlawed by the National Socialist regime in 1935.[39]

Schoeps adhered to the German Conservative Revolution movement that emerged in the aftermath of World War I. Among the influences on Schoeps from this milieu were Stefan George, Ernst Jünger, Arthur Moeller van den Bruck, Ernst Niekisch, Carl Schmitt, Oswald Spengler, Otto Strasser, and others. Schoeps never repudiated his Rightist sentiments in the post-1945 era, writing in 1960 that Spengler's Prussian socialism remained valid.[40]

---

39 Niewyk, op. cit., p. 176.

40 Richard Faber, *German Conscious Judaism and Jewish conscious Germans - The Historical and Political Theologian Hans-Joachim Schoeps* (King & Neumann, 2008), pp. 103.

Schoeps sought an accord between patriotic German Jews and National Socialism, writing in his newspaper The Vanguard that National Socialism can renew Germany, and that German Jews should be brought under a new organization representing them as German patriots.[41]

GERMAN JEWISH NATIONALIST WAR VETERANS

The German Jewish World War veterans had their own association, Reichsbund juedischer Frontsoldaten (RjF), that was, like the League of German Nationalist Jews, opposed to Zionism, Marxism and all other manifestations of subversion. From 1930 until 1934 Ludwig Freud, general secretary of the RjF, "gave lectures all over Germany with titles such as 'Community of the Frontlines – Community of the Volk' to audiences of non-Jewish veterans." They also opposed the influx of Ostjuden.[42]

RjF was founded in 1919 to counter claims that German Jews had shirked their military duty during the World War. Despite its repudiation of this basic National Socialist allegation, the RjF, like the Naumannites, hoped for an accommodation with the Hitler regime for German-Jews. Generally, fascism had arisen throughout Europe in the aftermath of the world war primarily from war veterans. It should be of no surprise that fascism also emerged from Jewish war veterans, and that Jewish veterans also joined fascist movements, especially in Italy where by the mid-1930s one-third of the adult Jewish population were members of the National Fascist Party, and 230 Jews participated in the March on Rome.[43] Ettore Ovazza, scion of a wealthy family who, with his two brothers and fifty-year-old father had enlisted with the Italian army to fight the world war, founded a "stridently pro-

---

41 Hans-Joachim Schoeps: *Ready for Germany: The German Jews Patriotism and National Socialism.* (Haude and Spener, 1970), pp. 106, 114

42 Gregory A Caplan, "Acknowledging German-Jewish Fascism," in "Amazing Differences": *Young Americans Experience Germany and Germans,* Alexander Von Humboldt-Stiftung/Foundation, Bonn, 2001, p. 3, http://www. humboldt-foundation.de/pls/web/docs/F30142/reflections_99.pdf

43 Roger Eatwell, *Fascism: A History* (London: Vintage, 1996), p. 66.

Friday, March 24, 1933, the headline "Judea Declares War on Germany" was splashed across the front page of the *Daily Express* newspaper.

fascist journal" and physically led an attack on Zionist Jews.[44]

While there is nothing inherent to fascist ideology that prohibits Jewish support, the anti-Semitic element of German National Socialism was a common feature of German romanticism which as noted, had reached its most cogent expression from Richard Wagner. The Hitlerites were heirs to that legacy, as well as to pre-war anti-Semitic and racial doctrines in Central Europe.[45]

The RjF, states Caplan in his study of the subject, "claimed to be models of the tough, self-confident, and disciplined ethos they believed to be necessary for the survival of German Jewry. As the first ever German-Jewish military elite, they sought to transmit their military masculinity to the rest of the German-Jewish community through youth and sports programs, the

---

44 Ibid.

45 Nicholas Goodrick-Clarke, *The Occult Roots of Nazism: The Ariosophists of Austria and Germany 1890-1935* (Northamptonshire: The Aquarian Press, 1985), pp. 33-216.

commemoration of the Jewish war dead, and the promotion of
Jewish cultivation of German soil.'[46] Unlike the Naumannites and
other German-Jewish nationalists, the RjF cannot be dismissed
as marginal. By the mid-1920s the RjF had 35,000 members and
was the third-largest organization of German Jews.[47]

Caplan writes of the generically fascist character of the Jewish
war veterans (as with other war veterans in Germany who
joined the Hitlerites, the Stahlhelm and the Freikorps), that they
"offered a popular platform for the battle against the pitfalls
of big city life at a time of rapid social transformation. Falling
birth rates, alcoholism, and the spread of nervous disorders had
already been diagnosed by the turn of the century as indicators
of social and cultural degeneration. The German military defeat
and its revolutionary aftermath exacerbated this sense of crisis
and added to the list of perceived symptoms.'[48]

RELATIONS WITH THE THIRD REICH

As indicated by the vehemence of the National Socialist campaign
against the esteemed head of the Stahlhelm, Lieutenant Colonel
Duesterberg, there was not much room for optimism that the
regime would accommodate even the most loyal of German
Jews, other than that Germans of partial Jewish descent were
categorized and some categories were granted a tolerable status
under the 1935 Reich Citizenship Law.

Caplan states that although the Hitlerites remained an enemy,
"nevertheless, the leaders of the RjF also subscribed to a
political ideology that incorporated all of the elements generally
associated with fascism - militarism, extreme nationalism,
anti-bolshevism, and middle class desires for a strong state
that would transcend divisive parliamentary structures.'[49] That

---

46 Caplan, op. cit. p. 4.

47 Ibid.

48 Ibid., p.p. 7-8.

49 Ibid., p. 8.

German Jewry ended up choosing Zionism rests squarely on the shoulders of the National Socialist regime, which favoured Zionism as a doctrine that likewise opposed assimilation of Jews into the national community.

With the assumption to Office of the National Socialists, the RjF believed that it was essential that they assume leadership of German Jewry. Despite their opposition to the Nazis from the start, due to the Nazi propaganda that sought to deny the Jewish role in the World War, the values the RjF espoused for German Jews, and especially for the young, were in accord with the doctrines the National Socialists expounded to "Aryan" Germans. As long "as the state seemed to honor the link between military service and German citizenship - and even longer, the RjF sought to cooperate with the Hitler regime in the construction of a viable Jewish community in the Third Reich.... the ideology, language, and tactics of the RjF reflected a fascist, anti-Zionist agenda that went above and beyond the rhetorical pandering of the oppressed to the oppressor."[50]

The RjF now proclaimed itself specifically against Zionism, dropping its hitherto neutral stance. The RjF become more active than ever in the first years of the regime, and its popularity increased at the expense of the oldest and largest of the Jewish organizations, the Centralverein Jews were increasingly antagonistic towards the Centralverein's "passivity in response to Zionism"[51] in a Jewish population where Zionism had never taken root. Liberalism was diminishing drastically among the German Jews also in line with the decline of Liberalism in Germany generally in the aftermath of the world war. With the demise of Liberal hegemony among German Jews, the choice was between Zionism and the fascism of the RjF.

While Ludwig Freud left Germany in 1934, Dr Leo Loewenstein,

---

50   Ibid., p. 8.
51   Ibid., p. 9.

chairman of the RjF, a scientist by profession, who had served as a captain in the Bavarian Army Reserve, attempted from 1933 to 1935 to "persuade Hitler by mail to allow patriotic Jews, and the young generation in particular, to be absorbed into the German Volksgemeinschaft," to allow Jewish youth to participate with German youth in athletic contests and to allow Jews to serve in the German Armed Force.[52] While there was no reply from Hitler, Loewenstein did succeed in April 1933, by appealing to President von Hindenburg, "in having Jewish civil servants with frontline service during wartime exempted from losing their jobs." However the exemption was revoked with Hindenburg's death later that year.[53]

When world Jewish organizations declared a boycott of German goods in 1933,[54] and established the World Jewish Economic Federation to starve Germany of foreign capital, the RjF reacted swiftly, condemning the actions of Jewish leaders far-removed from Germany, writing to the US Embassy in Berlin denying, "as German patriots," allegations that Jews in Germany were being subjected to "cruelties." While acknowledging that excesses had occurred, which are unavoidable in any kind of revolution, they commented that where able the authorities have sought to prevent these. The RjF also condemned the "irresponsible agitations on the part of the so-called Jewish intellectuals living abroad." These had "never considered themselves German nationals," but had abandoned those of their own faith" at a "critical time" while claiming to be their champions.[55] The same day the RjF issued a worldwide address to frontline veterans, stating that the propaganda against Germany was politically and economically motivated. They pointed out that the Jewish writers used as propagandists had hitherto been the same propagandists

52   W Angress, "The German Jews, 1933 – 1939," in: M Marrus, (ed.), *The Nazi Holocaust*, (Westport & London, 1989), Vol. 2, pp. 484 - 497.

53   Ibid.

54   "Judea Declares War on Germany," *Daily Express*, March 23, 1933.

55   Quoted by Udo Walendy, *The Transfer Agreement and the Boycott Fever 1933*, Historical Facts No. 26, 1987, p. 5.

who had "scoffed at us veterans in earlier years," and called on "honourable soldiers" to repudiate the "unchivalrous and degrading treatment meted out to Germany..."[56]

The choice of Germany's Jews between German nationalism and Zionism was decided by the regime for the Jews, in favor of Zionism. While approximately 600 newspapers were officially banned by the National Socialist regime during 1933, and others were pressured out of existence, *Jüdische Rundschau*, the weekly newspaper of the Zionist Federation of Germany (ZVfD) was permitted to flourish, and by the end of 1933 had a circulation of 38,000, four to five times more than in 1932. *Jüdische Rundschau* was even exempted from newsprint restrictions until 1937. The Zionist newspaper was not subjected to the same censorship as other German newspapers. They were the only newspaper in the Third Reich permitted to advocate a separate political doctrine. In 1935 the Zionist youth corps was the only non-Nazi body permitted to wear uniforms.

With the 1935 Nuremberg Laws Germans Jews were prohibited from raising the German flag, but could raise the Zionist flag.[57] German Jewish Nationalist were not wanted in the Reich, including the Jewish war veterans organization whose German nationalist doctrine could have won over at least a significant proportion of German Jews who had rejected Liberalism and had not been inclined towards Zionism.

Both the German Vanguard and the League of German Nationalist Jews were dissolved in late 1935, while the RjF endured until the end of 1938.

Schoeps' prior contacts with the anti-Hitler National Socialist Otto Strasser, and the "National Bolshevik" Ernst Niekisch made him suspect and he immigrated to Sweden in 1938. After the war

---

56   Walendy, ibid.

57   Edwin Black, *The Transfer Agreement – the Untold Story of the Secret Pact Between the Third Reich and Jewish Palestine* (New York: 1984), p. 175.

he established a celebrated career as a theological scholar. He also remained an active monarchist, as a leader of the National Association for the Monarchy (Volksbund für die Monarchie), called for the restoration of the State of Prussia in 1951, and was involved in forming subsequent conservative movements and periodicals. He died in 1980 in Germany.

Freund, of the RjF, was immigrated to the USA in 1934, and returned to Germany in 1961. So far from having repudiated his Germanness like the many Jews who turned to Zionism, he was one of the first of three men to be awarded the Adenauer Prize in 1961, by the German Foundation, for his work in the "revival of a healthy national feeling on the basis of necessary self-respect" and for the "protection of the rights of the German Volk, in spite of the wrongs done him in his own Fatherland,"[58] such nationalistic sentiments and awards being condemned by *Der Spiegel.*

CONCLUSION

German Jews had rejected liberalism for the same reasons as other Germans had turned to the Right, hoping for a national renewal of the Fatherland. Zionists had not made significant inroads, and while German-Jewish nationalist organizations such as those of Naumann remained small, they maintained a challenge to the mainstream Jewish organisations. The RjF was another matter however, and was gaining support for its form of fascism that sought to fully identify Jews with Germany. They were undertaking in particular a program among the Jewish youth of the type that had been sought by Rathenau, to recreate a Jewish youth that was robust, martial and patriotic. The German Zionists undertook a similar program in the interests of creating vigorous youth pioneers for Palestine.

If the RjF had been permitted to proselyze among German-Jews they would have captured the majority of that community

---

58   "Wahrung der Rechte," *Der Spiegel,* No. 11, pp. 22-24, quoted by Caplan, op. cit., p. 4.

for Germany, despite the anti-Semitism that existed to varying degrees of extremity among the National Socialists. Jews had for centuries started a process of acculturation reflected in the many Jews who fought for Germany during the world war. Unfortunately, the most conspicuous Jews, promoted no less by the anti-Semitic press as by their own followers, were the likes of Rosa Luxemburg, Willi Munzenberg, the wealthy publisher of the Communist press, Karl Radek, Kurt Eisner, et al., until Communism became synonymous in Germany,[59] as in much of the rest of the world, with Jews. However, only 4% voted for the Communist Party, and 28% for the Social Democrats. Most were moderate liberal-democrats.[60] There was also a widespread, vigorous dislike, one might say even hatred, for the "Eastern Jews" that were coming into Germany, especially after the war, whom Rathenau condemned with such vehemence. The "liberal" Jews were just as offended by the manners of the Ostjuden as anyone else.

The Jewish German nationalist sought acculturation, the continuation of a process that had been taking place for centuries. In the Zionists the National Socialists had allies, as opposed to assimilation as themselves. While the Zionists continued collaborating with the Third Reich even during the war, German-Jewish nationalists were suppressed, although a significant number of Mischlinge maintained their patriotism and were able to serve Germany, including Hitler's original bodyguard and SS commander Emile Maurice, who maintained an honored position despite the discovery of his Jewish descent.

The National Socialists maintained a type of Manichean outlook that saw the Aryan in mortal combat with the Jew as a conflict between God and the Devil, a synthesis of biology and theology that had since the late 19th century portrayed the Jews as less

---

59 "The Jews as the Apostles of Communism", in: *Jewish Domination of Weimar Germany*, op, cit., pp. 21-29.

60 Lenni Brenner, *Zionism in the Age of the Dictators* (Westport, Connecticut: Lawrence Hill, 1983), p. 27.

than human, or bestial spawn, expressed in the New Templar theosophy of Jörg Lanz von Liebenfels.

Where most German-Jews saw the Ostjuden as a danger to Germany, or at best an embarrassment to themselves, the National Socialists did not distinguish between them. While only a minority of Jews supported the Left, the National Socialists focused on the conspicuous Jewish presence in the Communist movement, and in other anti-German movements. Most particularly, the Third Reich did not accord status to Jewish war veterans, and the regime chose Zionism over German-Jewish nationalism.

The Red Face of Israel

Israel has for several decades presented itself as an "ally", and one of prime importance, to the "West" and specifically to the USA. This is based on subterfuge. While it has long served the interests of Zionism and of Israel to be presented as the "bulwark of democracy" in the Middle East, surrounded by intolerance and bigotry and theocratic dictatorship, the long arm of Zionism across the world will support or oppose any movement, individual and state depending upon how Zionist interests are served.

WHEN ZIONISM WAS RED

Several decades ago Israel began presenting itself as the "bulwark against communism" in the Middle East and as of vital strategic importune to the USA vis-à-vis the USSR in the region. Israel's supposed anti-Communism was of recent duration, and thoroughly self-serving.

The roots of modern Zionism go back to Moses Hess, who predated Herzl and mentored Karl Marx. Prof. Shlomo Avineri of the Hebrew University, Jerusalem, states in his biography of Hess:

> No other writer has similarly been honored in East Berlin and in Jerusalem just as no other writer has had his manuscripts scattered in such diverse places as the International Institute of Social History in Amsterdam and the Institute for Marxism-Leninism in Moscow as well as the Central Zionist Archives in Jerusalem.[1]

Avineri states that many of Hess' ideas were incorporated into *The Communist Manifesto*, with which he was involved in the

---

1   Shlomo Avineri, *Moses Hess: Prophet of Communism and Zionism* (New York: New York University Press, 1985), 246.

initial writing.[2] Hess was also deeply involved with the First International and served as Marx's spokesman when Marx could not attend conferences.[3]

Marxism and Zionism emerged from the same milieu. Sometimes they merged, and sometimes they were rivals for the allegiance of Jewry. Chaim Weizmann, who became first President of Israel, described these family splits where communist Jews would argue that Jewish emancipation had to be part of a universal emancipation of labor, while the "Zionist revolutionary group" although agreeing that world revolution was necessary insisted that full emancipation for the Jews would only be gained by a Jewish state. Weizmann related that his mother – expressing the general feeling of Jews at that time and place – would say: "Whatever happens I shall be well off. If Shemuel [the revolutionary son] is right, we shall all be happy in Russia; and if Chaim [the Zionist] is right, then I shall go to live in Palestine."[4]

Revolutionary socialism in Eastern Europe was centred on the General Federation of Jewish Workers, the Jewish Bund, a constituent of the Social Democratic movement. This was absorbed into the Bolshevik party, the Ukrainian bundists joining the Bolsheviks in 1919, the Russian bund in 1920, and the Polish in 1939.[5]

The relationship between the socialist revolutionaries and the Zionists is indicated by meetings that took place between Lenin and Chaim Weizmann in the home of the industrialist Daniel Schoni, in Switzerland, recorded by French intelligence agent Jacques Levy. They discussed a "Jewish blueprint for the East"

2   Ibid., 140

3   Ibid., 244.

4   Chaim Weizaman, *Trial and Error*, (New York: Harper and Brothers, 1949), 39.

5   George W Robnett, *Conquest Through Immigration: How Zionism turned Palestine into a Jewish State* (Pasadena, Ca.: Institute for Special Research, 1968), 98.

which had been formulated in Austria in 1908 by Jewish socialists and which called for a socialist state in Palestine, "which would serve as a base from which Marxist philosophy could then spread throughout the Middle East." Weizmann stated to Lenin that the opening of Palestine to Jewish immigration rested on the overthrow of the Russian and Ottoman empires.[6]

PALESTINE BECOMES CENTER OF MARXISM

Palestinians were not, and could not be, well disposed towards Marxism, despite the myth that continues to be perpetuated by Zionists, neo-conservatives, Christian fundamentalists, et al. The religiosity of Islam precludes any possible belief in atheistic creeds such as Marxism, and Islam has its own doctrines drawn from the *Koran* that encourage social justice alternatives to both Marxism and capitalism, such as that of Nasser's "Arab socialism" and Qaddafi's Third Universal Theory.

Marxism in Palestine does not have an Arab or Muslim background. One of the earliest Marxist groups in Palestine was the Socialist Workers Party, established in 1919 as a party of the Poalei Zionists. In 1920 the primary theoretician of the party, Yaakov Meiersohn, left for the USSR, indicating the communistic nature of the movement. The party's May Day demonstration was held under the slogan "Soviet Palestine."[7] There was a violent clash between the SWP cadres and the official May Day activists of Histadrut. In 1922 the SWP split into factions representing the historic Jewish quandary since the rise of Zionism and Marxism side-by-side, forming the pro-Zionist Palestine Communist Party and the anti-Zionist Communist Party of Palestine.[8]

---

6   Quoted from the December 1967 issue of *Atlas Magazine* by Issa Nakhleh of the Arab Higher Committee for Palestine, Palestine Arab Delegation, *Common Sense*, No. 560, May 15, 1970.

7   Leslie Stein, *The Hope Fulfilled: The Rise of Modern Israel*, (Westport, Conn.: Praeger, 2003), 154.

8   Fed Halliday, "Early Communism in Palestine," *Journal of Palestine Studies*, Vol. 7, No. 2 (Winter, 1978), 162–169.

The founder of the Egyptian Communist Party in 1922 was Joseph Rosenthal, whose daughter Charlotte, trained in Moscow, acted as a courier between Egypt and Palestine. The delegate of the "Egyptian communists" to the Congress of the Third international was Avigdor Weiss.[9] The Palestine Communist Party was formed in 1923, with Leopold Trepper as party leader. Although the party was obliged to adopt an anti-Zionist position to be accepted into the Comintern, Trepper had been a member of Hashomer Hatzair (Youth Guard), a Zionist socialist organization that had been a pioneer of the kibbutz movement in Palestine.[10] After being the head of a Soviet espionage network ("Red Orchestra") in Nazi occupied Europe, he spent time in Stalin's prisons and went to Poland in 1955 where he became head of the Jewish Cultural Society. Trepper returned to Israel in 1974 and although having maintained his revolutionary communist fervor, when he died in Jerusalem in 1982 his funeral was attended by Zionist and Government luminaries, including defense minister Ariel Sharon.[11]

It is interesting to note that the Arab general strike of 1936 divided the Jewish and Arab nationalist factions within the Palestine Communist Party, as the Jewish labour union Histadrut was supporting the displacement of Arab workers by Jews, and the Jewish faction of the Communist Party adopted a position less critical of Zionism in seeking not to alienate itself

---

9   Nesta H Webster, *World Revolution* (Devon: Britons Ltd., 1971), 345. Additional chapter by Anthony Gittens.

10 Hashomer Hatzair, although supporting a bi-national state in Palestine with equality between Palestinians and Jews, was nonetheless a significant factor in the creation of the Zionist entity, providing support for the Haganah and the Palmach military forces. The organization became affiliated with the International Revolutionary Marxist Centre that rejected both the social democratic Second International and the Stalinist Third International and was associated with Trotskyism.

11 Leopold Trepper, <http://en.wikipedia.org/wiki/Leopold_Trepper > Despite the general uselessness of Wikipedia as a reliable source, the information on Trepper is presumed to be accurate in this instance as the US site of Hashomer Hatzair directly links to the wiki entry.

from the Zionist socialist movement.[12] Another communist movement founded in Egypt was *Iskra*, established in 1942 by Hillel Schwartz. Interestingly, the organization did not have an Egyptian Muslim in its leadership until 1947, Shudi Atiya ash-Shafi, an academic who quit within the year.

Dr Eli Tzur, senior lecturer at the Kibbutz Seminary in Tel Aviv, wrote of the Marxist influence in Palestine as a product of Jewish emigration:

> The Soviet Union was an international counterpart of Zionist construction and created a feeling of affinity. One can find earlier signs of admiration for the Soviets in Ben-Gurion's eulogy for Lenin, written in 1923, where he shows Lenin the highest regard by comparing Lenin to himself. Hoping to destroy the British Empire, the Soviets believed the Jews in Palestine were a catalyst in this process and helped their effort for the establishment of the State of Israel.[13]

Reminiscent of the comments by Chaim Weizmann about his youth in Russia where there was a messianic sense engendered by both Zionism and Marxism,[14] Tzur states that the Jewish emigrants from Eastern Europe and Russia considered that they had "two motherlands," the USSR and Israel. Tzur writes of this nexus:

> A few years ago, a cave used by Jewish soldiers was discovered with the slogan, "Palmach-Red Army" written on a wall. The young members of Palmach were

---

12 Yossi Schwartz, "Arab-Jewish workers' joint struggles prior to the partition of Palestine – Part II, "*In Defence of Marxism*, June 16, 2003, International Marxist Tendency, <http://www.marxist.com/arab-jewish-partition-two160603.htm>

13 Eli Tzur, *Midstream: A Quarterly Jewish Review*, New York, the Theodor Herzl Foundation, October 1996.

14 Chaim Weizmann, op.cit.

indoctrinated to see themselves as part of a fighting camp to which the Vietnamese and the Chinese Communists belonged. When a party of all the Zionist left, Mapam, was established in 1948, it defined itself, "as an integral part of the revolutionary camp led by the Soviet Union."

"In this coming war, the international Left must accept commands from one center, which is in Moscow." The scenario envisaged was of the Soviet Army advancing from the north and reaching Israel's northern border.

Many hoped to greet it there and we have documented cases of young people who joined the northern Kibbutzim in order to be on the spot when the Red Army arrived. Some Mapam leaders feared that with the advance of the Red Army, the Western powers would try to utilize the Haifa harbor as a logistical base. One of them declared in the Knesset that in this case, the workers would paralyze the port facilities. Of course, the war never came.[15]

In the early days of the Israeli State, Haifa was referred to as "Red Haifa," states Tzur. On holidays Jewish youth would march through the streets flying the red flag, their fists clenched in the revolutionary salute.

The Palmach was not merely a fringe terrorist group; it was, according to Israeli journalist and author Tom Segev, "the Haganah's[16] crack military force" of 6000 "ideological fanatics."[17] The Palmach commander Yitzhak Sadeh, had been a founder of the Haganah. Segev confirms what Tzur has stated, "the Palmachniks also identified with the Red Army and admired Joseph Stalin."[18]

---

15   Eli Tzur, op.cit.

16   Haganah, the "official" Zionist military force.

17   Tom Segev, *One Palestine, Complete: Jews and Arabs under the British mandate* (London: Abacus, 2000), 452.

18   Ibid., 454.

The USSR provided the wherewithal for the Zionist underground, including not only weapons but also training. At the time *The New York Herald Tribune* ran a report on the "Stern Gang" which identified this extreme Zionist terrorist faction as having communist origins:

> ...Abraham Stern joined the communists near the end of World War II, but there was no indication that Sternists wanted to make Israel a puppet state of the Soviet Union, when they said they wanted to divorce Israel from its dependence on the West, to pursue an intense Jewish nationalism and to lean more heavily for international support on the Soviet Union. Their propaganda explained it by asserting the similar position of Sternists and communists. Henry A Wallace who visited the Holy Land last Fall became a Sternist hero because of his views towards Russia and because of his position as a dissident.[19]

A previous report also indicated communist involvement at the highest levels of Zionism in the creation of the Israeli state:

> A Communist dominated national Hebrew front is expected to emerge in Palestine within a few weeks after the British evacuation. Spokesmen for the Jewish Agency reluctantly admit that the Communists have been gaining strength in direct proportion to the terrorism reported by the Haganah and the other Zionist military organizations.

> A symptom of the drift towards totalitarianism is the behavior of the Haganah's former commander in chief, Moshe Sneh, who recently resigned from the Jewish Agency's executive committee and joined the pro-communist Hashomer Hatzair, the strongest of the five Hebrew "dissident" groups.[20]

---

19   F Turner, "Group Portrait of the Stern Gang," *New York Herald Tribune*, October 2, 1948.

20   *Newark New Jersey Star-Ledger*, dispatch from Jerusalem, February 25, 1948.

At the time of Israel's creation Philip Jessup, US Ambassador to the United Nations, reported to US Secretary of State George Marshall that:

> It is not apparent that Communism has any substantial following among the Arab masses. On the other hand, there are apparently a substantial number of Communists in the Irgun, the Stern Gang and other dissident Jewish groups. Beyond that, the Soviet Union, through its support of partition and prompt recognition of Israel, must be considered as having a substantial influence with the Provisional Government of Israel. The Communist influence is, of course, capable of substantial expansion through whatever diplomatic and other missions the Soviet Government may establish in Israel.[21]

At the time, the creation of the Israeli State was a Marxist *cause célèbre*. *The New York Times* reported in 1948 a 10,000 strong demonstration of communists and Leftist labor leaders singing "solidarity forever," as they marched under the banner of the United Committee to Save the Jewish State and the United Nations, the *Times* reporting it as a front for the "internationally minded communists" to take up "an intensely nationalistic cause, the partition of Palestine." The grand marshal of the parade was Ben Gold, "president of the communist-led International Fur and Leather Workers Union." The march ended as a rally in support of Henry Wallace, Progressive Party candidate for the presidency, who had served as Roosevelt's Secretary for Agriculture.[22]

By this time the World War II alliance between the USA and USSR had cracked up, the American dreams of a "new world

---

21 *FRUS 1948*, "The Acting United States Representative at the United Nations (Jessup) to the Secretary of State," Top Secret, Priority, New York, July 1, 1948, 4:16 p.m., p. 1182. The report is cited by Donald Neff, "Israel seeks 'neutrality' between US and Soviet Union," *Washington Report on Middle East Affairs* <http://wrmea.com/backissues/0195/9501036.htm>

22 Alexander Feinberg, "10,000 in protest on Palestine here," *New York Times*, March 12, 1948, 8.

Members of a Palmach military unit Palestine 1948.

order" via the UN, with the co-operation of the USSR, had been uncivilly scotched by Stalin, and the Cold War era had emerged rather than the era of One World Government.[23] The USSR was pursuing an imperialistic and nationalistic course and the method of gaining a Soviet foothold in the Middle East, where the Arabs were not susceptible to Communism, was through Israel; large numbers of Jewish emigrants, unlike the Arabs, being inclined towards Marxism and still grateful for the Soviet war effort against the Nazis. Stalin and the Soviet leaders thereafter pursued a policy of *realpolitik*, temporarily backing the creation of Israel as a means of ensuring instability in the Middle East.

The Zionist state wished to opt for a neutralist position during the Cold War era. There was nothing pro-Western or pro-American about the setting up of Israel. Israel is nothing if not pro-Israel, and that is all. Any alliance is purely pragmatic, dialectical and designed for nothing other than short or long term Zionist gain.

---

23 K R Bolton, "Origins of the Cold War," *Foreign Policy Journal*, June 1, 2010
    <http://www.foreignpolicyjournal.com/>

The New York Times reported at the time: "It is true that Israel cherishes the ideal of remaining 'neutral' between the United States and the Soviet Union, constantly referred to as 'our two powerful friends...'"[24]

Donald Neff writes in a comprehensive article on this subject:

> The policy's name in Hebrew was *ee-hizdahut*, "non-identification." Although the Cold War was in full force at the time, Israel hoped to remain friendly with both superpowers because both had assets that Israel needed—money, people and weapons. Israeli Foreign Minister Moshe Sharett said: "Israel will in no case become identified with one of the great blocs of the world as against the other."[25]

Neff alludes to the lack of Soviet influence in the region prior to Israel, which served as the means of Soviet entry rather than as a bulwark against Communism, as the Zionists and their Christian Fundamentalist and pseudo-conservative apologists had for several decades presented the issue.

> Before the Palestine problem grew acute after the end of World War II, the Middle East had been "virtually clean" of Soviet influence, in the words of one British general. But since then it had made some modest gains in Israel because of Moscow's support of partition, its quick recognition of the Jewish state, its decision to allow Jews to emigrate to Israel and its secret supply to Israel of weapons via Czechoslovakia during the fighting.

Neff continues in regard to the selling of weaponry to the region:

> But of more immediate importance were weapons. And it was here that the Soviet Union played a paramount

---

24   Anne O'Hare McCormack, *New York Times*, January 14, 1949. Cited by Donald Neff, *Washington Report on the Middle East*, op.cit.

25   Donald Neff, op.cit.

role at this time. Moscow had allowed Czechoslovakia to become Israel's major arms supplier in 1948. In that capacity, Czechoslovakia had provided Israel with all the Messerschmitts and Spitfires that formed its new air force, as well as other weapons and the training of 5,000 of its military personnel by the fall of 1948. And it remained Israel's major arms supplier in 1949.

The significance of the Czech connection to Israel rested on the fact that the U.S. had imposed an arms embargo on the area in 1947. Despite unrelenting pressure from Israel's supporters, the Truman administration continued to observe the embargo in 1949, as did subsequent administrations for more than a decade.

This attempt by the USA to stabilize the region in an effort to minimize Soviet influence was sabotaged by France's decision to displace the USSR as Israel's arms supplier, the strategy being to secure Israel as an ally against Arab nationalism. The USSR then stepped in and began to arm Nasser, and in 1955 the Egyptian statesman announced that "Czechoslovakia had agreed to provide Egypt with major weapons systems, including bombers, jet warplanes, tanks and artillery."[26] This had followed the February Israeli raids against an Egyptian military post in the Gaza Strip, where 36 Egyptian soldiers and two civilians had been killed.

Secretary of State John Foster Dulles commented that "we are in the present jam because the past Administration had always dealt with the area from a political standpoint and had tried to meet the wishes of the Zionists in this country and that had created a basic antagonism with the Arabs. That was what the Russians were now capitalizing on."[27]

---

26   Ibid.

27   *FRUS 1955-1957*, "Memorandum of Conversation with the Secretary of State," Washington, Oct. 18, 1955, p. 612. Neff, ibid.

CENTER OF GLOBAL SUBVERSION

With the change of circumstances vis-a-vis the USSR and Israel, the Zionists and their apologists changed track and presented Israel as the "bulwark of democracy " in the Middle East. The Soviet backing of the Zionists had always been pragmatic, as Stalin was no friend of Zionism or even particularly of the Jewish people.[28] The eminent British military figure and scholar John Glubb Pasha, who had commanded the Jordanian Legion, wrote in 1967 an exceptionally penetrating analysis of the Middle East situation in regard to Russian strategy. He remarked that none of the Arab countries wished to become Soviet satellites, but with the defeat of Egypt during the Six Day War, they became ever reliant upon the USSR. The West heralded the 1967 war as a defeat for the Soviet Union, which had "backed the losing side." However, "the British and the Americans have simple minds and accept events unquestioningly at their face value."[29] It was Glubb Pahsa's view that it was in Soviet interests that the West become totally committed to Israel and exclude the Arab world, and that the Arabs, with the devastating Egyptian defeat would turn completely to the Soviets as allies. Despite the hard realities of Soviet foreign policy in helping to contrive a situation that would force the Arabs into their arms, this is not to say that the USSR did not have a genuine commitment to opposing Zionism world-wide from the time of Stalin. While the USSR backed the formation of Israel in it embryonic stages, the Soviet bloc's internal policy was one of unremitting resistance to Zionism.[30] The position of some conspiracy theorists such as someone even as well-placed as King Feisal of Saudi Arabia that the USSR was Jewish controlled and in secret league with the Zionists is not tenable.[31]

---

28 Paul Lendvai, *Anti-Semitism in Eastern Europe* (London: MacDonald and Co., 1971). Arkady Vaksberg, *Stalin Against the Jews* (New York: Alfred A Knopf, 1994).

29 Glubb Pasha, *The Middle East Crisis: A Personal Interpretation* (London: Hodder and Stoughton, 1968), 12.

30 Paul Lendvai, Arkday Vaksberg, op.cit.

31 King Faisal, "A Grand Conspiracy," *Newsweek*, December 21, 1970.

While the Soviet bloc was supplying Israel, in Czechoslovakia, which also happened to be the precise source of Soviet weaponry to the Zionists, the "Prague Treason Trial" was purging the party of those accused of Zionism, a treasonous crime *per se*. The circumstances of the Prague Treason Trial are that in late 1951 Rudolf Slansky, Secretary General of the Communist Party in Czechoslovakia was arrested for "antistate activities." A year later, he and thirteen co-defendants went on trial as "Trotskyite-Titoist-Zionist traitors." They were accused of espionage and economic sabotage, working on behalf of Yugoslavia, Israel and the West. Eleven of the fourteen were sentenced to death, the other three to life imprisonment. Slansky and the ten others were hanged on December 3, 1952. Of the fourteen defendants, eleven were Jews, and were identified as such in the indictment. Many other Jews were mentioned as co-conspirators, implicated in a cabal that included the US Supreme Court Justice Frankfurter, described as a "Jewish nationalist", and Mosha Pijade the "Titoist Jewish ideologist" in Yugoslavia. The conspiracy against the Czechoslovak state had been hatched at a secret meeting in Washington in 1947, between President Truman, Secretary Acheson, former Treasury Secretary Morgenthau, and the Israelis Ben Gurion and Moshe Sharett. In the indictment, Slansky was described as "by his very nature a Zionist", who had, in exchange for American support for Israel, agreed to place "Zionists in important sectors of Government, economy, and Party apparatus". The plan included the assassination of President Gottwald by a "freemason" doctor.[32] These are not the actions and accusations of a system that is in secret league with the Zionists.

Did the rearrangement of alliances in the Middle East mean that there was a consequent change of strategy and perspective by Israel, in pursuing a pro-Western, anti-communist agenda?

To the contrary, Israel became, and remains, a center of global subversion on a scale reminiscent of the image the conservatives

---

32   Paul Lendvai, op.cit., 243-245.

presented for the USSR as the center of world communist subversion. While Soviet anti-Zionist propaganda was still somewhat encumbered by Leninist perceptions, or at least found it still convenient as a method of propaganda, in portraying Israel as a bulwark of Western imperialism, Israel had its own agenda of world-wide dimensions, seeking to fill the void created by European colonial scuttle after World War II. An early example was the training given to Waruhiu Itote (aka "Gen. China"), second in command of the Mau Mau insurgency against the British in Kenya. The General went to Israel in 1962 along with other East Africans:

> On the night of 13th November 1962 he left for Israel for further military training. The trip was not made public to avoid bringing it to the attention of the colonial authorities who would not have permitted it to go ahead. He left with Mzee Kenyatta's blessings. His studies covered a wide range of military principles and practices. On 26th July 1963 he, together with other participants from East Africa, graduated as an Officer. After his graduation, he remained in Israel until 26th November 1963 when he returned to Nairobi under heavy security. During his stay in Israel, the British government came to learn of his training and had expressed its displeasure at this development.... Shortly after independence, the government arranged for General China and other Kenyans who had been trained in Israel to be absorbed into the new Kenya Army as Officer Trainees.[33]

From the mid-1950s Israel began an earnest initiative to influence Black Africa, where in most of the countries there were "Israelis aiding the military and civil systems," according to Israel Lior, military secretary to Prime Minister Eshkol.[34] In Uganda, Israel

---

33 "Waruhiu Itote aka 'General China,'" *Africa Tribute*, 2002 <http://webcache. googleusercontent.com/search?q=cache:pGqCtS5csF8J:kenya740.tripod.com/ china.html>

34 Andrew and Leslie Cockburn, *Dangerous Liaison: The Inside Story of the*

began cultivating Idi Amin when he was assistant chief of staff under Pres. Obote. Baruch Bar Lev, head of the Israeli military delegation, explained to Lior that Amin, despite his oddities, was "our man," or "he would be."[35] In Zaire, Pres. Mobutu had a close friend in Mossad agent Meir Meyouhas, who had been part of the "Lavon Affair," the Israeli attempted to bomb British and US installations in Egypt and blame the Egyptians.[36] In 1971 the British MI-6 and the Israelis encouraged Amin to overthrow Obote, with advice from Israeli attaché Baruch Bar Lev.

Israel's subversive role in the Mediterranean region is indicated by the Israeli backing of the Red Brigades in Italy which were causing havoc during the 1970s. The strategy was to destabilize Italy to increase US dependence on Israel as the only "stable" state in the region. In 1982 Red Brigade leader Prof. Senzani and others were arrested for planning to massacre the leadership of the Christian Democratic Party at the party's council meeting. Magistrate Ferdinando Imposimato, who had headed the investigation into the 1978 kidnapping and murder of Prime Minister Aldo Moro by the Red Brigades, was reported by *Il Giorno* as stating:

> …At least until 1978 Israeli secret services had infiltrated the Italian subversive groups. He said that based on confessions by jailed guerrillas who turned police informer, there had been an Israeli plan to destabilize Italy. The plan aimed at reducing Italy to a country convulsed by civil war so that the United States would be forced to count on Israel for the security of the Mediterranean, the judge said.[37]

This is not to say that Zionism is "Red" *per se*; Zionism is whatever complexion serves Zionism. The attempted alliances

US-Israeli Covert Relationship (New York: Harper Collins, 1991), 11.

35   Ibid.

36   Ibid., 112.

37   "Arrest wrecked Brigades' plan for massacre," NZPA-Reuter, Wellington, New Zealand, *The Evening Post*, January 18, 1982.

with Fascism are better known than the relationship with Communism, including the effort of the Stern Gang to establish a military alliance with Nazi Germany before settling on a pro-Soviet orientation.[38] The wartime Nazi rebuff did not dissuade Zionists from lending support to neo-Nazis in more recent years.

Israel's long connection with street gangsters[39] also provides a good background for dealings with gangsters who can capture entire states, General Manuel Noriega of Panama being particularly close to Israel. Noriega's chief adviser was Michael Harari, who had been funded with $20,000,000 by Israel according to an ABC News report. Narcotics were sent under the name of "Dr Harari", marked vaccine. He is referred to by ex-Mossad agent Victor Ostrobvosky as second only to Noriega in Panama.[40]

Initial reports that Harari had been caught when the US invaded Panama in 1989 were apparently incorrect, or something was amiss shortly thereafter, as Harari was able to escape back to Israel. Noriega had been trained in Israel, owned a villa in Tel Aviv and sent his children to a kibbutz. Israel's associations with arms and narcotics marketing in the Americas is extensive and involves the infamous Colombian drug cartels and more, just as Israel itself is a major source of narcotics for worldwide distribution while attention is focused on Afghanistan.

---

38 Lenni Brenner, *Zionism in the Age of the Dictators* (London: Croom Helm, 1983) 267-268.

39 For example in 1945 a meeting took place between Bugsy Siegel and Reuven Dafne, an emissary for the Haganah, after which Siegel supplied $50,000 cash. Jewish Virtual Library, "Jewish Gangsters." In 1948 the Meyer Lansky mob, of which Siegel was a part, was involved in securing arms for Israel. Dennis Eisenberg, Uri Dan and Eli Landau, *Meyer Lansky* (New York: Paddington Press, 1979), 295-296. In 1985 Moe Dalitz, head of the Mayfield Road Gang, received the Anti-Defamation League's "Torch of Freedom Award" for his large donations to Israel.

40 Meir Doron, "The Dark Side of Israeli L.A.," *Jewish Journal of Greater Los Angeles*, August 2, 2002.

General Manuel Noriega military dictator of Panama from 1983 to 1989.

Israel has presented itself before the world as a "bulwark of democracy' in the Middle East, first during the Cold War –after relations with the USSR soured, and now in the battle against "Islamofascism," a term coined by the neo-trotskyite-neo-cons. An alternative view is that the state is a center of pestilence from which emanates a world-wide subversive network, based around an ideology that has sought alliances with communists, nazis and fascists, and with narco-peddlers and street gangsters such as Meyer Lansky and Bugsy Siegel; whose luminaries saw no evil in dragooning the USA into World War I to secure the Balfour Declaration,[41] thereby extending hostilities, where previously Zionist efforts to secure Palestine had centered round a pro-German policy. The perfidy represented by the Balfour Declaration brought an end to the goodwill of the Arab people

---

41 Samuel Landman, *Great Britain, the Jews and Palestine* (London: New Zionist
    Organisation, 1936). Landman was Hon. Secretary of the Joint Zionist
    Council of the United Kingdom 1912, Joint Editor of the *Zionist* 1913-14 and
    1917 – 1922 Solicitor and Secretary to the Zionist Organisation, and at the
    time of writing the pamphlet Legal Adviser to the New Zionist Organisation.
    The pamphlet can be read online at: <http://www.itk.ntnu.no/ansatte/
    Andresen_Trond/kk-f/2005/0036.html>

towards Britain and the West generally that had been heroically cultivated by T E Lawrence; abruptly ended, moreover, by back room deals among corrupt statesmen, and neo-messianists. That is the legacy from which the "West" has not only not recovered, but is further removed than ever from doing so.

The Zionist Factor in Africa

During the 1980s when the offensive against South Africa was at its height the Right was focused on the prospect of the USSR taking over the mineral wealth and strategic position of SA. I recall this because I was among those in New Zealand speaking in favour of SA, and using this spectre as the main reason for opposing the anti-SA campaigns, albeit among the few who also defended White self-determination. As with much else during that time and before, the USSR and the spectre of "communism" were red-herrings. While the USSR naturally had its own strategic interests in being involved in Africa, certainly of far greater influence in Europe's scuttle from Africa, and the surrender of the Afrikaners and Rhodesians, were the subversion and pressures emanating from the USA and from international capital. The USA wanted to fill the power vacuum left by White scuttle, and international capital regarded the old colonialism and race segregation as hindrances to what became "globalization."[1]

Another major factor in the decolonization and White surrender process was the geopolitical interests of Israel. That was even less understood at the time of White scuttle and surrender than the role of the USA and international finance, although a certain amount of information was documented by the sterling work in particular of A. K. Chesterton,[2] and the journalist Ivor Benson, who served as information advisor to the Rhodesian Government.[3] Now more about Israel's role in backing "Black liberation" in Africa is known.

---

1   See: K. R. Bolton, *Babel Inc.: Multiculturalism, Globalisation and the New World Order* (London: Black House Publishing, 2013), pp. 41-77.

2   A. K. Chesterton, *The New Unhappy Lords* (Hampshire: Candour Publishing House, 1975). The book remains in print.

3   Ivor Benson, *The Zionist Factor* (Bullsbrook, Western Australial: Veritas Publishing Co., 1986).

NELSON MANDELA TRAINED BY MOSSAD

In 2013, the year of Nelson Mandela's death, *Haaretz* published reports from the Israeli state archives that referred to him as having been trained in weapons and sabotage by Mossad in Ethiopia in 1962. This was a few months prior to his being arrested as part of a sabotage cell in South Africa, and during a visit of African states, including Ethiopia, Algeria, Egypt and Ghana, to obtain support for the military wing of the African National Congress. The *Haaretz* article states, "During his training, Mandela expressed interest in the methods of the Haganah pre-state underground and was viewed by the Mossad as leaning toward communism,"[4] according to a "top secret" letter sent from the Mossad to the Foreign Ministry in Jerusalem, deposited in the Israeli state archives, dated October 11, 1962, shortly after Mandela was arrested in SA:

> As you may recall, three months ago we discussed the case of a trainee who arrived at the [Israeli] embassy in Ethiopia by the name of David Mobsari who came from Rhodesia," the letter said. "The aforementioned received training from the Ethiopians [Israeli embassy staff, almost certainly Mossad agents] in judo, sabotage and weaponry." The phrase "the Ethiopians" was apparently a code name for Mossad operatives working in Ethiopia.[5]

The letter noted that "David Mobsari" "showed an interest in the methods of the Haganah and other Israeli underground movements." "He greeted our men with 'Shalom', was familiar with the problems of Jewry and of Israel, and gave the impression of being an intellectual. The staff tried to make him into a Zionist. In conversations with him, he expressed socialist worldviews and at times created the impression that he leaned toward communism."[6]

---

4   Ofer Aderet and David Fachler, "Mandela Received Weapons Training From Mossad Agents in Ethiopia," *Haaretz*, December 20, 2013.

5   Ofer Aderet and David Fachler, ibid.

6   Mossad letter cited by Ofer Aderet and David Fachler, op. cit.

What is just stated in passing and without reference by *Haaretz* or the other media who picked up the story in 2013, was the reference to Mandela's interest in the methods not only of the Haganah, the so-called "official" Zionist underground, but of "other Israeli underground movements."[7] This can only refer to the likes of the Stern, Irgun and Palmach. Mandela's interests in the "other Israeli underground movements," even if one accepts the official Zionist line that the Haganah was a legitimate military force, undermines his image as a man of peace, who brought tranquillity between all races and created the "rainbow nation." The claim of Mandela's interest in these terrorist organizations is perfectly plausible, as Irgun/Stern/Palmach tactics were put into practise by the ANC's military wing, *Umkhonto We Sizwe*; "Spear of the Nation." While it is often said, to the point of being a cliché, that "one man's 'terrorist' is another man's 'freedom fighter'," an apt definition might be the use of violence that does not take regard of civilian casualties. Mandela's cell was terroristic, and so was the Israeli underground, if that definition is accepted.

The Stern organization was a split from the Irgun. Among Stern's 18 principles was the creation of Israel extending from the Nile to the Euphrates; i.e. the "Deed of Covenant" of Genesis 15:18.[8] The Zionist terror organizations saw themselves as part of an anti-imperialist struggle (other than imposing their own imperialism over Arabs). Their primary enemy, even more so than Hitler, for Stern and Irgun, was Britain. They identified with the Irish Republican Army,[9] and considered sending a detachment to fight the British in India.[10] Among the actions of Stern were the assassination of Lord Moyne, Colonial Secretary for Palestine, in 1944; and Count Bernadotte, U.N. Middle East mediator, in 1948, noted for his assistance to Jews during the

---

7   Emphasis added..

8   Lenni Brenner, *Zionism in the Age of Dictators* (Connecticut: Lawrence Hill, 1983), p. 265.

9   "The Michael Collins of Israel," http://www.hankewitz.com/shamir.html

10   Lenni Brenner, op. cit., p. 266.

war. The Irgun, whose leader, Menachem Begin, became an Israeli prime minister, blew up the King David Hotel in 1946, killing British, Jewish and Arab civilian workers. In 1947 the infamous killing and hanging up of the booby-trapped bodies of sergeants Martin and Paice caused wide outrage. Martin and Paice were hung-up on account of their "anti-Hebrew activities." Rabin, another prime minister, was a Palmach commander. Palmach saw themselves as part of the "national liberation" armies. They identified themselves with the Chinese Red Army and the Vietcong, according to Tom Segev. They were the "crack military forces, 6000 strong," of the official Haganah. [11]

These organizations served as inspiration and guidance for the Israeli training of Black insurgents. With the establishment of Israel and the scuttling of Europe from Africa, it was a short step for Israel to portray itself as a fellow African state, albeit one that would lead all the others, and part of the "neutralist" alliance. On January 13, 1949, *"The New York Times* reported Israel sought to steer a neutral course between the United States and the Soviet Union. Correspondent Anne O'Hare McCormick reported from Jerusalem that "It is true that Israel cherishes the ideal of remaining 'neutral' between the United States and the Soviet Union, constantly referred to as 'our two powerful friends...'" [12] It subsequently became opportune for Israel portray itself as the bulwark against Soviet penetration into the Middle East. Part of this image was Israel's backing of the Red Brigades in Italy as part of a regional destabilization program. [13]

---

11   Tom Segev, *One Palestine, Complete: Jews and Arabs under the British Mandate* (London: Abacus, 2000), p. 452.

12   Donald Neff, "Israel Seeks 'Neutrality' Between U.S., Soviet Union," *Washington Report on Middle East Affairs,* January/February 1995, Pages 36-38; https://www.wrmea.org/1995-january-february/middle-east-history%E2%80%94it-happened-in-january-israel-seeks-neutrality-between-u.s.-soviet-union.html

13   Ferdinando Imposimato, investigating magistrate into the 1978 kidnapping of Prime Minister Aldo Moro, stated that "at least until 1978 Israeli secret services infiltrated the Italian subversive groups. He said that based on confessions of jailed guerrillas who turned police informers there had been an

It was the sabotage plans of the ANC cell headquartered at the Lilisleaf Farm, near Johannesburg, that resulted in the famous Rivonia Trial and the jailing of Mandela et al, which became a *cause célèbre* for the sundry factions the world over that wanted the destruction of White South Africa.

Israel Maisels (1905-1994) "a major Jewish and Zionist leader [was] one of the lead defense attorneys at the 1958-61 Treason Trial of Mandela and others."[14] The Maisels law firm eulogises its founder's role:

> ... In the 61st year since the Treason Trial, Isie's leadership will forever be memorialised in the letter penned by the struggle stalwarts he represented which hangs in the foyer of the building which bears his name. Of him, they said: 'throughout the long dreary years of our trial we have been proud to have been defended by you, not only because we know that in you we have had the best defence that this land could supply, but we have been proud because we know of the magnificent legal battles you have fought to preserve the rule of law, to prevent it from being whittled away by the unscrupulous machinations of the Government'. The Maisels Group is proud to carry his name and legacy and to continue the finest traditions of the Bar which Isie's life exemplified throughout his extraordinary career.[15]

Maisels served as president of the South African Jewish Board of Deputies, and the South African Zionist Federation.[16]

Israeli plan to destabilise Italy. 'The plan aimed at reducing Italy to a country convulsed by civil war so that the U.S. would be forced to count on Israel for the security of the Mediterranean," the judge said." "Arrest wrecked Brigades' plan for massacre," NZPA-Reuter, *Evening Post* (Wellington, New Zealand), January 18, 1982.

14   David Fachler, "Mandela and the Mossad: How Israel courted Black Africa," *Haaretz*, December 20, 2013.

15   "Remembering Isie Maisels," The Maisels Group, http://maiselsgroup.co.za/remembering-isie-maisels/

16   "Maisels, Israel Aaron," https://www.encyclopedia.com/religion/

While it is now denied by South Africa that Mandela underwent Mossad training, there was a cryptic allusion by Mandela at the Rivonia sabotage trial to having received "military training" when he was on his tour of African states in 1962, having been acquitted of "treason." [17] The official leasees of Lilisleaf Farm, the headquarters of *Umkhonto We Sizwe*, were Arthur Goldreich and lawyer Harold Wolpe. In a tribute to Goldreich the *Jerusalem Post* states that during the raid on the farm "The 19 persons arrested and charged with sabotage included five whites – all Jews, namely Goldreich, Rusty Bernstein, Dennis Goldberg, Bob Hepple and Hilliard Festenstein." Considered by security police to be "the arch-conspirator" of the sabotage campaign Goldreich escaped to Israel before the Rivonia trial, and lived there until his death in 2011. Goldreich was a veteran of Palmach.[18] Mandela, closely associated with Goldreich at the farm, "wrote in his autobiography how he turned to Goldreich as one of the few in the ANC's nascent guerrilla army who knew how to fight because of his experience in Israel." Again, such an allusion suggests the plausibility of Mandela's interest in learning Israeli terror tactics.[19]

Another of the *Umkhonto We Sizwe* "high command," and Rivonia defendant, Denis Goldberg, was released from jail in 1986 as the result of Zionist pressure. While it is said that Goldberg, like other Jewish communists, did not regard themselves primarily as "Jews," nonetheless, when Goldberg was in jail his daughter, Hilary, organized a committee on a kibbutz where she lived, to lobby for her father's release. He was and remains critical of Israel, as many Jewish Marxists always have, but it was Israeli diplomats who secured his release. He stayed for several months on the

---

encyclopedias-almanacs-transcripts-and-maps/maisels-israel-aaron

17   Lauritz Strydom, *Rivonia Unmasked*, p. 78; http://www.rhodesia.nl/
      rivoniaunmasked.pdf

18   Roy Isacowitz, "Mandela's Jewish comrades," *Haaretz*, July 30, 2013.

19   Maurice Ostroff, "Appreciation: Arthur Goldreich," *The Jerusalem Post*,
      May 29, 2011; https://www.jpost.com/Opinion/Op-Ed-Contributors/
      Appreciation-Arthur-Goldreich

kibbutz where his daughter lived, and regarded the collective as "pure communism," according to the *Chicago Tribune*. Speaking to an Israeli magazine, *Koteret Rashit*, just after his arrival in Israel, Goldberg reiterated his belief in "terrorism": "It is very possible that innocent people will get killed, but that is the price."[20]

Again, we might discern something that does not accord with the cultivated image of Nelson Mandela's noble struggle. As Goldberg pointed out, he gave a commitment to eschew personal involvement with violence to secure his release from jail, while Mandela never did, and Goldberg respected that. The deaths of the innocent, as Goldberg stated, were acceptable to the "high command" of *Umkhonto We Sizwe,* including Mandela.

ISRAEL AND AFRICA

Israel had been cultivating relations with Black Africa as the European powers were retreating. In 1958, Israel established the Agency for International Development Cooperation (MASHAV) to support the emerging independent African states.

During the 1960s "Israel was keen to court the recently decolonized African states and so went out of its way to show solidarity with the latter by consistently voting in UN resolutions condemning the apartheid state and the regime behind it. ... The ANC itself, then led by Oliver Tambo, penned a letter from London to Israel's President Yitzhak Ben Zvi thanking him for Israel's actions at the United Nations."[21] Steven Gruzd of the South African Institute of International Affairs, states: "There was a kind of anti-colonial affinity because the Israelis had gotten rid of British colonialization and Africa was doing the same."[22]

---

20 Jonathan Broder, "Apartheid fight still his passion," *Chicago Tribune*, March 21, 1985; http://www.chicagotribune.com/news/ct-xpm-1985-03-21-8501160166-story.html

21 David Fachler, "Mandela and the Mossad: How Israel courted Black Africa," op. cit.

22 "Is Israel Africa's new best friend?," *Deutsche Welle*, https://www.dw.com/en/

Among the first of the Black terrorist organizations was the Mau Mau in Kenya, whose very name at the time conjured images of blood-curdling savagery; albeit today feted as freedom fighters against the brutal British. At around the time (1962) that Mandela was receiving training from the Mossad in Ethiopia, "General China" (Waruhiu Itote), who had been second in command of the Mau Mau, was in Israel with other East Africans, receiving military training.[23] In July 1963 he and other East Africans graduated as officers. They served as the basis of the post-British Kenyan army officers corps.

From the mid-1950s, that is, at the start of the White scuttle from Africa, Israel had an intensive program to influence Black Africa, and they were "aiding the military and civil systems," according to Israel Lior, military secretary to Israeli prime minister Eshkol.[24]

The Israelis were able to take advantage of a certain fascination Africans had for Israel as a new state that had attained independence from the British, and Israel was able to take advantage of its anti-colonial status, as it subsequently did as a newfound bulwark against the Soviet bloc from the 1970s, and now as a bulwark of "Western democracy" against "Islamism," or of the present supreme cynical irony of its mixture of atheists and Talmudists being lauded by Christian Fundamentalists as being the defenders of Christianity in the "Holy Land." Each image has been based on a profound myth, and adjusted according to the needs of the time. The initiative towards Black Africa was intended to make Israel the leader of non-Muslim Africa. Jomo Kenyatta, the secret leader of the Mau Mau, wrote in the introduction of the Hebrew edition of his book, *Facing Mount Kenya*:

---

is-israel-africas-new-best-friend/a-41777233

23 Steven Carol, *From Jerusalem to the Lion of Judah and Beyond: Israel's Foreign Policy in East Africa* (Bloomington: iUniverse Inc., 2012), p. 68.

24 Andrew and Leslie Cockburn, *Dangerous Liaisons: The inside story of the US-Israeli covert relationship* (New York: Harper Collins, 1991), p. 11.

You [Israelis] have built a nation with Jews coming from all the corners of the world; we want to build a unified Kenya composed of a multitude of tribes joined together through *Harambee* ["working together"].[25]

Dr. Steven Carol, a highly experienced - pro-Israel - historian, comments that, "These sentiments go far to explain the thinking behind the symbol of progress that Israel represented to the people of Kenya and to the developing nations of East Africa. To them Israel represented the attainable dream..."[26] Carol shows that after Kenya's independence links with Israel in terms of training, development and technical expertise were extensive. [27]

The situation was similar in Uganda. Yusuf Lule, president of Uganda in 1979, after the ouster of Idi Amin, had gone to Israel. Milton Obote, prime minster, had visited in September 1962, the month prior to independence, to discuss assistance from Israel. A Technical Cooperation Agreement was signed in 1963, and many scholarships were granted, while Israel sent advisers.[28] While Idi Amin is remembered for later his anti-Jewish and anti-Israel sentiments, Israelis started cultivating Amin when he was chief of staff under Obote. Baruch Bar Lev, Israeli military attaché, stated that Amin was "our man." Israelis, headed by Lev, backed Amin's overthrow of Obote in 1971.[29]

In Tanganyika/Tanzania Israeli delegations started examining how they could fill the void of the White colonials even before independence in 1961. The focus was on water development, and agriculture, Israel's agriculture minister then being General Moshe Dayan. Joint ventures and training programs ensued. Although the focus was on technical ventures and training in

---

25   Quoted by Steven Carol, op. cit., p. 68.

26   Carol, ibid., pp. 68-69.

27   Carol, ibid., p. 69.

28   Ibid., p. 72.

29   Andrew and Leslie Cockburn, op. cit., p. 11.

Black Africa, monetary loans were made to Kenya and Tanzania. Dr. Carol comments that this indicated how important East Africa was to foreign policy makers in Israel.[30] As is often the case with Israel's relationships, its associations with White ruled South Africa and Rhodesia were duplicitous. While Israel profited from White South Africa and Rhodesia, it simultaneously continued its subversion. It is a necessary part of Left-wing fantasy to believe that there was a symbiotic relationship between Israel and "the apartheid regime."

As with its consistent vote against South Africa at the United Nations, while profiting from trade deals, on the international diplomatic level Israel also acted against Rhodesia. Israel opposed Rhodesia's declaration of independence, while assiduously backing the "winds of change" of white scuttle. Black Africa could be manipulated and used. The thinking not only of Israel but of the USA, USSR, China and international finance, was that White ruled states could not, especially given the Afrikaners long history of antagonism against an oligarchy they referred to as the "Hoggenheimers." At the time of Rhodesia's UDI, The *Jewish Telegraphic Agency* reported:

> The Israel Government formally denounced today Rhodesia's declaration of independence as an "illegal, unilateral act violating the elementary rights of the overwhelming majority of the population." The official Israeli communique said Israel would not recognize the Rhodesian regime, had already acted to interrupt relations, including economic ties, and that it would support United Nations actions on the declaration. The Foreign Ministry today requested the Ministries of Finance and Commerce and Industry to withhold approval of any further trade exchanges with the British colony, Israel's exports to Rhodesia last year totaled some $600,000.[31]

---

30 Carol, op. cit., p. 76.

31 "Israel supports U.N on Rhodesia; severs economic ties with colony," Jewish Telegraphic Agency, November 15, 1965.

One surely has to wonder whether the drafters of the Israeli declaration were rolling about with laughter when they included: "illegal, unilateral act violating the elementary rights of the overwhelming majority of the population." The following month the Israeli delegate reiterated Israel's stand against Rhodesia and added an attack on South Africa:

> Israel's unqualified opposition to the apartheid program of the South African Government and to the "illegal regime" in Rhodesia was reaffirmed here today by Joel Barromi, Israel's delegate to the General Assembly's Special Political Committee.
>
> Speaking in debate on the South African apartheid policy, Mr. Barromi declared that Israel and the Jewish people reacted "instinctively" against the apartheid program as a threat not only against Africa, or against any given race but one against all mankind.
>
> He said that to be a citizen of Israel "means to take a position" in the struggle against racial discrimination. As far as Israel is concerned, he told the committee, its place is in the "anti-racist front," which is the front of human rights and fundamental freedoms.
>
> Israel, he said, hoped that all members of the United Nations would be ready to make the sacrifices necessary to meet the challenge. He reported that on November 13, Israel advised the Security Council of its decision not to recognize "the illegal regime" of Rhodesia and to take immediate steps to sever ties with the breakaway regime of Ian Smith economically "or otherwise." He also said that Israel was ready to "consider earnestly" any proposal for further "serious and responsible international action."[32]

---

32 "Israel takes stand at U.N. against Rhodesia and South African policy," JTA, December 3, 1965.

Body of white missionary Pamela Joyce with three month old baby killed by
Mugabe terrorists at Elim Mission, Rhodesia on 23 June, 1978

It is evident here that Israel was seeking to ingratiate itself
with Black Africa in furthering its aim of establishing a neo-
colonialism in the name of anti-colonialism. While details still
seem obscure, Israel was backing Black terrorist groups in
Rhodesia, as it had elsewhere (along with the USA[33]). In their
anti-Rhodesia book *The Struggle for Zimbabwe* journalists
David Martin and Phyllis Johnson refer to the expenses of
running Robert Mugabe's ZANU-PF offices in Dar es Salaam
being funded by the Israeli embassy.[34] Already in 1951 ANC
General Secretary Walter Sisulu, with Duma Nokwe (president
of the ANC Youth League) although not having passports, were
able to attend an international conference in Romania, courtesy
of Israel's *El Al* airlines. Stopping over for several weeks in
Israel, they were widely feted as heroes, although having a
preference for Israel's Communist Party rather than Zionism,
met General Moshe Dayan, and approvingly noted the popularity
of Communism among Israelis.[35]

33 Bolton, *Babel Inc.*, op. cit., pp 58-68.

34 David Martin and Phyllis Johnson, *The Struggle for Zimbabwe*, (London:
    Faber and Faber 1981).

35 Elinor Sisulu, *Walter and Albertina Sisuulu: In Our Lifetime* (Claremont, SA:

REVERSES

Unsurprisingly, Israel's posturing as the leader in "the anti-colonialist struggle" soon became unconvincing, as Israel's own colonialism became obvious (although one could wonder why it was not always obvious). The 1973 Yom Kippur War was the defining event when Black Africa broke its relationship with Israel, although there had been disquiet in 1967, and Israel had nowhere left to go other than the other pariah states, South Africa and Rhodesia. Geoff Sifrin, writing in *Haaretz* states of the time:

> Then, when African nations severed ties after the 1973 Yom Kippur war, Israel drew closer to South Africa – another international "pariah." South African Prime Minister John Vorster even made an official visit to Israel at the height of apartheid, causing disquiet among the local Jewish community. Then in 1987, with South Africa ablaze in violent protests, Israel followed other Western nations and restricted ties. Black South Africans still remember, though, that throughout their struggle the PLO helped the liberation movements, forging bonds which still endure.

> The affair was tinged with irony, coming soon after the UN World Conference Against Racism in Durban, which turned into an open display of anti-Semitism, and Water Affairs Minister Ronnie Kasrils'[36] attempt to get local Jews to sign a declaration against Israel called "Not in my name."[37]

Israel has been restoring its relationship with Black Africa in recent years. While Mandela is widely cited as having condemned Israel as an "apartheid state," this is incorrect; the result of a

---

David Philips Publisher, 2006), pp. 160-162.

36 Ronnie Kasril's, a leader of the South African Communist Party, of Jewish descent.

37 Geoff Sifrin, "Coming in from the cold: can Israel and South Africa restore warm ties?," *Haartez*, August 7, 2013.

spoof letter supposedly written by Mandela, but actually written by Arjan el Fassed, a Palestinian activist.[38] Zionists are still eager to present their credentials as supports of Mandela, and as heirs to an anti-colonial legacy.

Prime Minister Netanyahu said in 2016 that a new diplomatic initiative with African states was one of his top priorities, and that "Israel is coming back to Africa, and Africa is returning to Israel." Yoram Elron, deputy director general and head of the Africa division of the Israeli foreign ministry, commented on the continuing importance of Israel's role in Africa: "The reason why Africa is gaining so much importance in our foreign policy is its growing economic and political importance. The other component is the instability of northern African countries that are of concern to us. We would like to see more countries disengage from the positions of the African Union and vote against anti-Israeli resolutions in international forums. This is work in progress, this is not something that happens overnight, but the trend is positive." There are 54 African votes to be had at the U.N. General Assembly. [39]

CONCLUSION

Dr. Carol refers to Israel's agenda in East Africa as a mixture of altruism and strategic interest, as well as a sense of messianic mission. Critics of Zionism will be more cynical in regard to any altruistic motive, and one might contend that a sense of messianic mission does not extend to humanitarian gestures other than when they also serve a messianism that is based on Jewish world supremacy.

Theodor Herzl wrote in a novel *Altneuland* (Old-New Land, 1898) through the novel's hero Professor Steineck, referred to the

---

38 Ben Cohen, "Nelson Mandela and Zionism," Jewish News Syndicate, December 5, 2013; https://www.jns.org/opinion/nelson-mandela-and-zionism/

39 "A history of Africa-Israel relations," *Deutsche Welle*, https://www.dw.com/en/a-history-of-africa-israel-relations/a-43395892

suffering of the Negro race through slavery, and the desire to see the renaissance of the Negro, as he had seen the renaissance of the Jews. That is why he – the fictional character – was engaged in the "development of Africa."[40] However, while Zionist lobbies are active in promoting open borders and multicultural agendas over the world, Israel remains the exception. Israel's reaction to the "refugee crisis," inflamed by the destruction of Libya as Europe's bulwark against Black Africa, has been to reach an "international agreement" to deport 40,000 Africans, described as "infiltrators," and to shut down the Holot migrant detention center, allowing their removal without delay. The Israeli Public Security Ministry issued a statement saying the options were to leave or to be jailed.[41]

---

40 Cited by Carol, op. cit., p. 37.

41 Israel to deport 40,000 African refugees without their consent," *Deutsche Welle*, https://www.dw.com/en/israel-to-deport-40000-african-refugees-without-their-consent/a-41443084

The Alliance Between China and Zionism

The Zionist state's relationship with China is something that has come to public attention with a new Chinese documentary on Israel, although the relationship between Communist China and Israel is of long and strategic duration.

Walk into Israel – the Land of Milk and Honey has been produced by China's national TV channels in co-operation with Israel state authorities. The title should be a giveaway as to the nature of the series: one of the sustaining myths of Israel is that the superior Jewish settlers made Palestine flourish where once it was just sand occupied by a pack of rag-heads; never mind that Palestine was, before being blessed by the presence of Irgun, Haganah, Palmach and Stern, a land of plenty. The *People's Daily* reports of the event launching the series:

> An event to mark the launch of the TV documentary series "Walk into Israel – The Land of Milk and Honey," the first comprehensive TV series about the Jewish civilization and the State of Israel produced by CCTV, was held at the National Center for the Performing Arts in Beijing on July 29.

> "The TV documentary series 'Walk into Israel – The Land of Milk and Honey' is the most important TV series ever produced in China about Israel and the Jewish People, and it offers the viewer an historical, comprehensive and systematic introduction to the Jewish civilization and Israel," said Guy Kivetz, Director of Communications and Public Diplomacy at the Embassy of Israel in Beijing.

"Through this amazing program, which explores and unveils the wonders of the State of Israel and the contributions of the Jewish Civilization to the world, we are now able to present the real and bountiful Israel to the Chinese public. We are sure that this program will enhance the understanding of Israel in China and will therefore further promote friendly relations between the two peoples," he said.

Amos Nadai, Ambassador of Israel to China, delivered a speech during the launching event.

He said "Israel and China are two great civilizations known for their contributions to mankind and two modern states that share a rich history and many modern challenges. After watching the TV series, people may have a better understanding of the history and development of the 4000-year-old Jewish civilization as well as the rapid development of the modern State of Israel. This series has the potential to enhance mutual understanding and traditional friendship between Chinese and Jewish nations, promote cooperation between the two peoples and jointly build a better future for all."

Around 450 people, including CCTV Vice President Gao Feng and foreign diplomats were present at the event. The 12-episode HD TV series is now being broadcasted by the CCTV-2 and will be broadcast by CCTV's other leading channels in the future.[1]

Arutz Sheva, reporting on the documentary, stated:

Ties between Israel and China were virtually non-existent prior to the 1980s due to China's support for the Muslim

---

1   Liang Jun, "China-made documentary series spotlights Israel," *People's Daily Online*, July 30, 2010. (http://english.peopledaily.com. cn/90001/90782/90873/7087171.html)

world and the Palestinian Liberation Organization (PLO). The two nations developed military ties in the 1980s, and formally established diplomatic ties in the early 1990s.

Trade between the countries has since surpassed $4 billion per year.[2]

LONG HISTORY OF SINO-JEWISH RELATIONS

The *Arutz Sheva* claim that Sino-Zionist relations are something new is not accurate. There is a long history between Maoist China and Israel, both states emerging at about the same time, and with the same revolutionary Marxist zeal.[3] Israel's Ambassador to China, Amos Nadai, was more accurate when he referred, as quoted above by the *People's Daily*, to the "traditional friendship between Chinese and Jewish nations."

Rabbinic tradition claims an ancient association between "Jews" and China. Rabbi Jacob S Raisin, writing of the Chinese Jews, stated that "Some medieval commentators state that when Isaiah[4] forecasted the restoration of 'the land of Sinim' by the Jews," he had in mind Hebrews who had crossed the Jordan and who had travelled through the Caucasus, Turkestan and Tibet up to the Yellow River.[5]

During the 1640s there was a revolt against the Ming Dynasty, a dynasty that protected the Jews. The city of Kai-Fung-Foo fell and its Synagogue was destroyed (indicating the revolt was against Jewish influence). A "Jewish Manadarin" named Chao-Yng-Cheng, led an army that retook the city, and he rebuilt the

---

2   Maayana Miskin, "Chinese TV Features Israel, Jewish History," *Arutz Sheva: IsraelNationlaNews.com*, July 30, 2010. (http://www.israelnationalnews.com/News/News.aspx/138868)

3   K R Bolton, "The Red Face of Israel," *Foreign Policy Journal*, August 2, 2010. http://www.foreignpolicyjournal.com/2010/08/02/the-red-face-of-israel/all/1

4   *Isaiah* 6:12.

5   Rabbi Jacob S Raisin, *Gentile Reactions to Jewish Ideals*, (New York: Philosophical Library, 1953).

Ashkenazic Jews reached China via the Silk Road as traders and merchants.

synagogue in 1663. This history appears in engravings on the Synagogue and attests to the great political, commercial and military influence the Jewish community had in China[6] (unless the engravings are an "anti-Semitic forgery").

The Anglo-Chinese Opium Wars of 1839 and 1858-60 were attempts to kick out the Sassoon dynasty that controlled the opium trade under the protection of the British Empire. The Manchu emperor attempted to stop the trade but the Opium Wars only ended in defeat and the extension of the trade throughout China.

T V. Soong[7] head of Sassoon's Bank of China, held numerous important posts in the Kuomintang Government, including

---

6   "China," *Jewish Encyclopaedia*, (New York, 1903) Vol. IV. See: http://www.jewishencyclopedia.com/view.jsp?artid=461&letter=C

7   Soong's Jewishness is assumed by the fact that Sassoon "only employed Jews," according to the *Jewish Encyclopaedia*, 1944.

those of Governor of the Central Bank of China and Minister of Finance (1928–31, 1932–33); Minister of Foreign Affairs (1942–45); President of the Executive Yüan (1945–47), and premier in 1949. After failing to reconcile Communist and Nationalist factions he moved to the USA.

Soong's sister, Soong Ch'ing-ling, became prominent in revolutionary politics, and in 1914 she married Sun Yat-sen, the revolutionary leader. After Sun's death (1925) she was elected (1926) to the Kuomintang central executive committee, resigning in 1927 in protest at the expulsion of the Communists. The outbreak (1937) of the Sino-Japanese War reconciled her with the Kuomintang until 1946. From 1949 she served as Vice Chairman of the Government of Communist China.

Another sister, Soong Mei-ling, married Dr Sun's successor, Chiang Kai-shek in 1927. In 1945 she became a member of the central executive committee of the Kuomintang.[8]

When Dr Sun died in 1925, the Sassoon interests sent T V Soong to offer Chiang Kai-shek $3,000,000 cash, Soong's own sister as a wife (although Chiang already had a wife and family) and the offer of support for the presidency of China in succession to T V Soong's late brother-in-law.[9]

Under Chiang Kai-shek, Jewish refugees from Germany filled prominent posts. Dr Bernhard Weiss, former vice president of the police in Berlin presided over the reorganisation of the Chinese police. The *Castilian Jewish Encyclopaedia* states: "Many German officers of Jewish origin enlisted in Chiang Kai-shek's army." Miriam Karnes founded the Chinese women's battalion. General Moshe Cohen organised the supply for the army.[10]

---

8   *The Columbia Encyclopaedia*, Sixth Edition, 2002 Columbia University Press.

9   E C Knuth, *The Empire of "The City"*, (Milwaukee: Knuth, 1946), reprinted 1982, no further publication details, 45, 46, 82.

10   *Castilian Jewish Encyclopaedia*, Mexico, 1948, "China."

Sino-Zionist Relations

In 2002 Israel and China commemorated ten years of diplomatic relations. This is deceptive. The relationship goes back since the early days of the founding of both Israel and Red China. The *People's Daily* reported:

> Israel and China have jointly issued a postal souvenir on Thursday to mark the 10th anniversary of the establishment of diplomatic ties between the two countries.

> Israeli Minister of Communication Reuven Rivlin said at the issuing ceremony in Tel Aviv that he was pleased that Israel and China chose a postal and philatelic medium to mark this important event. The minister said: "I believe that the common values that our two ancient nations share, alongside with the cooperation that we have established in so many fields will ensure that our relationship will continue to flourish in the decades to come."....

> Rivlin just came back this week from China after signing an agreement for the sale of two communication satellites for broadcasting and the telecommunications for the 2008 Olympic Games in Beijing....

> Chinese Ambassador to Israel Pan Zhanlin said he was very pleased to witness the significant development of the profound relations between the two countries. He added that it demonstrates the friendship between the two peoples forged during long-standing contacts and the achievements of cooperation made during the past 10 years.

> Peres said in his message, "Israel is full of appreciation and gratitude for the warm relations and friendship that China has expressed to the Jewish people over the years."[11]

---

11   "Israel, China Celebrate 10 Years of Diplomatic Ties," *People's Daily*, January 25, 2002.

Professor Guang Pan outlined China's role in the Middle East, of which the following are some of the salient facts in relation to Israel:

During the period 1949-1955, with the exception of Israel, none of the independent Middle Eastern states recognised Red China. In 1950 the Arab League voted to recognise Taiwan rather than the Red China as the legitimate representative of the Chinese people. The Arab states generally also voted against Red China's admission to the UNO, while Israel supported China. China referred to Middle Eastern leaders as "the anti-revolutionary rulers" and "feudal dictators." "Even after Egypt's July Revolution of 1952, Beijing continued to refer to "the anti-revolutionary military dictators" of that country... *The only exception to this pattern of condemnation was Israel with its socialist leaders. The Chinese press welcomed the establishment of the State of Israel in 1948* and accused the British of "agitating" the Arab "anti-revolutionary rulers" to launch an anti-Jewish war. During the 1950s and 1960s China sought to influence the Arab states as they became increasingly estranged from the West, due to the pro-Israeli stance of the USA and other states. From the mid-1980s China presented itself as pro-Arab and anti-Israel. However, with the Sino-Soviet break of 1960-61 China's attitude towards the Soviet allies Egypt and Syria cooled. An anti-Russian attitude was the basis of Chinese relations during the decade of 1966-76. Professor Guang Pan states:

As an active Middle East diplomacy developed on the basis of anti-Soviet goals, Beijing established diplomatic ties with three pro-Western countries between August and November 1971: Turkey, Iran, and Lebanon. It did not, however, restore contact with Israel, for fear of this harming relations with the Arab world. Nonetheless, China and Israel had in the Soviet Union a common opponent and at one time both were fighting Soviet soldiers—Chinese infantry on the common border with Russia, Israeli pilots over the skies of Egypt and Syria. *In 1971, Zhou even told Senator Henry Jackson (Democrat of Washington) that China supported Israel in its efforts against Soviet expansion in the Middle East.* After 1971, Beijing backed Egypt's Anwar as-Sadat, Sudan's Ja'far an-Numayri, and other Arab leaders as they expelled Soviet forces from their countries." [Emphasis added].From 1977 onward China sought to establish contact with all Middle Eastern states, culminating in the establishment of formal relations with Israel in 1992.[12]

It should be kept in mind that even as China was fostering relations with the Arab states, this anti-Russian strategy was serving Zionist interests in countering the USSR, which had become increasingly antagonistic towards Zionism since Stalin. In particular, Israeli sources were covertly arming China through Shaul Eisenberg, an agent of Mossad,[13] and "the richest man in Israel." According to Mossad defector Victory Ostrovsky, Eisenberg was "Mossad's tie-in with China."

Uri Dan, writing in the New York Post, March 30, 1997, reported that back in 1979 then-Israeli Prime Minister Menachem Begin got U.S. approval for authorising Shaul Eisenberg to undertake a $10 billion 10-year deal to modernise the Chinese armed forces thereby "strengthening the counterbalance to Soviet military might." Dan describes this deal as "one of the most important in Israeli history" and that "the Chinese insisted on absolute secrecy."[14]

---

12 Guang Pan, "China's Success in the Middle East," *Middle East Quarterly*, Vol. IV, No. 4, December 1997. Guang Pan is professor of political science and history at the Institute of European and Asian Studies in Shanghai, and director of the Chinese Society of Middle East Studies, with a special interest in Jewish, Middle Eastern, and international studies.

13 Victor Ostrovsky, *By Way of Deception: The Making & Unmaking of a Mossad Officer*, (New York: St Martin's Press, 1990), `26.

14 Michael Collins Piper, "Chinese Espionage and Israel," an open letter to Congressman Christopher Cox, May 6, 1999. http://www.mail-archive.com/

Israel's role as a major supplier of arms for China, including sophisticated military equipment originating from the USA, has become a public scandal on several occasions over the past decade.

In 1999 the *New York Times* reported: "Israel has long had a close, secretive military relationship with China that arms experts say has resulted in billions of dollars of weapons sales in recent years and raised a variety of concerns in the United States."[15] Note that *The Times* stated the Sino-Israeli relationship is close, secret, and of long duration. Elta, a subsidiary of the Israeli Aircraft Industry, designed Phalcon, a sophisticated radar system for the Chinese Air Force.[16] In 1999 Howard Phillips reported:

> *Israel is China's second-largest supplier.* A recent report by Kenneth W. Allen and Eric A. McVadon of the Henry L. Stimson Center, a research organization in Washington, said *Israel had provided China with a range of weapons– including electronic components for tanks, communications and optical equipment, aircraft and missiles–during a relationship that began at least two decades ago.* Full diplomatic ties were not established until 1997.

> "*Both China and Israel appear to gain military and political benefits from the arms and technology transfer relationship,*" the report said. "Besides seeking money from China, some Israeli officials claim the sale of military technology to China will secure Beijing's agreement not to sell specific weapons to Israel's enemies in the Middle East."[17]

---

ctrl@listserv.aol.com/msg12562.html

15   "Clinton Administration Presses Israel to Stop Aiding Red China," *New York Times*, November 11, 1999, 1.

16   "Taiwan at risk from transfer of US originated technology," *Howard Phillips Issues & Strategy Bulletin*, July 31, 1999. For numerous examples see: http://www.conservativeusa.org/redchina-military-old.htm

17   "Israeli-Chinese military Co-operation is Bad for America," *Howard Phillips,*

Note above that the report states that although full diplomatic relations were not established until 1997, a covert relationship involving weapons and technology transfers had been going on since the 1970s.

U.S. protests at Israel's transfer of advanced military systems to China rings hollow. Those typically lame protests from the world's leading Israel-fawning state are of the kind typical for public consumption, since the USA was itself engaged at the time in the same relationship with China (as well as having long since approved the secret arms deals with Eisneberg) one report at the time stating of the Clinton Administration:

> Unlike his predecessors Democrat or Republican, Mr. Clinton transferred primary legal authority for approving export licenses for advanced U.S. technology from the security-conscious State Department to the politically conscious Commerce Department for the purpose of making such exports easier.

> Mr. Clinton is also the first and only president to approve an export waiver authorizing two companies — Loral Space and Communications and Hughes Electronics — to transfer technological secrets in the face of a criminal investigation involving their prior alleged export violations. Mr. Clinton approved personally the export of their data relating to satellite and missile-launch technology to China over the objections of his secretary of state, the Pentagon and others.[18]

After a deal between China and Israel on advanced weapons technology became public and resulted in cancellation, Israeli and Chinese diplomats met to overcome difficulties. A Jewish newspaper reported:

---

ibid.

18   Mark Levin, *Washington Times*, May 27, 1999, A1.

JERUSALEM — Defense Minister Binyamin Ben-Eliezer met with Chinese Ambassador Pan Zhanlin in Tel Aviv Monday to discuss the cancellation of Israel's sale of the Phalcon advanced radar system.

Ben-Eliezer appraised relations between the two countries and glossed over the affair. "We have to see it as *an incident inside the family* and not as a crisis between two states," he told Zhanlin. *Ben-Eliezer promised to work to strengthen the defense ties with Beijing.*

Zhanlin told Ben-Eliezer that he believes *China knows how to overcome the difficulties and strengthen the ties*, according to a statement issued by the Defense Ministry. *China is fully prepared to cooperate with Israel.*[19] [Emphasis added].

The deal only fell through because of public concern expressed in the USA. Note the fraternal relations expressed between the two; "an incident inside the family." In 2009 a new Israeli consulate was established in Guangzhou, capital of the flourishing Guangdong province, where much trade between Israel and China is undertaken.[20]

Against such a background of Sino-Israeli relations, that a major Chinese documentary on the wonders and glories of Israel is to have such an extensive airing among the Chinese people and over such a duration of time, launched with much ado by leading Israeli and Chinese luminaries, it seems pertinent to ask whether there are major developments afoot in regard to extending Sino-Zionist collaboration.

---

19 "China, Israel meet on foiled radar system," *Jewishweekly.com*, January 4, 2002. http://www.jweekly.com/article/full/17020/china-israel-meet-on-foiled-radar-system-sale/

20 Malkah Fleisher, "New Israeli Consulate in China to Boost Partnership, Prosperity," *Arutz Sheva* July 6, 2009. http://www.israelnationalnews.com/News/News.aspx/132226

Sino-Zionist collaboration, often covert, and of long-duration, again contradicts the widely-propagandised view that Israel is the brave little defender of Western interests, and even of Western culture, against a sea of alien, anti-Western interests. As we have already seen from the preceding chapters, Israel will deal with any interest, doctrine, state or power that serves Israel, and stab anyone in the back if that serves their interests, regardless of the supposed closeness of prior relationships.[21]

---

21 For example the 1967 sinking of the USS Liberty in international waters by
     Israeli air fighters, resulting in 34 deaths and many wounded U.S. sailors. Any
     other state would have been demonised, embargoed, and then obliterated.
     See: The U.S. reaction to this Israeli atrocity against Americans however,
     was to try and muzzle those who survived. http://whatreallyhappened.com/
     WRHARTICLES/ussliberty.html
     One might also recall the more recent murder of Rachel Corrie in Israel:
     "Rachel Corrie was a 23-year-old American peace activist from Olympia,
     Washington, who was crushed to death by an Israeli bulldozer on 16 March
     2003, while undertaking nonviolent direct action to protect the home of
     a Palestinian family from demolition." Rachel Corrie Foundation, http://
     rachelcorriefoundation.org/rachel

Walkout on Ahmadinejad at U.N.

While it is all very easy for the news media, sundry interest groups, and government functionaries throughout the world to dismiss Dr Ahmadinejad as a Mad Mullah beyond the ken of rational debate, perhaps that is because Iran's president poses questions that are too near the mark to allow a sensible hearing.

As if it weren't enough being the leader of a large Islamic nation that does not kowtow to the USA and to Israel, Dr Ahmadinejad put himself beyond redemption for eternity by suggesting that "holocaust revisionism" should be subjected to the same standards of scholarly scrutiny as any other historical matter,[1] and like the Left-wing Jewish academic Prof. Norman G Finkelstein, suggested that the holocaust was being exploited for political and economic motives.[2] Being Jewish, Left-wing and the son of parents who had survived both the Warsaw Ghetto and Nazi concentration camps,[3] didn't save Finkelstein from the Zionist smear-brigade, so Dr Ahmadinejad is not about to be cut any slack.

When Dr Ahmadinejad reached the UN podium on September 24, it is certain that Israel, the USA and sundry lackeys to both states, waited with baited breath to see what the president would do this time to try and expose their corrupt system before what remains of states that have any sense of national sovereignty and dignity. The reaction of the delegates from the USA, Australia,

---

1   Ahmadinejad at Holocaust Conference: Israel will soon be 'wiped out,'" Haaretz.com December 12, 2006, http://www.haaretz.com/news/ahmadinejad-at-holocaust-conference-israel-will-soon-be-wiped-out-1.206977

2   Norman G Finkelstein, *The Holocaust Industry: Reflections on the Exploitation of Jewish Suffering* (New York: Verso, 2001).

3   Ibid., 5.

President Mahmoud Ahmadinejad gestures as he attends the United
Nations General Assembly

New Zealand, all 27 delegates from the EU states, Canada, and
Costa Rica was to walk out en mass — the response of those who
have nothing thoughtful or honest to offer. In New Zealand's
case, our state relies on moral posturing at world forums to
compensate for national impotence. Dr Ahmadinejad suggested
before the General Assembly in regard to 9/11 that scenarios
might include:

- That a "powerful and complex terrorist group" which
  is "advocated by American statesmen," penetrated US
  intelligence and defences.

- "That some segments within the US Government orchestrated
  the attack to reverse the declining American economy and its
  grip on the Middle East in order to save the Zionist regime.
  The majority of the American people as well as other nations
  and politicians agree with this view."

- That the attack was the work of "a terrorist group but the

American government supported and took advantage of the situation."[4]

According to media reports, "Ahmadinejad said the US used the September 11 attacks as a pretext to invade Afghanistan and Iraq, killing hundreds of thousands of people."[5]

Media reports incredulously claim that Dr Ahmadinejad did not explain the logic behind blaming the US for the terror attacks but state there were three theories (as listed above). Well surely the three theories are three explanations for the "logic behind blaming the US"?

While it might be questionable for Dr Ahmadinejad to have stated that "the majority" of Americans support the view that 9/11 was a Zionist jack up somewhere along the line, as well as the view of other nations and politicians, the view – of course dismissed by orthodox academia, media and government functionaries as "conspiracy theory" – is certainly one that is at least very widespread, including among many professionals in the relevant sciences for investigating such matters.

There are also many oddities about events before and after 9/11, such as the large number of Israelis who were acting suspiciously and were rounded up and deported from the USA, albeit quietly, and the antics of five Israeli "moving company" employees[6] dancing atop a warehouse roof in New Jersey at the time of the Twin Towers collapse, arrested and questioned for several months by the FBI, at least two of whom were found to

---

4   "Ahmadinejad's speech leads to walkout at UN," *The Dominion Post*, Wellington, New Zealand, September 25, 2010, A21.

5   Ibid.

6   Urban Moving Systems, found by the FBI to be a Mossad front, the owner quickly departed back to Israel after initial questioning by the FBI. Marc Perelman, "Spy rumors on gusts of truth," *Forward*, New York, March 15, 2002.

be Mossad operatives.[7] These matters will not concern us here however, as the internet has abundant details. What we will consider here is:

- Have such methods, as suggested by Dr Ahmadinejad been used before to justify wars?

- Was there a long-range plan to use conflict scenarios as justification for the invasion of states in order to secure "regime change" in the interests of Israel?

FALSE FLAG OPERATIONS

The 9/11 attacks have been called "False Flag operations." Media and others bleat about this "conspiracy theory" as though the concept has just been conceived by paranoid mentalities. The False Flag operation has been frequently used to instigate conflicts, and many such incidents are recognized by orthodox academe and media. Therefore, what makes 9/11 so inconceivable as a False Flag operation?

Examples of False Flag operations accepted as such by orthodox academe include:

- The Manchurian Incident, 1931, when Japanese officers contrived a pretext for invading Manchuria by blowing up part of the Japanese owned railway.[8]

- Gleiwitz, Poland, 1939. German soldiers dressed in Polish uniforms attacked and occupied a German radio station near the Polish border. Several German prisoners dressed as Polish soldiers were left dead at the scene. The incident was used to justify the invasion of Poland. Other incidences under "Operation Himmler" occurred simultaneously along the border.[9]

---

7   Marc Perelman, ibid.

8   C Peter Chen, "Mukden Incident and Manchukuo," World War II Database, http://ww2db.com/battle_spec.php?battle_id=18

9   Andrzej Jarczewski (Steward to the Gliwice Radio Station), Radio Station

- Mainila, Russia, 1939. The Soviets shelled this Russian town near the Finnish border, claiming that it had been bombed by the Finns, using this as a pretext for invasion.[10]

- Cairo and Alexandria, 1954, The Lavon Affair. Israeli agents bombed American and British properties in Egypt for the purpose of blaming the Egyptians. The nine Egyptian Jews involved were honoured in 2005 by the Israeli Government, despite the operation supposedly being of a "rogue" nature.[11]

- USA-Cuba, 1962. Operation Northwoods, conceived by the Joint Chiefs of Staff and signed off by Gen. Lyman Lemnitzer. The plan included the sinking of a US ship near Cuba, aeroplane hijackings, and bombings throughout the USA, which would be made to appear to be of Cuban origin. The plan was scotched by Kennedy, but was later exposed by James Bamford via the Freedom of Information Act. The purpose of this plan is instructive in the context of 9/11: The desired result from the execution of this plan would be to place the United States in the apparent position of suffering defensible grievances from a rash and irresponsible government of Cuba and to develop an international image of a Cuban threat to peace in the Western Hemisphere.[12]

Gliwice Museum, http://www.radiostacjagliwicka.republika.pl/foldery/FoldeRAng.htm

10   Robert Edwards, *White Death: Russia's War on Finland 1939–40*, (London: Weidenfeld & Nicolson, 2006), 105.

11   "Israel honors nine Egyptian [sic] spies, "Reuters, March 30, 2005, http://www.ynetnews.com/Ext/Comp/ArticleLayout/CdaArticlePrintPreview/1,25 06,L-3065838,00.html#n

12   "September 11 – Another Operation Northwoods?," (from chapter 4 of Bamford) http://www.blythe.org/nytransfer-subs/2001cov/11_Sept_2001_-_Another_Operation_Northwoods_
James Bamford, *Body of Secrets: Anatomy of the Ultra-Secret National Security Agency From the Cold War Through the Dawn of a New Century* (New York: Doubleday, 2001). The Operation Northwoods memorandum can be found at The National Security Archive, George Washington University, http://www.gwu.edu/~nsarchiv/news/20010430/northwoods.pdf

The destruction of the USS Arizona at Pearl Harbor - 7th December 1941.

While not a "False Flag" operation, Pearl Harbor is worth mentioning in this context. It has long been contended by many well placed individuals, including ex-military commanders on Hawaii, that the Roosevelt Administration was forewarned of the Japanese attack due to having broken the Japanese naval codes, but failed to warn the Pearl Harbor command of the attack so that maximum propaganda could be obtained. Col. Curtis Dall, President Roosevelt's son-in-law, was on the inside of what went on in Washington at that time. In a scenario familiar to those who consider 9/11 to be a False Flag operation, Dall cites the November 25, 1941 entry from US Secretary of War Henry L Stimson's diary:

> The question was how we should maneuver them [the Japanese] into firing the first shot, without allowing too much damage to ourselves. It was a difficult proposition.[13]

The Stimson comment follows the strategy recommended by

---

13   Ibid., 11. Dall relates that Kimmel told him that US Secretary of State Marshall got around to telegraphing Kimmel via regular commercial channels about the "impending" attack two hours after the event. Dall, ibid., 15-16.

Lt. Commander Arthur H McCollum, director of the Office of Naval Intelligence, Fear East Asia section, who had on October 7, 1940, over a year prior to Pearl Harbor, drafted a memorandum, suggesting methods of goading Japan into attacking the USA to justify America's entry into the war, and move public opinion which was overwhelmingly isolationist. McCollum outlined eight points of policy that might provoke Japan into an action against the USA, the problem as McCollum stated it being that, "It is not believed that in the present state of political opinion the United States government is capable of declaring war against Japan without more ado..."[14] McCollum concludes by unequivocally stating: "If by these means Japan could be led to commit an overt act of war, so much the better. At all events we must be fully prepared to accept the threat of war."[15]

ZIONIST STRATEGY FORMULATED IN 1996

While the USA, Israel and their hangers-on feign ignorance as to why there would be any rational explanation for a False Flag operation in regard to 9/11, the US strategy that was subsequently pursued after the Twin Towers topplings follows a scenario that was formulated in 1996, five years previously. The strategy document entitled *A Clean Break* was prepared by the Study Group for a New Israeli Strategy Toward 2000, a group set up by the think tank, the Institute for Advanced Strategic and Political Studies headquartered in Jerusalem.[16] Its authors described as "prominent opinion makers," were listed as follows:

Richard Perle, American Enterprise Institute, study group leader; James Colbert, Jewish Institute for National Security

---

14 Arthur H McCollum, "Memorandum for the Director, Subject: Estimate of the Situation in the Pacific and Recommendations for Action by the United States," October 7, 1940, Point 9. http://en.wikisource.org/wiki/McCollum_memorandum

15 McCollum, ibid., Point 10.

16 "A Clean Break: A New Strategy for Securing the Realm," Institute for Advanced Strategic and Political Studies, 1996, http://www.iasps.org/strat1.htm

Affairs; Charles Fairbanks Jr., Johns Hopkins University, Douglas Feith, Feith and Zell Associates; Robert Loewenberg, President, Institute for Advanced Strategic and Political Studies; Jonathan Torop, The Washington Institute for Near East Policy; David Wurmser, Institute for Advanced Strategic and Political Studies; Meyrav Wurmser, Johns Hopkins University.

Of these, in the Bush Administration Perle became director of the Defense Policy Board; Feith, Under-Secretary of Defense for Policy at the Pentagon; and David Wurmser, personal assistant to Chief Policy Adviser John Bolton, another Zionist.

The strategy document, *A Clean Break* focused primarily on removing Syria and Iraq as obstacles to Israeli hegemony in the Middle East, with the focus specifically being as a first step to remove Saddam, "an important Israeli strategic objective in its own right." Of particular interest is the recommendation that "Cold War" type rhetoric be utilized for propaganda purposes in order to garner US support for an expanded Israeli role in the region in destabilising and "rolling back" regimes that are obstacles to Israel:

> To anticipate U.S. reactions and plan ways to manage and constrain those reactions, Prime Minister Netanyahu can formulate the policies and stress themes he favors in language familiar to the Americans by tapping into themes of American administrations during the Cold War which apply well to Israel.

Hence, the oft-used references in the document to how Israel has a shared vision with the USA based on "Western values" and how it is a bulwark for those values surrounded by hostile regimes. This strategy has been pursued of course with vigor since Zionist David Frum, White House speechwriter for Bush, coined the term "axis of evil."

This document also reiterated the need for Israel to resume the aggressive policy of "pre-emption" rather than just "retaliation," for the purpose not only of overcoming Israel's enemies but of "transcending" them.[17]

In 2002 the Project for a New American Century presented a policy document in the form of a letter to George W Bush amongst whose signatories was again Richard Perle.[18] This coterie reiterated the common bond between Israel and the USA in the wake of 9/11 as fellow "free and democratic" nations, adding: "We are both targets of what you have correctly called an 'Axis of Evil,'" a term which was itself a Zionist contrivance, as referred to above.

> Israel is targeted in part because it is our friend, and in part because it is an island of liberal, democratic principles — American principles — in a sea of tyranny, intolerance, and hatred. As Secretary of Defense Rumsfeld has pointed out, Iran, Iraq, and Syria are all engaged in "inspiring and financing a culture of political murder and suicide bombing" against Israel, just as they have aided campaigns of terrorism against the United States over the past two decades. You have declared war on international terrorism, Mr. President. Israel is fighting the same war.

Here we have for the most part Zionists defining what are "American principles," declaring those principles to also be Israel's and identifying the common enemies that must be destroyed in a "war on international terrorism," those enemies being Iran, Iraq and Syria, in addition to a subsequent reference to Afghanistan.

The nightmare scenario of attacks on the USA by Iraq – and Iran – is then emphasized, by the familiar but entirely discredited

---

17   Ibid.

18   William Kristol et al, letter to President Bush, April 3, 2002, Project for A New American Century, http://www.newamericancentury.org/Bushletter-040302.htm

theme of "weapons of mass destruction."

> Furthermore, Mr. President, we urge you to accelerate plans for removing Saddam Hussein from power in Iraq. As you have said, every day that Saddam Hussein remains in power brings closer the day when terrorists will have not just aeroplanes with which to attack us, but chemical, biological, or nuclear weapons, as well. It is now common knowledge that Saddam, along with Iran, is a funder and supporter of terrorism against Israel....

> ...Israel's fight against terrorism is our fight. Israel's victory is an important part of our victory. For reasons both moral and strategic, we need to stand with Israel in its fight against terrorism.

The rhetoric is that of Cold War type propaganda recommended in 1996 in the *Clean Break* document. In fact the founding statement of the Project for a New American Century unequivocally states that it has been formed amidst what it attempts to project as a new "Cold War" type world crisis scenario, precisely as the Study Group for a New Israeli Strategy Toward 2000 had recommended the year previously as a propaganda ploy to get the American public behind an aggressive US-Zionist alliance.

> As the 20th century draws to a close, the United States stands as the world's preeminent power. Having led the West to victory in the Cold War, America faces an opportunity and a challenge: Does the United States have the vision to build upon the achievements of past decades? Does the United States have the resolve to shape a new century favourable to American principles and interests?[19]

That same year – 2000 – also, the Project for a New American Century, issued an agenda for post-Cold War foreign policy

---

19   Project for a New American Century, "Statement of Principles," June 3, 1997, http://www.newamericancentury.org/statementofprinciples.htm

doctrine.[20] The PNAC report emphasizes the need to maintain US weapons supremacy. The PNAC, as the name of the organization implies, is unapologetically dedicated to maintaining the USA as the center for world control; an American world empire whose hegemony is unchallenged; to not only "preserve but to 'enhance' what is called "American peace,"[21] "Pax Americana," as it is called.[22] The neo-Cold Warriors of the PNAC emphasize in their document that a major concern is that with the demise of big power rivalries after the collapse of the Soviet bloc, the USA will become complacent, and there will be an ongoing process of military stagnation, rather than seeking not only to preserve but to "enhance" (sic) US hegemony. Again, like the concerns of the architects of the *McCollum Memorandum* and Operation Northwoods, the problem is to overcome this complacency, since "that solely pursued capabilities for projecting force from the United States, for example, and sacrificed forward basing and presence, would be at odds with larger American policy goals and would trouble American allies."[23] Here again we come to the crisis scenario that is needed to shock the USA and its allies out of complacency and justify the USA's global military supremacy: "Further, the process of transformation, even if it brings revolutionary change, is likely to be a long one, absent some catastrophic and catalyzing event – like a new Pearl Harbor."[24]

The current "war on terrorism" has been long in the making. The propaganda has been contrived to generate a new Cold War type hysteria, "Islamofascism" being among the new propaganda terms for the purpose. One of the primary goals of eliminating Saddam Hussein has been achieved. There remains Iran, with

---

20   Thomas Donnelly, *Rebuilding America's Defenses: Strategy, Force and Resources for a New Century*, Project for a New American Century, September 2000, http://www.newamericancentury.org/RebuildingAmericasDefenses.pdf

21   Ibid., iv.

22   Ibid., 1.

23   Ibid, 50-51.

24   Ibid., 51.

the war drums being beaten in that direction for the past several years, utilizing the same discredited allegations about "weapons of mass destruction" that were used to justify the invasion of Iraq; while Syria has been listed as the next victim. For UN delegations led by the USA to walk out on Iran's President in feigned moral indignation that anyone could suggest that 9/11 could have been an inside jack-up, promptly followed by President Obama chastising Dr Ahmadinejad for such blasphemy is of course merely disingenuous humbuggery, given that such False Flag operations have been planned often enough previously both by the USA and Israel.

Manipulation of Islam

Globalists and U.S. policy-makers are playing a duplicitous game in regard to Islam: The so-called 'Jihadists' or 'Islamists,' are paraded as the universal bogeymen that justify the 'global war on terrorism'; the 'Arab Spring' (another batch of well-planned and funded 'spontaneous' 'colour revolutions')[1] and the invasion and occupation of 'rejectionist' states. On the other hand, funding from globalist organisations and agencies of the U.S. government have supported 'Islamists' such as the Mujahideen when 'Islamists' were used to dislodge the Russians from Afghanistan, and similar organisations in Libya, Albanian Muslim terrorists in Serbia and the same types presently in Syria. These 'Islamists' can be called 'terrorists' or 'freedom fighters' as requirements dictate. The Kosovo Liberation Army had been designated originally by the U.S. State Department as terrorists and gangsters but, when needed, were armed to topple the Yugoslav state. The globalists have been playing the same game in supporting Muslim terrorism against Russia in Chechnya.

Today's 'Islamists' are a product of U.S. Cold War policy against Russia. Graham Fuller, when Deputy Director of the CIA's National Council on Intelligence, spawned the Mujahideen during the 1980s, recruiting fundamentalist Muslims for training in guerrilla insurgency against Soviet forces in Afghanistan. One of these trainees was Osama bin Laden. Al Qaeda was the product. Fuller, worked at the Pentagon, and at the RAND Corporation globalist think tank. Swiss journalist and author Richard Labévière cited a 1999 memo of Fuller as a basis for U.S. policy:

The policy of guiding the evolution of Islam and of helping

---

1   K. R. Bolton, *Revolution from Above*, 'The Global Democratic Revolution,'

them against our adversaries worked marvellously well in Afghanistan against [the Russians]. The same doctrines can still be used to destabilize what remains of Russian power, and especially to counter the Chinese[2] influence in Central Asia.[3]

Russia's main pipeline route out of the Caspian Sea basin transits through Chechnya and Dagestan. The 1994–1996 Chechen war, instigated by the main rebel movements against Moscow, served to undermine secular state institutions. The adoption of Islamic law in the largely secular Muslim societies of the former Soviet Union serves U.S. strategic interests in the region, as a means of destabilisation. Elsewhere, conversely, U.S./globalist policy pursues secularisation against Islam and all other traditional religions, as explained by Ralph Peters. The Soros networks are particularly assiduous in funding movements and individuals against traditional cultural, ethnic and national principles. 'Feminism' including so-called 'reproductive' rights' (abortion), is especially promoted by such globalist NGOs. 'Feminism' next to multiculturalism, is one of the most useful tools for globalist subversion in subverting traditional national and cultural structures.[4]

However, it is notable that while Islamic states are targeted for their alleged mistreatment of woman due to the supposed harshness of Islamic laws, nothing is said about the laws on women in Orthodox Judaism and in Israel.[5] The Orthodox Jewish view, according to Evelyn Kaye, who was raised under

---

2   In this writer's opinion, the United States will not act against China. The two have symbiotic economies and the globalists headed up by Rockefeller, Soros and Goldman Sachs interests are profiting well from the Chinese status quo. Russia under Putin remains the primary globalist irritant. See Bolton,

3   Richard Labévière, *Dollars for Terror: The United States and Islam* (New York: Algora Publishing, 2000), 5–6.

4   K. R. Bolton, 'Feminism,' in *Revolution from Above.*

5   See: Evelyn Kaye, *The Hole in the Sheet: A Modern Woman Looks at Orthodox and Hasidic Judaism* (New Jersey: Lyle Stuart, 1987).

Orthodox Judaism, which is reflected in Israeli laws, is that 'women are wicked, unreliable sexual temptresses, who are put on earth to lead men into evil ungodly ways and tempt them to stop observing the laws and commandments of Judaism. Women are not human beings able to cope with the demands of real life. They are strange people who must be bound by stern rules so that they know what to do, and who must be kept strictly within bounds, lest they upset the established male order'.[6]

One of the numerous subversive organisations established to encourage 'regime change' in 'rejectionist' regimes is the American Committee for Peace in the Caucasus (ACPC), originally founded as the American Committee for Peace in Chechnya. This is a project of Freedom House, one of the primary globalist NGOs promoting 'regime change' around the world, in tandem with the Soros 'Open Society' network, USAID, the National Endowment for Democracy, *ad infinitum.*[7] ACPC, which is based at Freedom House, states of itself:

> Founded in 1999 to advocate for a political solution to the conflict in Chechnya that erupted into a war for independence with Russia in 1994, ACPC was at the helm of international NGO efforts to galvanize the U.S. and international policymaking community on the implications of the conflict for human rights in Chechnya. As violence spread into other republics in the North Caucasus— Ingushetia, Dagestan, Kabardino-Balkaria, Karachay-Cherkessia and North Ossetia—ACPC concentrated its efforts on supporting human rights and rule of law, monitoring the trajectory of violence in the region, and advocating for peace and stability in the North Caucasus.[8]

The rhetoric about 'human rights' follows exactly the same

---

6   Evelyn Kaye, ibid., p. 19.

7   Ibid., 218–33.

8   'About ACPC,' http://www.peaceinthecaucasus.org/about.

agenda as the myriad of other NGOs, think tanks, and funds etc., in targeting any 'rejectionist' regime, from apartheid South Africa, to Milosevic's Serbia, to Assad's Syria to Putin's Russia. Whenever a state or statesman hinders some globalist objective, a sudden hue and cry goes up about 'human rights.' The formula does not change. The purpose is to undermine Russian policy in a patchwork of multi-ethnic republics by appeals to 'human rights,' 'civil society, and 'democracy.' Hence in Dagestan, plagued by Muslim militancy, ACPC concluded in 2011:

> Magomedov's appointment signalled the Kremlin's renewed reliance on clan politics as an instrument of control. His inability to launch a meaningful dialogue with adherents of Salafi Islam underscore the pitfalls of his limited mandate, made accountable to the federal centre as opposed to the Dagestani population. In the Russian political landscape, any attempts at changes by North Caucasus leaders will go awry without the Kremlin support, which suggests that the central government continues to favor ironfisted policies as opposed to reconciliation and aborts local efforts at practicing alternative approaches.[9]

After the bombing at the Boston marathon in 2013 allegedly by two Chechen 'Islamists,' the anti-Russia campaign of the ACPC received some criticism for portraying Russia as a villain in the region, and for spurning Russian warnings about Chechnyan terrorism. William Kristol, a seminal spokesman in favour of U.S. global hegemony, and a member of ACPC,[10] stated that although the Russian authorities had offered the United States 'a pretty detailed dossier of [bombing suspect Tamerlan Tsarnaev's] contacts,' he stated that the Russians were 'trying to get us to be suspicious of every Chechen who came to the U.S., especially of

---

9   Dagestan at Tipping Point, American Committee for Peace in the Caucasus, 2011, http://www.peaceinthecaucasus.org/sites/default/files/pdf/ACPC_paper_Dagestan.pdf.

10   ACPC, members, http://www.peaceinchechnya.org/about_members.htm.

everyone who came as a political refugee.'[11] That is a dilemma of multiculturalism even for its chief backer, the United States: the chickens come home to roost. Many of those on the Chechnya-aiding ACPC, such as William Kristol, were also founders of the Project for a New American Century,[12] which drew up the blueprints for 'regime change' throughout the Middle East, a plan which is still unfolding. They were also enthusiasts for war against Serbia.[13]

However, there is another major factor in regard to globalisation and Islam. The globalists are manipulating Islam by different and in several respects, contradictory, means; which is to say, they are pursuing a *dialectical* strategy:

As we have seen, a certain type of Muslim, the 'Islamists' or 'Jihadists' have been created by the globalists via their American proxies, to produce controlled crises—the 'war on terrorism'—to justify globalist intervention in states that are regarded as 'rejectionist,' such as Iran, Iraq, Libya, and Syria.

Conversely, those states that were or are fighting 'Islamists,' namely Serbia, Libya, Iraq, and Syria, and Russia vis-à-vis Chechnya, are targeted by the globalists as tyrannical for trying to suppress or contain their own Muslim militants, who receive globalist support.

Muslim migrants,[14] especially to Europe, are used to establish ethnic enclaves and break down any remnants of European

---

11   David Weigel, 'We Are All Russians Now,' *Skate*, 22 April 2013, http://www. slate.com/articles/news_and_politics/politics/2013/04/russia_warned_the_ fbi_about_tamerlan_tsarnaev_how_american_neocons_originally.html.

12   Project for a New American Century, 'Statement of Principles,' 3 June 1997, http://web.archive.org/web/20070810113753/www.newamericancentury.org/ statementofprinciples.htm.

13   Project for a New American Century, 'Balkans/Caucasus,' http://www. newamericancentury.org/balkans.htm.

14   Asians in New Zealand and Australia, Hispanics in the United States, etc., serve the same purposes.

pride, while justifying increasingly oppressive measures against the European populations through 'human rights' laws and mass re-education of the young to discard the 'xenophobia' of their elders and embrace 'multiculturalism' as the exciting new wave of the future.

Having considered the first two points, we shall now turn our attention to a specific example of the globalist plan to destroy a European cultural and national identity by pushing multiculturalism in France via the use of Muslim migrants and their offspring.

TARGET: FRANCE

During 19–22 October 2010, Charles Rivkin, U.S. Ambassador to France, invited a 29-member delegation from the Pacific Council on International Policy (PCIP) to a conference in France, the stated purpose of which was to discuss Arab and Islamic relations in the country.[15] The meeting was part of a far-reaching subversive agenda to transform that entire character of France and in particular the consciousness of French youth. This programme focuses on the use of France's Muslim youth in a typically manipulative strategy behind the façade of 'human rights' and 'equality.' The PCIP report stated of the conference:

> The delegation further focused on three key themes. First, the group examined Franco-Muslim issues in France through exchanges with Dr Bassma Kodmani, Director of the Arab Reform Institute, and Ms Rachida Dati, the first female French cabinet member of North African origin and current Mayor of the 7th Arrondissement in Paris. A trip to the Grand Mosque of Paris and a meeting with the Director of Theology and the Rector there provided additional insight. Second, meetings with Mr Jean-Noel Poirier, the Vice President of External Affairs at AREVA (a highly innovative French energy company), and with Mr

---

15   '2010 France Country Dialogue,' PCIP, http://www.pacificcouncil.org/page. aspx?pid=583.

Brice Lalonde, climate negotiator and former Minister of the Environment, highlighted energy and nuclear policy issues and the differences between U.S. and French policies in these arenas. And finally, the delegation explored the connections between media and culture in California (Hollywood) and France in meetings at the Louvre, the Musée D'Orsay, and at FRANCE 24—the Paris-based international news and current affairs channel.[16]

The primary purpose was obviously on matters of a multicultural nature, including not only Arab and Islamic relations in France, but also importantly, a discussion on the impact of Hollywood 'culture' on the French; i.e. a major part of the 'culturally lethal' virus that Ralph Peters described as the most pervasive and subversive element of globalisation. Obama appointed Rivkin due to his role as a major fund-raiser for the President. His career has been in business, becoming head of two entertainment companies and gaining 'powerful friends' in Hollywood.[17]

The PCIP, of which Rivkin is a member, was founded in 1995 as a regional appendage of the omnipresent globalist think tank, the Council on Foreign Relations (CFR).[18] It is headquartered in Los Angeles, 'with members and activities throughout the West Coast of the United States and internationally.' Corporate funding comes from, among others: Carnegie Corporation of New York, Chicago Council on Foreign Relations, City National Bank, The Ford Foundation, Bill and Melinda Gates Foundation, The William & Flora Hewlett Foundation, Rockefeller Brothers Fund, The Rockefeller Foundation, United States Institute of

---

16 '2010 France Country Dialogue,' ibid.

17 Nicholas Kralev, 'Being good at raising money doesn't make you a good diplomat,' *The Atlantic*, 19 March 2013, http://www.theatlantic.com/international/archive/2013/03/being-good-at-raising-money-doesnt-make-you-a-good-diplomat/274148/.

18 'Founded in 1995 in partnership with the Council on Foreign Relations,' PCIP, Governance, http://www.pacificcouncil.org/page.aspx?pid=373.

Peace.[19] The PCIP is therefore yet another big player in the globalist network comprising hundreds of interconnected organisations, lobbies, 'civil society' groups, NGOs, and think tanks, associated with the U.S. Government, and with banks and other corporations.

Early into his appointment as Ambassador, *The Los Angeles Times* described Rivkin as a '48-year-old Yale alum and Harvard Business School graduate with Russian Jewish parents,' who aims to promote American-style multiculturalism among France's bellicose *banlieues*[20] as the way of the future.[21] Prior to his appointment as Ambassador, Rivkin was California finance co-chair of the Obama Presidential campaign, raising $500,000— in a campaign that was heavily funded by the United States' oligarchy.[22] He had run an entertainment company, Wildbrain, and prior to that the Jim Henson Company,[23] and has stated that 'I do feel I understand the power of media.'[24]

WHY FRANCE?

France has long been a thorn in the side of U.S. globalism because of its frequent (although not invariable) adherence to French interests around the world, rather than those of the manufactured 'world community.' France has followed the dictum of President Charles de Gaulle that they 'don't have friends, but only interests.' France is one of the few states left in Western Europe with the remnant of a national consciousness. She is therefore

---

19   Corporate and Foundation funding: http://www.pacificcouncil.org/page. aspx?pid=513.

20   France's ghettoised Third World ethnics.

21   Devorah Lauter, 'U.S. envoy in France is making the most of his opportunity,' *Los Angeles Times*, 24 April 2010, http://articles.latimes.com/2010/apr/24/ world/la-fg-france-ambassador-20100425.

22   K. R. Bolton, *'Obama—cat's-paw of international capitalism,'* www.rense.com/ general83/cats.htm

23   Producers of the Sesame Street series that inculcated multiculturalism into preschoolers, with funding from the Ford Foundation.

24   Lauter, op. cit.

General De Gaulle in a BBC radio broadcast during WW2.

regarded as 'xenophobic' and in need of change. The best way of destroying any such sentiment is to weaken ethno-national consciousness and identity by means of 'multiculturalism.' Was it only a coincidence that the 1968 student revolt, sparked by the most puerile of reasons, occurred at a time both when the CIA was very active in funding student groups around the world, and when President de Gaulle was giving the United States a lot of trouble? De Gaulle did little to play along with American's post-war plans. He withdrew France from NATO military command. Even during World War II as leader of the Free French, he was distrusted by the United States.[25] Of particular concern would have been De Gaulle's advocacy of a united Europe to counteract U.S. hegemony,[26] especially as de Gaulle's vision of a united Europe included the Soviet Union. In 1959 he stated at Strasbourg: 'Yes, it is Europe, from the Atlantic to the Urals, it is the whole of Europe, that will decide the destiny of the world.' The expression

---

25 Simon Berthon, *Allies at War* (London: Collins, 2001), 21.

26 Aidan Crawley, *De Gaulle: A Biography* (London: The Literary Guild, 1969), 439.

implied détente between a future neutralist Europe and the USSR. In 1967 he declared an arms embargo on Israel and cultivated the Arab world. This is the type of statesmanship that globalists fear. With constant tension among disaffected Muslim youth, a backlash could see an intransigently anti-globalist, 'xenophobic' regime come to power, such as that of the Front National. Of note in regard to the 2010 PCIP delegation is their interest in the influence of Hollywood on French culture. This might seem at first glance to be an odd concern. However Hollywood, as the symbol of international cultural excrescence, is an important factor in globalisation, in what amounts to a world culture-war, as discussed previously in regard to the Ralph Peters analysis. It is notable that the instigators of the 'Arab Spring' that swept through North Africa, reaching into Iran, were secularised youths without strong traditional roots, and enamoured by the products of global consumerism. These modernised youths are precisely the type that Ralph Peters described as being infected by the 'lethal culture' of Hollywood, MTV, etc., who could be mobilised and manipulated into overthrowing not only 'rejectionist' regimes such as that of Libya, but even regimes such as the Egyptian, that had traditionally been pro-U.S. but which did not accord with longer term aims for Africa and the Middle East. I have described elsewhere precisely how this was done during the 'Arab Spring' with a generation of North Africans as obsessed with 'social media' as their rootless counterparts in the West, at the instigation of U.S.-based globalists.[27]

So what are Rivkin and the U.S. State Department up to in France, that they should be so interested in the place of Hollywood and of Muslims in that nation?

---

27   K. R. Bolton, 'Twitters of the World Revolution: The Digital New-New Left,' *Foreign Policy Journal*, 28 February 2011, http://www.foreignpolicyjournal. com/2011/02/28/twitterers-of-the-world-revolution-the-digital-new-new-left/.
Tony Cartalucci, 'Google's Revolution Factory—Alliance of Youth Movements: Color Revolution 2.0,' *Global Research*, February 23, 2011, http:// www.globalresearch.ca/index.php?context=va&aid=23283.

THE RIVKIN PROJECT FOR SUBVERTING FRENCH YOUTH

When Rivkin invited a delegation of fellow PCIP members to France in 2010 he had outlined a program for the globalisation of France that involves the use of the Muslim minorities and the indoctrination of French youth with multiculturalism. The slogan invoked was the common commitment France and America historically had to 'equality.' Wikileaks released the 'confidential' Rivkin programme. It is entitled 'Minority Engagement Strategy.'[28] Here, Rivkin outlines a program that is a far-reaching interference in the domestic affairs of a sovereign nation and, more profoundly, seeks to change the attitudes of generations of Muslim and French youth so that they might be merged into a new globalist synthesis; or what might be called a new humanity: *Homo economicus*, or *Homo globicus*; what the financial journalist G. Pascal Zachary calls 'The Global Me.'[29] Rivkin begins by stating that his Embassy has created a 'Minority Engagement Strategy,' that is directed at Muslims in France. Rivkin states as part of the programme: '. . . We will also integrate the efforts of various Embassy sections, target influential leaders among our primary audiences, and evaluate both tangible and intangible indicators of the success of our strategy.'[30]

Rivkin is confident that France's history of ideological liberalism 'will serve us well as we implement the strategy outlined here . . . in which we press France. . . .' Note the phrase: 'press France.' America's global agenda is linked by Rivkin to his blueprint for transferring France into 'a thriving, inclusive French polity [that] will help advance our interests in expanding democracy and increasing stability worldwide.' The program will focus on the 'elites' of the French and the Muslim communities, but will also involve a massive propaganda campaign directed at the 'general population,' with a focus on the young.

---

28   C. Rivkin, 'Minority Engagement Report,' U.S. Embassy, Paris, http://www.wikileaks.fi/cable/2010/01/10PARIS58.html.

29   G. Pascal Zachary, op. cit.

30   Rivkin, op. cit.

The programme includes redefining French history in the school curricula to give attention to the role of non-French minorities in French history. It means that the Pepsi/MTV generation of Americans and their mentors in academe will be formulating new definitions of French culture and rewriting French history to accord with globalist agendas. Towards this end: '. . . we will continue and intensify our work with French museums and educators to reform the history curriculum taught in French schools.' The U.S. 'elite' arrogates to itself the prerogative to refashion culture and the very collective consciousness of another people, in order to reshape France for globalisation. This revision of French history and culture to accord with a multicultural, anti-national agenda has already been imposed within the United States itself for decades, to ensure that Euro-American consciousness is obliterated, in favour of the American 'melting pot,' while conversely 'Black Pride' and 'Hispanic Pride' (*La Raza*) have been promoted as a dialectical battering ram against American Whites. Ultimately the aim remains to create a nebulous mass called 'Americans' out of a melting pot.

'Tactic Number Three' is entitled: 'Launch Aggressive Youth Outreach.' As in other states targeted by the U.S. State Department and their allies in the Soros network, Freedom House, Movement. org, the National Endowment for Democracy, Solidarity Center,[31] and so forth, disaffected youth are the focus for change. Leading the charge on this effort, the Ambassador's inter-agency Youth Outreach Initiative aims to 'engender a positive dynamic among French youth that leads to greater support for U.S. objectives and values.' Can the intentions be stated any plainer? It is cultural and political Americanisation. It is here that we can most easily get past the cant and see what is behind the strategy: to form a generation 'that leads to greater support for U.S. objectives and values' (*sic*). These 'U.S. objectives and values' will be sold to the French as 'French values' on the basis of the liberal-humanist

---

31   K. R. Bolton, 'The Globalist Web of Subversion,' *Foreign Policy Journal*,
      7 February 2011, http://www.foreignpolicyjournal.com/2011/02/07/the-
      globalist-web-of-subversion.

ideals that instigated both the 1776 American Revolution and the 1789 French Revolution. The young French will be taught to think that they are upholding French traditions, rather than acting as the useful idiots of Americanisation, and the concomitant *idiocracy*[32] of the global shopping mall. A far-reaching program incorporating a variety of indoctrination methods is outlined by Rivkin:

> To achieve these aims, we will build on the expansive Public Diplomacy programs already in place at post, and develop creative, additional means to influence the youth of France, employing new media, corporate partnerships, nationwide competitions, targeted outreach events, especially invited U.S. guests.[33]

The program directed at youth in France is similar to that directed at the youth that formed the vanguard of the 'velvet revolutions' from Eastern Europe to North Africa. Potential leaders are going to be recruited by the U.S. State Department in France and cultivated to play a part in the future Americanised France:

> We will also develop new tools to identify, learn from, and influence future French leaders. As we expand training and exchange opportunities for the youth of France, we will continue to make absolutely certain that the exchanges we support are inclusive. We will build on existing youth networks in France, and create new ones in cyberspace, connecting France's future leaders to each other in a forum whose values we help to shape—values of inclusion, mutual respect, and open dialogue.[34]

---

32   Coined from the 2006 movie, *Idiocracy*, where the United States' population has been dumbed-down dysgenically; the most intelligent pursuing careers rather than having families, while the idiots proliferate and are addicted to the banality of mass entertainment. The United States is led by a ghetto Black and his Cabinet includes a youngster who won the post in a game-show. 'Advertising, commercialism, and cultural anti-intellectualism have run rampant and dysgenic pressure has resulted in a uniformly stupid society.' 'Idiocracy,' http://en.wikipedia.org/wiki/Idiocracy.

33   Rivkin, op. cit.

34   Ibid.

Here Rivkin is advocating something beyond influencing Muslims in France. He is stating that a significant part of the programme will be directed towards cultivating French youth in 'American' ideals, behind the façade of French ideals. The State Department and corporate allies and allied NGOs intend to 'shape their values.' The globalist programme for France is stated clearly to be the re-education of French youth. One would think that this is the most important role of the French state, the Catholic Church and the family; the latter two in particular.

As in the states that are chosen for 'velvet revolutions' part of the strategy includes demarcating acceptable political boundaries. In the context of France it is clear that the demarcation of French politics cannot include any elements of so-called 'xenophobia' which in today's context would include a return to the grand politics of the De Gaulle era. Hence, 'Tactic 5' states:

> Fifth, we will continue our project of sharing best practices with young leaders in all fields, including young political leaders of all moderate parties so that they have the toolkits and mentoring to move ahead. We will create or support training and exchange programs that teach the enduring value of broad inclusion to schools, civil society groups, bloggers, political advisors, and local politicians.[35]

Rivkin is outlining a programme to train France's future political and civic leaders. While the programmes of U.S. Government-backed NGOs such as the National Endowment for Democracy are designed to develop entire programs and strategies for political parties in 'emerging democracies' (*sic*), this can be rationalised by stating that there is a lack of experience in liberal-democratic party politics in certain states. The same can hardly be used to justify America's interference in France's party politics. Towards this end Rivkin states that the 1,000 American English language teachers employed at French schools will be provided with the propaganda materials necessary to inculcate the desired ideals

---

35   Ibid.

into their French pupils: 'We will also provide tools for teaching tolerance to the network of over 1,000 American university students who teach English in French schools every year.' The wide-ranging programme will be coordinated by the 'Minority Working Group' in 'tandem' with the 'Youth Outreach Initiative.' One of the issues monitored by the Group will be the 'decrease in popular support for xenophobic political parties and platforms.'[36] This is to ensure that the programme is working as it should, to block the success of any 'extreme' or 'xenophobic' party that might challenge globalisation. Hence, one might conclude that the Front National, is or will be the target of agencies of the U.S. Government.

Rivkin clarifies the subversive nature of the programme when he states: 'While we could never claim credit for these positive developments, we will focus our efforts in carrying out activities, described above, that prod, urge and stimulate movement in the right direction.'[37] What Rivkin is describing is a covert operation to fundamentally change the character of French youth and society and to interfere with the French political process.

What would the reaction be if the French Government through its Embassy in Washington undertook a program to radically change the United States in accordance with 'French national interests,' inculcating through an 'aggressive outreach program' focusing on youth, 'French ideals' under the guise of 'American ideals on human rights'? What would be the response of the U.S. Administration if it were found that the French Government was trying to influence the attitudes of Afro-Americans, American-Indians, and Latinos? What if French officials were ordered to take every opportunity to 'press' U.S. officials to ask why there are not more American Indians in Government positions? What would be the official U.S. reaction if it were found that French-language educators in American schools and colleges were

---

36 Ibid.
37 Ibid.

trying to inculcate American pupils with ideas in the service of French interests, and to reshape attitudes towards a pro-French direction in foreign policy?

MULTICULTURAL PROGRAMMES
SPONSORED BY U.S. GOVERNMENT

What the globalist agenda is for French youth can be seen in what the United States has for decades imposed upon American youth with programmes such as 'Black History Month' (February) in which a history of Africans and Afro-Americans is invented, where Cleopatra and Hannibal are portrayed as Black Africans. Black History Month was formally recognised by the U.S. Government in 1976.[38] Black History Month has been extended to Canada,[39] Britain,[40] and France, and is being extended throughout the world via UNESCO. Black History Month in France in February 2013 featured events held by 'the mainstay American cultural institutions such as The American Church, The American Library, The American Embassy, or Dorothy's Gallery' (American Center for the Arts).[41] A feature of Black History Month in France is the denigration of its colonial heritage, which, as with apartheid in South Africa, slavery and segregation in the United States, and colonialism in other European states, serves as a convenient method of social engineering; namely the inculcation of a guilt complex especially among the young. Hence in 2013 the public activities of the 'Beyond Colonialism' Association were organised to coincide with Black History Month.[42]

---

38 'President Gerald R. Ford's Message on the Observance of Black History Month,' 10 February 1976, *Gerald R. Ford Presidential Library and Museum*, University of Texas, http://www.ford.utexas.edu/library/speeches/760074. htm.

39 Citizenship and Immigration Canada, http://www.cic.gc.ca/english/ multiculturalism/black/background.asp.

40 Black History Month UK, http://www.black-history-month.co.uk/sitea/ BHM_FAQ.html.

41 'Spirit of Black Paris,' http://spiritofblackparis.blogspot.co.nz/2013/02/whats-focus-of-black-history-month-in.html.

42 Ibid.

US Ambassador Rivkin speaking at event for Black History Month in Paris.

In 2010, the year that the Rivkin memo was issued, the U.S. Embassy in Paris sponsored a symposium featuring Afro-American expatriate Dr. Monique Wells, who runs a travel agency called 'Black Paris.' She spoke on the theme 'Black Paris and the Myth of a Color Blind France.' The lecture and discussion were evidently of the type structured to promote a guilt complex among the Europeans present, while promoting a sense that French culture owes much to American Negro input.

The lecture was given in three parts: part one—physical traces of African Americans in Paris (i.e. names on buildings, street signs, etc.); part two—the African-American presence in Paris which continues to permeate the city sometimes impalpably so. During this segment Dr. Wells also confronted the question 'Is France Color Blind?,' examining it from both a cultural and historical perspective; part three—was a slide show of images of the contemporary Diaspora in Paris.[43]

---

43   Monique Wells, 'Black Paris and the Myth of a Colorblind France,' Embassy of the Untied State, Paris, 9 February 2010, http://france.usembassy.gov/events100209.html.

Wells stated that Paris and France culturally owe much to Africans: 'Paris has changed and is the way it is because we continue to be here. We're not the only force that drives the French way of life but the African-American contribution is definitely not insignificant to the culture of this city and by extension of this nation.'[44]

Music, particularly jazz, made major inroads into French culture, and now a new generation of French youth are being Africanised via hip hop:

> Gospel music is very much appreciated in France; however the biggest contribution from African-Americans was jazz music. The famous jazz club *Caveau de la Huchette* has attracted many top jazz musicians such as Lionel Hampton, Art Blakey, and Sidney Bechet. Hip-Hop is another genre that has permeated French youth culture, not only in music but in fashion, slam poetry/spoken word, graffiti, and dance.[45]

Note that Wells states this corporate-generated Afro-American ghetto subculture has 'permeated' French youth not only in music, but in fashion and in speech, which the French have so assiduously attempted to preserve in its purity.

Wells' presentation concluded with a discussion, seemingly as a type of 'group therapy' session long popular in the United States among corporate and government organisations, and political and religious cults, as a method of imposing conformity of opinions through induced guilt.[46] Hence, 'The positive feed-back allowed audience members from different racial backgrounds to interact and discuss racial inequalities experienced in Paris; not just among Blacks but among others outside the traditional

---

44 Ibid.

45 Ibid.

46 K. R. Bolton, *The Psychotic Left* (London: Black House Publishing, 2013), 190–92.

US backed Hip-Hop rapper Sphinx (right) performed in Egypt calling for President Hosni Mubarak to stand down.

construct of mainstream French.'[47] The *a priori* assumption is that 'the traditional construct of mainstream French' is still not sufficiently open to cultural subversion from alien sources.

One project of particular concern that was exposed in France was the U.S. backing of an immigrant lobby. Such U.S. sponsorship of NGOs via the National Endowment for Democracy, Freedom House, USAID, and many others, is generally directed at states marked for 'regime change,' such as Libya, Syria, Iraq, Serbia, former Soviet bloc states, etc. However, in 2011 Abdelaziz Dahhassi, described like many U.S. dupes as a 'human rights activist,' set up a 'think tank to find new ways of fighting ethnic and religious discrimination in France,' with 'backing from the U.S. State Department.'[48]

---

47   M. Wells, op. cit.

48   Anita Elash, 'U.S. accused of meddling in France's immigration policies,' *Globe & Mail*, 17 February 2011, http://m.theglobeandmail.com/news/ world/europe/us-accused-of-meddling-in-frances-immigrant-policies/ article1910663/?service=mobile.

The *Globe & Mail* specifically points to the support given by the United States to groups as part of the Rivkin programme, and pointed to the cultivation of Muslim youth by the United States. Such 'leadership programs' are a long-used method of influencing potential leaders of states marked for 'regime change,' and have been used since the days of the Cold War, when the U.S. was trying to take over from Europe's colonial rule in Africa and elsewhere, as we have previously seen. The *Globe and Mail* report states of the programme:

> A U.S. embassy official in Paris said the program focused on building relationships with potential leaders in Muslim groups and other minorities, mainly by inviting young up-and-comers to participate in the U.S.-sponsored International Visitor Leadership Program. The program has traditionally sent members of the white French elite on educational visits to the United States. Last year, about a third of French participants belonged to minority groups, mostly Muslims.[49]

It also seems that U.S. diplomats actually encourage discontent and legitimise insurgency from within Muslim enclaves in France by visiting 'troubled immigrant suburbs' and inviting youths to U.S. Embassy functions. It might well be asked whether the U.S. Embassy is recruiting radical Muslim youth leaders for direction as cadres against France, just as youths in Serbia, Ukraine, Georgia, Egypt, Morocco, Tunisia, Libya, and so forth, have been selected, funded, and trained to agitate in states marked for 'regime change'? In 2009, the U.S. Embassy helped fund a mural project in the Paris suburb of Villiers-le-Bel, where there had been violent riots in 2007.[50] Three wall daubings included two other suburbs, undertaken under the direction of three muralists from the Mural Arts Program (MAP) of Philadelphia, which the U.S. Embassy described as having worked for 25 years on

---

49   Ibid.
50   Ibid.

murals that bring urban populations together;[51] a euphemism for what in liberal-speak is called 'empowering' ethnic enclaves. Rivkin inaugurated the first of the murals in September 2009 before 200 guests at Martin Luther King Middle School, the first mural honouring King.[52] Hence, the message of U.S. officialdom to volatile ethnic minorities in France is to look to the example of Martin Luther King, whose sit-downs and other so-called 'passive resistance' strategies were designed to provoke violent confrontations with the authorities of local communities.[53]

Note the fact that there is even a 'Martin Luther King Middle School' in France. King was just the type of Black 'Uncle Tom' that the globalists love; an integrationist, in contrast to 'Black separatists' and the 'Nation of Islam' that also emerged among Blacks, repudiating assimilation in favour of Black racial consciousness,[54] with a widespread belief that the 'Whites' who were responsible for Black woes, including slavery, were often Jews.[55] When King (and now also President Obama) is upheld by the United States as a beacon towards which the non-White ethnic minorities of the world can turn, they are providing a black face—as with Nelson Mandela also—for an oligarchical slavery of all races.

---

51 'A dialogue between local citizens, artists and urban spaces: Three murals are born in Bagnolet, Bondy and Villiers-le-Bel,' U.S. Embassy in Paris, http://france.usembassy.gov/event090726.html.

52 'Ambassador inaugurates in Paris suburbs Franco-American exchange program on mural art,' U.S. Embassy in Paris, 19 September 2009, http://france.usembassy.gov/event090919.html.

53 Martin Luther King, 'Letter from a Birmingham Jail,' 1963, http://mlk-kpp01.stanford.edu/index.php/resources/article/annotated_letter_from_birmingham/.

54 'A Summing Up: Louis Lomax Interviews Malcolm X,' 1963, http://teachingamericanhistory.org/library/document/a-summing-up-louis-lomax-interviews-malcolm-x/. Here Malcolm X refers to Martin Luther King as an 'Uncle Tom' subsidised by 'whites.'

55 *The Secret Relationship Between Blacks and Jews*, vol. 1 (Boston: Historical Research Department, Nation of Islam, 1994).

American news media have referred to the U.S. State Department as a primary influence in pushing multicultural agendas in France. In a report for *The Christian Science Monitor*, Anita Elash wrote that 'The U.S. embassy in France has become a key promoter of Muslim and minority rights as part of a long-term strategy to ease the threat of terrorism.'[56] As we have seen from the Rivkin memo, the U.S. strategy goes well beyond the globalist catchphrase of heading off Muslim radicalism, which, as we have also seen, has been backed by the U.S. in Serbia, Afghanistan, Chechnya, Libya, Syria, and elsewhere. Islamic migration and the support of Muslim enclaves in Europe are used to fundamentally change the character of Europe.

Returning to the activities of Abdelaziz Dahhassi, Elash states that 'it was the U.S. State Department that helped Mr. Dahhassi's Lyon-based Association for the Convergence of Respect and Diversity finally get off the ground. . . . "I'm not saying we couldn't have done it without them, but their support is very important," he says. "The Americans have a very interesting vision which can be very enriching for France."'[57] Here we have an example of how the globalists are channelling Muslim migrant discontent in multicultural Europe into an 'American vision'; that is, a cosmopolitan vision designed to make the 'American Dream' of accumulating consumer goods the Universal Dream in a Global Shopping Mall, as alluded to with pride by the Afro-American expatriate in Paris, Dr. Wells at her U.S. Embassy-sponsored seminars. Elash reported in 2011:

> Over the next several months, U.S. embassy staff will work with Dahhassi to secure funds and expertise from public and private U.S. sources to help establish the think tank's

---

56 Anita Elash, 'In France, U.S. advocacy for Muslim rights raises more than a few hackles,' *Christian Science Monitor*, 17 February 2011, http://www. csmonitor.com/World/Europe/2011/0217/In-France-US-advocacy-for-Muslim-rights-raises-more-than-a-few-hackles?nav=topic-tag_topic_page-storyList.

57 Ibid.

program. Dahhassi says the focus will be to 'find another approach' to addressing racism directed at all minority groups in France, and that it will likely include a debate over the divisive issue of whether France could benefit from an affirmative-action program.[58]

Such a programme of Affirmative Action, based on the U.S. model, would see ethnic minorities given favouritism in employment and university placements, with lesser qualified applicants being promoted over better qualified French Whites. Such a programme would also likely see applicants to medical schools, for example, be selected on the basis of their minority ethnicity rather than their academic accomplishments. That is a price of 'ending racism.'

The Rivkin offensive is part of a long-time programme of undermining French identity. France, like much of the rest of the world, is however fighting a losing battle against globalisation. Jeff Steiner's column 'Americans in France' refers to the manner by which the French at one time resisted the opening of the fast food franchise McDonald's as 'part of an American cultural invasion.' Steiner wrote:

> That seems to be past as McDonald's has so become a part of French culture that it's not seen as an American import any longer, but wholly French. In short, McDonald's has grown on the French just like in so many other countries.

> I've been to a few McDonald's in France and, except for one in Strasbourg that looks from the outside to be built in the traditional Alsacien style, all McDonald's in France that I have seen look no different than their American counterparts.

> Yes, there are those that still curse McDonald's (They are now a very small group and mostly ignored.) as the symbol

---

58   Ibid.

American filmmaker Zachary Taylor and co-founder of
Discover Paris! Monique Y. Wells

of the Americanization of France and who also see it as
France losing its uniqueness in terms of cuisine. The menu
in a French McDonald's is almost an exact copy of what
you would find in any McDonald's in the United States.
It struck me as a bit odd that I could order as I would in
the United States, that is in English, with the odd French
preposition thrown in. If truth were told, the French who
eat at McDonald's are just as much at home there as any
American could be.[59]

This seemingly minor example is actually of much importance
in showing just how a culture as strong as that of, until recently,
an immensely proud nation, can succumb, especially under
the impress of marketing towards youngsters. It is an example
par excellence of the standardisation that American-imposed
corporate culture entails. It is what the globalist oligarchy desires
on a world scale, standardisation right down to what one eats. It is

---

59   Jeff Steiner, "Americans in France: Culture: McDonald's in France," http://
www.americansinfrance.net/culture/mcdonalds_in_france.cfm.

notable that the vanguard of the initial resistance to the opening of McDonald's came from farmers, a traditionalist segment of Europe's population that are becoming increasingly anomalous, and will under the globalist regime become an extinct species in the process of agricultural corporatisation, where the family farm becomes extinct.

Nonetheless, given France's historical role of maintaining sovereignty in the face of U.S. interests, she remains one of the few potentially annoying states in Europe; hence her being first on the line of the globalist offensive using multiculturalism. However, the concern remains, as alluded to in the Rivkin memo, that the French, despite their acceptance of McDonald's, and their liking for American trash TV, will translate the remnants of their 'xenophobia' into the election to office of a stridently anti-globalist party, as reflected in the electoral ups and downs of the Front National, whose policy would not be in accord with either U.S. foreign policy, or with privatisation and cultural Americanisation. Hence the Front National, like other anti-globalist parties, can be attacked with red-herring slogans about 'racism' and 'hate' to deflect from the real concern, which is opposition to globalisation. The militants of the Left with slogans such as 'Open Borders' hardly credit being regarded as opponents of globalisation, when they accept the fundamentals of globalist ideology. This is a major reason for Rivkin's far-reaching subversive and interventionist program to assimilate Muslims into French society, which in so doing would also have the result of casting French consciousness into a more thoroughly cosmopolitan mould. The intention is clear enough in the Rivkin Embassy documents where it is stated that the Embassy will monitor the effects of the 'outreach' program on the 'decrease in popular support for xenophobic political parties and platforms.'

Some conservative observers immediately recognised the U.S. agenda, criticising the United States for trying to undermine French values by imposing failed U.S. policies on how to deal with ethnic minorities:

'They are criticizing us because we are not the United States, or more precisely, because we do not resemble them,' blogger Christine Tasin wrote on a website for The Republican Resistance, a non-partisan group established last year to defend what it sees as French values. '[It] is a strategic plan to get France to do whatever the U.S. wants'[60]

Ivan Rioufol, of the conservative newspaper *Le Figaro*, stated that 'The American analysis, which seems to say that the France of the future will be the France of the immigrant suburbs, is very disparaging to native French people.'[61]

ZIONIST FACTOR

One might think that Zionists would react with alarm at the growing 'Islamisation' of Europe. Yet this is not the case. Zionism operates dialectically, like their usually allied U.S. globalists. Zionism sees the Islamisation of Europe as part of a broader multicultural agenda to impose plural states over the West, in the name of 'democracy' and 'human rights', because they feel that Jewish interests are most secure, and especially inconspicuous, in states that have no sense of national identity. In such states, the Zionists and other Jewish strategists reason, Jews are just regarded as one community among many, and in this instance, as a harmless religious community, like Baptists, Catholics, Mormons, Presbyterians, etc.

On the other hand, Jewish communities are kept in a constant state of unease by their Zionist leaders, as the primary means of maintaining Jewish commitment to Israel and Zionism. As we have seen in regard to the symbiotic relationship with anti-Semitism, which has always provided the *raison d'être* for Zionism, when Muslim vent their frustrations at synagogues of Jewish graves in France or Argentina, the Zionist leaders can remind the local Jewish communities that 'anti-Semitism' is

---

60   Elash, *Globe & Mail*, op. cit.

61   Ibid.

continually on the rise, and the only way to ensure protection is to support Zionism and Israel, which remain the insurance policy of Diaspora Jewry.[62]

The role of organised Jewry in pushing multicultural agendas onto Europe has recently been described by Barbara Lerner Spectre, 'founding director' of the state funded organisation, Paideia (The European Institute for Jewish Studies in Sweden):

I think there is a resurgence of anti-Semitism because at this point in time Europe has not yet learned how to be multicultural. And I think we are going to be part of the throes of that transformation, which must take place. Europe is not going to be the monolithic societies they once were in the last century. Jews are going to be at the centre of that. It's a huge transformation for Europe to make. They are now going into a multicultural mode and Jews will be resented because of our leading role. But without that leading role and without that transformation, Europe will not survive.[63]

More explicitly the strategy of Jews in promoting pluralistic, multicultural states, is described by Miriam Faine, an editorial committee member of the Australian Jewish Democrat:

The strengthening of multicultural or diverse Australia is also our most effective insurance policy against anti-Semitism. The day Australia has a Chinese Australian Governor General I would feel more confident of my freedom to live as a Jewish Australian.

A Chinese Governor general for Australia, in this instance, would mean that Australia would have become so bereft of a sense of identity that Euro-Australians are no longer conscious

---

62 Jews living outside Israel, who are nonetheless expected to retain loyalty to Israel and to Jewry first.

63 *Barbara Lerner Spectre, IBA-News, 2010.*

that different ethnic communities even exist, or of their own identity. Hence, Organised Jewry maintain a duplicitous role, and one that is difficult to justify, in insisting on being a special people, 'God's Chosen People', no less, while at the same time also insisting that they are no different from any other religion or community.

The Zionist dual, or dialectical strategy, can be starkly seen by referring again to Spectre who conversely stated of Jewish identity:

> We need a Jewish community in Europe. Israel needs a Jewish community in Europe. Israel cannot exist, both economically and politically, without Europe. They are necessary advocates for Jewish issues.[64]

Spectre, typically, also enthuses over the way Jews in Eastern and central Europe are rejecting assimilation:

> While the rest of the Jewish world is facing assimilation and apathy among the generation of 20-30, in Central and Eastern Europe with that same generation we are encountering a striking and significant resurgence of the desire to be Jewish.[65]

Hence the existence of Europe for Zionism, as in all else, only has meaning insofar as it serves Israel and the 'Jewish community'.

At the same time, Jewish leaders must be careful to ensure that Jews do not react to the Islamisation of the West by joining organisations of the Nationalist-Right that resist this Islamisation rather than supporting both Zionism and multiculturalism. However, a perverse by-product of these twists and turns of

---

64   *Barbara Lerner Spectre, 'Jewish Peoplehood and Identity', The Peoplehood Papers, New York: United Jewish Communities, 2007), 15, http://www.bh.org.il/Data/ Uploads/Peoplehood%20Papers%201-%20November%202007.pdf*

65   Spectre, ibid., 14.

Zionist policy is that 'extreme Right' organisations that are smeared by Organised Jewry as being 'neo-Nazi' are increasingly responding to Muslim immigration by becoming pro-Zionist. A most extreme example of this pro-Zionist outlook by a 'fascist' is that of Anders Breivik, whose case will be considered in the following chapter. One of the most militant of these anti-Muslim organisations has been the English Defence League, whose demonstrations include the conspicuous appearance of the Israeli flag. However, even such pro-Zionist organisations among the 'extreme Right' is not in accord with Zionist policy, which is based on multiculturalism and pluralism for Gentile states.

Anders Breivik: Neo-Conned

The news media had a field day in headlining Anders Breivik's actions as those of someone from the "far Right," and as actions that are a consequence of Rightist ideology. Yet Breivik is an avid Zionist whose motives were predicated on Islamophobia. His ideological influences are libertarian and "neo-conservative." He was playing his part, albeit as a loose cannon, in the "clash of civilizations."

Although the news media has focused on his previous membership in the Progressive Party, his ideological commitment is to Zionism. Why then did not the news media headline Breivik's atrocity as being that of a "Zionist," and as a "stanch supporter of Israel"? As is often the case, the fictional "far Right" connection is a red herring. Headlines could have read "Zionist extremist on shooting spree," "Israel supporter massacres youngsters at Labour camp in Norway," and the like.

While Breivik advocates banning the Islamic religion from Europe, he seems to have been totally oblivious to the intrinsically anti-Christian nature of Orthodox Judaism,[1] and while he wrote at length on the supposed enmity between "Judaeo-Christianity" and Islam, he wrote nothing of the anti-Christian record of Israel,[2] including the demolition of Christian holy sites, and the common practice of spitting on Christian clergy in the Holy Land. Although he did recognize the historical predominance of Jews in Leftist movements, this is an acknowledgement of the rivalry within Jewry between liberals and leftists on the one side and "neo-conservatives" on the other, the latter being

---

1   Israel Shahak, *Jewish History, Jewish Religion: The Weight of Three Thousand Years* (London: Pluto Press, 1994).

2   Israel Shahak and Norton Mezvinsky, *Jewish Fundamentalism in Israel* (London: Pluto Press, 1999).

considered by Breivik to be his best potential allies in the fight against Islam. Breivik is Judaeophilic to the extent that he is Islamophobic, writing in his manifesto:

> Regardless of what the Jewish communities motives are I think it's imperative that they take a stance on multiculturalism and Muslim immigration as soon as humanly possible. They have to recognize that "multiculturalism" is the system that allows Europe to be Islamised and it's obviously not in their interest to contribute to this. Jews will in a much larger degree start to support the 'new right' (just like everyone else), who oppose multiculturalism as a means to stop Islamisation, at least this is my hope. In the back of their minds they realize that a Muslim Europe will be more "anti-Semitic" than a Christian Europe. Muslims don't have the guilt complex that Europeans have. Many Jews feel they are trapped between the 'bark and the wood', they are both sceptical of Muslim immigration on one side and of the nationalist far right wing movements on the other side. Nevertheless, time is off [sic] the essence and it is imperative that the European Jewish community without delay take a stance on the ongoing Islamisation. Neutrality on this issue is not an option. The only way of doing this is to back the new right wing (anti-multiculturalism, pro-Israel) groups and political parties (also manifested through views such as by moderate Jewish writers such as Daniel Pipes and Bat Ye'or).[3]

Breivik's opposition to Jewish leftists, as with his opposition to liberals and leftists of any type, is no more antagonistic towards Jews *per se* than the opposition of Jewish neo-cons towards Jewish leftists. The above passage from Breivik is in total accord with the pro-Zionist neo-con party-line.

---

3   A Breivik, *2083: A Declaration of European Independence* (London, 2011) p. 1372.

ISRAEL & ISLAM

The only "Right" that Breivik can be said to identify with is the Zionist extreme Right. This calls to mind the likes of the Jewish Defense League, Likud, the settler movement, etc. Breivik's support for the expansion of Israeli borders north and south also reminds one of the "Greater Israeli Empire" that has always been a basis of the Zionist "extreme right." He sees Israel as the vanguard in the fight against Islam, writing:

> While most people refer to Israel's security fence as a 'wall', the fact remains that less than 5 percent of the barrier is actually concrete slab. The rest is a network of fence and sensors. The fence has cut terrorism incidents by more than 90% since its completion. What was the reason for establishing the Security Fence Area? The Security Fence is being built with the sole purpose of saving the lives of the Israeli citizens who continue to be targeted by the terrorist campaign that began in 2000[4]

His justification for the "security wall" is the same party line as that of other pro-Zionists, including the neo-con ideologues. The main difference is that Breivik is happy to call this situation 'apartheid', while the neo-cons recoil at the word.[5] Was Breivik inspired in his shooting rampage of Norwegian youths more by the example of the Israeli security forces than by the crusader knights whose legacy he claimed to be reviving, albeit only with a handful of members who included two atheists and an agnostic, by his own account?

THE CLASH OF CIVILIZATIONS

Breivik is a product of the "clash of civilizations," formulated by neo-con ideologues and used by American and Zionist interests to philosophically justify the so-called "war on terrorism." He is the product of a legacy that is anything but "conservative" in

---

4   A Breivik, ibid., p. 1215.

5   "Wall of Lies," *Front Page*, 25 February 2011, http://frontpagemag. com/2011/02/25/ucla-daily-bruin-prints-centers-wall-of-lies/

the Western historical sense: he sees himself as an underground resistance fighter against the Islamic occupation of Europe, who, in other circumstances, would be honored as a war hero. He sees Islamic laws and customs taking the place of Western laws. The attitude is no different from that of Sarkozy's attempts to ban the Burka in public, Breivik writing:

> Several recent incidents have demonstrated that Muslims are now trying to apply these dhimmi rules to the entire Western world. The most important one was the burning of churches and embassies triggered by the Danish cartoons depicting Muhammad. This was, down to the last comma, exactly the way Muslims would treat the persecuted non-Muslims in their own countries. The cartoon Jihad indicated that Muslims now felt strong enough to apply sharia rules to Denmark, and by extension NATO.[6]

The Muhammad cartoon saga was symptomatic of the "clash of civilizations." The cartoons published in Denmark were a contrived provocation against Muslims in order to create a climate of tension. It is such a strategy of tension that Breivik sought in a more dramatic way. The American neo-con magazine *Human Events*, which by-lines itself as 'leading conservative media since 1944', was among the Western media that republished the cartoons.[7] It is of added interest in that one of those instrumental in the 2006 Muhammad cartoon provocation was Daniel Pipes, cited as one of Breivik's ideological gurus, whom he calls a 'moderate Jewish writer' along with Bat Ye'or. Christopher Bollyn, writing for *American Free Press*, stated of this:

> The anti-Muslim cartoon scandal has turned out to be a major step forward for the Zionist Neo-cons and their long-planned 'clash of civilizations', the artificially constructed conflict designed to put the so-called Christian West against the Islamic world.

---

6   A Breivik, op. cit., p. 677.

7   "Muhammad cartoon gallery," *Human Events*, 2 February 2006, http://www. humanevents.com/article.php?id=12146

Bollyn wrote that Flemming Rose, the "cultural editor" who commissioned the cartoons for his newspaper *Jyllands Posten*, visited the Philadelphia office of Daniel Pipe's website *Middle East Forum* in 2004. "Rose then penned a sympathetic article about Pipes entitled 'The Threat from Islamism,' which promoted his extreme anti-Islamic views without mentioning the fact that Pipes is a rabid Zionist extremist." Bollyn cited references by the individual whom Breivik recommends as a "moderate Jewish writer," Pipes having written that a "change of heart" of the Palestinians can only be achieved by their "being utterly defeated." After three days of Muslim rioting in Denmark USA's CNN TV network turned to Pipes as their pundit on the situation, who then blamed 'Islamic extremists'. At the time, neo-con US Secretary of State Condoleezza Rice condemned the Syrian and Iranian governments for protests in those states. Pipes appealed to Western liberal secular values in regard to the tumult that was sparked by his Danish comrade:

> Will the West stand up for its customs and mores, including freedom of speech, or will Muslims impose their way of life on the West? Ultimately, there is no compromise. Westerners will either retain their civilization, including the right to insult and blaspheme, or not'.[8]

This is the Breivik line that he learned at the metamorphical knees of his neo-con and Zionist gurus. Pipes at the time cited in support another Breivik ideological hero, Robert Spencer of *Jihad Watch*, which is part of the network of neo-con luminary David Horowitz. Pipes wrote: "Robert Spencer rightly called on the free world to stand 'resolutely with Denmark.' The informative *Brussels Journal* asserts, 'We are all Danes now.'"[9]

Now Pipes states of Breivik that "authors and artists" such as

---

8   D Pipes, "Cartoons and Islamic Imperialism," cited by C Bollyn, ibid.

9   D Pipes, "Cartoons and Islamic Imperialism," danielpipes.org, http://www.danielpipes.org/3360/cartoons-and-islamic-imperialism Originally published in the New York Sun, 7 February 2006.

himself cannot be held responsible for the actions of those they inspire and, like Robert Spencer and other neo-cons, he reiterates what seems to be their party-line on the matter by giving the example, among others, of how The Beatles' "Helter Skelter" influenced Charles Manson.[10] However, the connection is just not that cryptic: the neo-con coteries, including Daniel Pipes, have been promoting the "clash of civilizations" and when a foot solider goes rogue and gets out of control they protest: "don't blame me." Pipes is more than a street corner agitator. He is a visiting fellow of the Hoover Institution of Stanford University, with columns appearing in newspapers around the world. He has lectured at the US Naval War College, Harvard, and others, and appears on leading TV networks. His *Middle East Forum* has a budget of $4,000,000.[11] In a 2010 interview with the *Washington Post*, Pipes stated that he is no longer regularly criticized as Islamophobic because of the proliferation of more extreme Islamophobes. This means that Pipes' and others such as Spencer and Horowitz now look 'moderate' because of the shifting of the center of Islamophobic gravity by years of propaganda. The interview also mentions a particularly interesting phenomenon; the support Pipes had given to the Dutch "right-wing" politician Geert Wilders who, like Breivik, wants to ban the *Koran* in The Netherlands. While regarding the "new crop of bloggers" as "unsophisticated", a *Washington Post* interview states:

> Pipes says he shares "the same enemies" with people like Wilders and the new crop of bloggers. "We're in the same trench but we have different views of what the problem is. We both see an attempt to impose Islamic law, sharia, in the West. We are both against it, and want to maintain Western civilization. But we understand the nature of the problem differently."

---

10   D Pipes, danielpipes.com 24 July 2011, http://www.danielpipes.org/blog/2009/12/why-did-nidal-hasan-read-the-middle-east-forum

11   http://www.danielpipes.org/bios/

IMPORTANT DISTINCTION, IN YOUR EYES?[12]

It is just this type of alliance between the neo-cons, Zionists and the European so-called 'right-wing' that Breivik regards as a basis for the anti-Islamic civil war he hoped to foment in Europe. It is not an isolated phenomenon. The well-publicized English Defence League's anti-Muslim demonstrations and riots are marked by the number of Israeli flags appearing amidst their shaven headed ranks.[13] Breivik regards the EDL as one of the better organizations, writing:

> The British EDL seems to be the first youth organization that has finally understood this. Sure, in the beginning it was the occasional egg heads who shouted racist slogans and did Nazi salutes but these individuals were kicked out. An organization such as the EDL has the moral high ground and can easily justify their political standpoints as they publicly oppose racism and authoritarianism.[14]

According to the anti-Zionist former Israeli Gilad Atzmon, the EDL has formed a "Jewish Division," which the *London Jewish Chronicle* states immediately drew "hundreds" of followers. The Division is led by Roberta Moore, who was interviewed by the Israeli newspaper *Ha'aretz*, and boasted of how the 'Jews were exploiting' the EDL:

> Roberta Moore, aged 39, the leader of the Jewish Division, admitted this week to *Ha'aretz* that it is 'actually the Jewish Division that exploits the EDL'. In an interview with the Israeli newspaper on 13 July 2010, she said: "They [the EDL] think the league is exploiting us, while it is really we who initiated the Jewish Division. If anything, we are

---

12   Michelle Boorstein, "Once Considered Anti-Islam, Senior Scholar says he's now in the Middle," *The Washington Post*, 18 August 2010. http://www.danielpipes.org/8777/in-the-middle

13   http://mondoweiss.net/2009/09/the-enemy-of-my-enemy-is-my.html
     http://deisraellobby.blogspot.com/2010/08/british-zionists-join-far-right.html

14   A Breivik, op. cit., p. 1240.

English Defence League protestors in Birmingham, England.

exploiting them."[15]

Of the previously mentioned Bat Ye'or, a Jewish woman of Egyptian birth, resident in Britain, she specializes in writing of Jewish experiences in Muslim states.[16] Her theme of "Eurabia" is a condemnation of relations between Europe and the Arab states.[17] It is a concept that was taken up by Breivik. Ye'or contends that Eurabia is a development of 'Nazi' and 'fascist' origins in alliance with radical Arabs, and has placed European states in a foreign policy position inimical to the interests of both Israel and the USA. In other words, it is indicative of Europe as a new force rather than as a lackey to the USA. This Eurabia was formalized in 1974 in Paris in an association called Euro-Arab

15   G Atzmon, "British Zionists Join Far Right Organisation to Promote Islamophobia and Racism in UK," 17 August 2010, http://deisraellobby.blogspot.com/2010/08/british-zionists-join-far-right.html

16   Bat Ye'or, *The Dhimmi: Jews and Christians Under Islam*, (New Jersey: Fairleigh Dickinson University Press, 1985).

17   Bat Ye'or, *Eurabia: The Euro-Arab Axis*, (New Jersey: Fairleigh Dickinson University Press, 2005).

Dialogue. Ye'or has outlined her views in many articles, one of which was published in the neo-con *National Review*.[18] She has attracted the support of neo-cons such as Robert Spencer. From a Western cultural perspective, the concept of Eurabia so abhorred to Ye'or and other neo-cons, plutocrats and Zionists, is hopeful. The relations souring the Arab states and the West are of intrusive origins and could be addressed diplomatically. The origins of poisoned relations between the West and the Arabs will now be considered.

SOURING OF ARAB AND WESTERN RELATIONS

Israel has existed for much of its history since 1948 by maintaining the fiction that it is the only reliable state in the Middle East that is Western-orientated amidst a sea of states hostile to "Western values." The dichotomy is misleading. Israel was for the first years of its existence largely a center of Marxist agitation in the Middle East, and even before the declaration of Israel in 1948, Zionist settlers in Palestine were conveyers of the Marxist creed that has never found fertile ground in any form among the Arabs.[19] Israel is neither pro-Western nor anti-Western; it is pro-Israel, no more and no less. Israel has always played a duplicitous game diplomatically. For example, it has for decades maintained a largely covert relationship with Red China to the point of contravening US restrictions on weapons transfers.[20] As for the souring of relations between the West and the Arabs, this is of a particularly treacherous nature, and is a festering sore that the West has the responsibility to heal.

As we have seen, the origins of this perfidy are in World War I at a time when the Arabs were under Ottoman rule, fighting for the

---

18 B Ye'or, "Eurabia: The Road to Munich," *National Review*, 9 October 2002, http://old.nationalreview.com/comment/comment-yeor100902.asp

19 K R Bolton, The Red Face of Israel', 2 August 2, 2010, op. cit.

20 K R Bolton, "Chinese TV Series Lauds Israel: The Alliance Between China and Zionism," *Foreign Policy Journal*, 18 August, 2010, http://www.foreignpolicyjournal.com/2010/08/18/chinese-tv-series-lauds-israel-the-alliance-between-china-and-zionism

Entente with promises of independence, while the Zionists had connived to do a backroom deal with the British War Cabinet.

TARGET

This background of Western duplicity towards the Arabs, along with the Zionist wire-pulling, is directly relevant to the present 'clash of civilizations', the 'war on terrorism', and the Breivik atrocity as a manifestation of these. Leading up to the Breivik massacre of Labour Party youth, the neo-cons had been agitating against the Labour Government that was indicating it would adopt a more strident policy towards Israel's treatment of the Palestinians. In particular, the youth wing of the party was lobbying for a Norwegian economic boycott of Israel. Joseph Klein, posting on Horowitz's *Front Page Mag* two days before Breivik's rampage, described the Norwegian Government as "Quislings" and called them the "the latest example of Norwegian collaboration with the enemies of the Jews." Is the language any less inflammatory than Breivik's *European Declaration of Independence* that the news media and their pundits are scrutinizing for signs of "right-wing extremism"? Klein stated:

"Norwegian Foreign Minister Jonas Gahr Stoere declared during a press conference this week, alongside Palestinian President Mahmoud Abbas, that 'Norway believes it is perfectly legitimate for the Palestinian president to turn to the United Nations' to seek recognition of an independent Palestinian state."[21] An agreement was signed giving Palestine's representative in Norway full ambassadorial status. Stoere also appealed for financial help for Palestinians. Other transgressions by the Norwegians, according to Klein, include a Labour Member of Parliament stating that Jews exaggerate the Holocaust; socialist leader Kristin Halvorsen having participated in an anti-Israel demonstration while serving as minister of finance; the Norwegian Government's divesting of funds from two

---

21 J Klein, "The Quislings of Norway," *Front Page Mag*, 20 July, 2011, http://frontpagemag.com/2011/07/20/the-quislings-of-norway/

Israeli companies in 2010; the claim that "anti-Semitism is alive and well" among the Norwegian political, cultural and academic elite; pro-Hitler sentiments expressed by Muslim students in Norway, and more. Klein stated that part of the reason for this rise in anti-Semitism is because of the toleration of multiculturalism by the Norwegian Establishment. He ends by writing: "Norway is repeating its Quisling treachery of the Nazi era, this time in league with a growing radical Muslim population. And once again the Jews are the victims."[22]

A Hebrew website, Rotter, states that two days before the massacre, the leader of the Norwegian Labour Party Youth, Eskil Pederson, said in an interview that it was time to end dialogue with Israel and undertake tough measures, including an economic boycott by Norway. The youth at the Labour camp aimed to lobby their party for a boycott. The site describes the Labour youth camp:

48 hours before the shooting attack on the island, the youth met the Norwegian Foreign Minister. Some called for a boycott of Israel.

On Wednesday, the second day of the ruling party youth conference on the island, the youth holiday camp discussed with the Norwegian Foreign Minister Jonas Gahar Store, and ordered him to support Palestine. About 48 hours later, many of them were killed, Anders Bering Breivik launched a shooting crazy.

Labour Youth Movement demanded recognition of a Palestinian state, and foreign minister have said that the Palestinians get their own state. 'The occupation must end, the wall should be demolished and it has to happen now,' said Ghar Store to the audience. Some of the youngsters in the camp waving a placard with the word 'boycott Israel',

---

22   J Klein, ibid.

demanded an economic embargo on Israel. The Summer camp ended in the massacre.

Leader, Askyl Pedersen, said that young people require imposition of an economic embargo on Israel. 'Our policy on the Middle East is to be more active and demand recognition of Palestine. There is also the peace process back on track,' said Pedersen. The Foreign Minister agreed with him, but said that a boycott is not the right approach: 'This will make dialogue become a monologue.' [23]

The media pundits have waxed indignant about the 'extremists' who have posted on 'far Right' websites in support of Breivik's actions, Dr Matthew Goodwin, writing for the *Telegraph*:

Make no mistake: Breivik has already become a heroic figure for sections of the ultra far right, much in the same way Timothy McVeigh became a hero for sections of the militia movement in the United States. In Britain, his anti-Muslim, anti-immigrant and anti-establishment ideas are easily found in a far-right scene that has become fragmented and chaotic.[24]

Yet it does not seem to have been pointed out that Breivik's action has generated enthusiasm in Israel. Some of the posts on the Israeli Hebrew website *Rotter*, state:

- Because I waited with this response until after it became clear that there was indeed a conference which explicitly called for the Boycott of Israel. I am very happy and pleased about the massacre that took place in the camp of the enemies of Israel.

- Hitler Youth members killed in the bombing of Germany

---

23 http://rotter.net/forum/scoops1/25606.shtml#38

24 M Goodwin, "Norway Killer: many within Far-Right share Anders Breivik's ideas," *The Telegraph*, London, 26 July 2011, http://www.telegraph.co.uk/news/worldnews/europe/norway/8658417/Norway-killer-many-within-far-right-share-Anders-Breiviks-ideas.html

were also innocent. Let us all cry about the terrible evil bombardment carried out by the Allies...We have a bunch of haters of Israel meeting in a country that hates Israel in a conference that endorses the boycott. So it's not okay, not nice, really a tragedy for families, and we condemn the act itself, but to cry about it? Come on. We Jews are not Christians. In the Jewish religion there is no obligation to love or mourn for the enemy.

- It's stupidity and malice not [to] want the death of those who call to boycott Israel.

- I have no sympathy for those who want the destruction of Israel.

- Not looking for excuses but it's not our mourning. Like not mourning at the time the 50 thousand dead in the bombing of Dresden.

- May all our enemies be paid with such speed.

- At least now they have more important things to worry about than Israel.

- Maybe we can arrange a badge of honor on behalf of the International Headquarters for Saving People and the Land.[25]

It seems that Breivik's actions made a lot of "sense" from a pro-Zionist perspective, but the motives have nothing to do with ideologies of the "far Right," and much to do with supporting Israel.

CONCLUSION

The "clash of civilizations" now taking place in the name of the "war on terrorism" is a second Cold War foisted upon the world in order to achieve American global hegemony and Zionist aggrandisement. With the eclipse of the first Cold War following the implosion of the Soviet bloc, the USA required another world

---

25   http://rotter.net/forum/scoops1/25606.shtml#38

bogeyman to justify its global adventures. The same ideologues undertook a new Cold War, this time against Islam, using the same type of sloganeering. Islamophobia is the new anti-Sovietism, and is serving the same interests. Trotskyites and other Marxists disaffected by the rise of Stalin created the ideological foundations for the Cold War. That is where the so-called "neo-conservative" movement has its origins.[26] Anti-Soviet rhetoric has been altered to apply to the new "menace of radical Islam." The slogan now is "Islamofascism," coined by neo-con ideologue Stephen Schwarz, director of the Center for Islamic Pluralism. Schwartz's background, like most of the neo-con founders, is as a Trotskyite, and he reiterated to *National Review* that he would defend the legacy of Trotsky to his "last breath."[27]

Relations between the West and the Arab states were evolving past the very old antagonisms until Zionist machinations entered the scene during World War I. It is not too late to correct the distorted relationships that have occurred between the West and the Arabs, and then an amicable solution can be found to the problems of Muslim immigration. As for Breivik, he is a product of the forces that are inimical to the traditional West. He is no more a "conservative" than the neo-cons who sprang from the bowels of Trotskyism, plutocracy, Zionism and the CIA during the first Cold War.

---

26 K R Bolton, "America's 'World Revolution': Neo-Trotskyist Foundations of US Foreign Policy'"*Foreign Policy Journal*, 3 May 2010, http://www.foreignpolicyjournal.com/2010/05/03/americas-world-revolution-neo-trotskyist-foundations-of-u-s-foreign-policy

27 S Schwartz, "Trotskycons?," *National Review*, 11 June 2003: http://faceoff.nationalreview.com/comment/comment-schwartz061103.asp

What's Behind 'The Innocence of Muslims'?

What motivated an Egyptian-born Coptic Christian, "Sam Bacile," (real name Nakoula Basseley Nakoula[1]) whose notability as a criminal, a bankrupt, and an ex-convict,[2] rather than as a committed activist for any cause other than his own financial well-being, to make a film that was guaranteed to inflame Muslims across the world?

What sparked the riots and violence across the Muslim world was not the movie, per se, which is called "Desert Warrior," "which was a bust, a wash," according to "consultant," Steve Klein,[3] but the more widely seen YouTube trailer called "Innocence of Muslims."

The frontman and hence the fall-guy for an action that was obviously also going to place him in extreme danger, must surely have been offered a sizable financial incentive considering the personal risks to a man who has hardly been known for his selflessness. Nakoula had been declared bankrupt in 2000 and had been involved in criminal schemes before and since. A Los Angeles Times report states of Nakoula:

> ...Some of those activities were criminal. He was convicted on state drug charges in 1997. In 2010, he was convicted

---

1   A Nagourney and S F Kovaleki, "Man of many names is tied to a video," *New York Times*, September 13, 2012, http://www.nytimes.com/2012/09/14/us/origins-of-provocative-video-are-shrouded.html?_r=1

2   Ibid.

3   M Basu, "New details emerge of anti-Islam film's mystery producer," CNN, September 14, 2012, http://edition.cnn.com/2012/09/13/world/anti-islam-filmmaker/index.html

in an identity theft scheme. According to the court file, Nakoula, who ran gas stations in Hawaiian Gardens, operated under a dizzying array of aliases, including Kritbag Difrat. He was sentenced to 21 months in federal prison and was released last summer.[4]

The individual that soon emerged as the "significant other" behind Nakoula is Steve Klein, a leading neocon Zionist associated with Robert Spencer, Pamela Geller, and Daniel Pipes, in what one Jewish investigative journalist, Max Blumenthal, calls the "Axis of Islamophobia."[5] Klein is stated to be the script consultant.[6]

Klein, a Vietnam veteran, has made a name for himself doing what he calls finding "al Queda cells" in California and leading "anti-Islam protests outside of mosques and schools." Klein claimed to journalist Jeffrey Goldberg that he did not know Bacile's real name but that Bacile had sought him out due to his prominence in agitating against Islam. For someone who claims that ferreting out Muslim terrorist cells in the USA is "a piece of cake,"[7] Klein's feigned ignorance about Bacile seems unlikely. The more likely scenario is that Nakoula (aka Bacile) was selected by Zionist handlers as someone who could be paid to do their bidding. Klein told Goldberg: "After 9/11 I went out to look for terror cells in California and found them, piece of cake. Sam found out about me. The Middle East Christian and Jewish communities trust me." Klein sounds like more than the usual two-bit neocon Islamophobic agitator, and we are entitled to ask, "Who looked for whom?" Klein assured Goldberg that "Israel is

---

4   H Ryan and J Garrison, "Christian charity, ex-con linked to film on Islam," *Los Angeles Times*, September 13, 2012, http://www.latimes.com/news/local/la-me-filmmaker-20120914,0,6397127.story

5   M Blumenthal, Monodoweis, AP reported anti-Islam film that sparked protests was made to help Israel, but questions surround producer of the film http://mondoweiss.net/2012/09/ap-says-anti-islam-movie-was-conceived-as-effort-to-help-israel.html

6   H Ryan and J Garrison, op. cit.

7   J Goldberg, op. cit.

Scene from The Innocence of Muslims.

not involved" and stated that Nakoula's original claim to having been an "Israeli Jew" "is a disinformation campaign." So does this mean that Klein, the pro-Zionist Islamophobe, is claiming that he was willingly (or unwillingly?) part of a Muslim-serving "disinformation campaign?" Was the man who is so canny that he finds "uncovering al Qaeda cells in California," "a piece of cake," duped by a low-class crim? Or is it a more plausible possibility that Klein recruited Nakoula?

It seems clear that the film was intended to be a provocation that would incite anti-Israel sentiments just as much as anti-American, with the aim being to generate a mass wave of resentment against Muslims. Nakoula was claiming "that he raised the $5 million to make the film from 'more than 100 Jewish donors'."[8] Why was Nakoula deliberately inciting Muslims to anti-Israel sentiment, along with anti-US sentiment, if not to provide a pretext for an American-Israeli military reaction? In particular, why were the two main Copts behind the film creating a situation that could only place their fellow Copts in Egypt and elsewhere in extreme danger from Muslims?

---

8   "Original Post," Mondoweiss, op. cit.

Somehow Nakoula had sufficient contacts, we are supposed to believe, to bring together a multinational task force of some Copts but mostly "Evangelicals" from Syria, Turkey, Pakistan, and Egypt.[9] However, it is Klein who states that he is "trusted" by "Middle East Christians," which presumably means Copts, and hence it would not be difficult for Klein to search out a dubious character with financial troubles, who could be induced to take the wrap for enough cash. If nothing else, he could have simply consulted his Coptic colleague Nassralla, whose company, Media for Christ, made the movie.

WHO IS STEVE KLEIN?

Max Blumenthal reports that Steve Klein writes on Pamela Geller's anti-Muslim, Zionist website Atlas Shrugs,[10] Geller apparently being a bit of a name in the neocon movement.[11]

Klein is also supported by Robert Spencer's "Jihad Watch," which promoted a "9/11 Rally at Ground Zero" involving Klein, as "founder of the Concerned Citizens for the First Amendment" and, of particular interest, "The courageous Coptic Christian activist Joseph Nassralla," founder of The Way TV satellite network.[12] Klein is also "founder of Courageous Christians United."[13]

Klein, despite the suggestive character of his name, is not Jewish, as far as can be ascertained. He would appear, rather, to be yet another Evangelical Shabbez Goy.

---

9   Ibid.

10   Atlas Shrugs, http://atlasshrugs2000.typepad.com/atlas_shrugs/2012/09/
     despite-ugly-revolt-at-dnc-democrat-party-of-jumah-and-right-of-retun-
     restores-references-to-god-jer.html

11   Pamela Geller, "Biography," http://atlasshrugs2000.typepad.com/about.html

12   Jihad Watch, http://www.jihadwatch.org/2011/07/los-angeles-sheriff-baca-
     press.html

13   "Anti-Islam film made by Media for Christ, directed by pornographer," *Times
     Live*, September 15, 2012, http://www.timeslive.co.za/world/2012/09/15/
     anti-islam-film-made-by-media-for-christ-directed-by-pornographer

However, despite the amateur nature of the film, which is in fact a 14 minute "trailer," Nakoula-Bacile was backed by a well-established Evangelical media production company, Media for Christ run by Joseph Nassralla Abdelmasih, although Abdelmasih is in hiding and denying involvement, while simultaneously stating he was "logistics manager." The company claims to be upset and repudiates the film, "But Duarte's deputy city manager said she had been told by sheriff's officials that the permits to shoot the movie had been issued to Media for Christ."[14]

As stated above, Robert Spencer's "Jihad Watch" has referred Joseph Nassralla of the Way TV, which the L.A. *Times* reports is the satellite network for Media for Christ. The L.A. *Times* reports of Steve Klein that his "views have been tracked by Muslim groups and others for years. One of his platforms was a weekly show on Media for Christ's satellite network, The Way TV."[15] Hence there is a close association between Klein and the pro-Israeli Copt Nassralla of Media for Christ, both of whom were involved in a "9/11 Remembrance Rally." The L.A. *Times* further states:

> While Media for Christ public filings describe it as an evangelical organization working to spread the Gospel, Nassralla has devoted himself in recent years to criticizing Islam in speeches and interviews. With Klein, Nassralla joined in accusations that Sheriff Lee Baca was embracing the Muslim Brotherhood by allying with a prominent Muslim American civil rights group.

> "I fled to America with my family because of the violence directed against me for my Christian faith," Nassralla was quoted as saying last year on an anti-Islamic website. "Sheriff Baca must be fired, and the County must apologize to all of us who have suffered at the hands of the Muslim Brotherhood."

---

14   H Ryan and J Garrison, op. cit.

15   Ibid.

In a 2010 speech in New York, Nassralla criticized violence against Christians in Egypt and deplored plans to build a mosque near the former World Trade Center site in New York. "Wake up, America. Stop Islamicization of America," he said.[16]

Surely one might ask just how Nassralla, who "fled to America" to get his family away from the murderous Muslims, thinks that such a film would serve his Coptic brothers and sisters in Egypt and elsewhere? Just how "Christian" the motivation behind the film is can be surmised from its director, Alan Roberts, being a veteran of the "soft porn" movie genre.[17]

As for Klein, despite at first seeming to downplay his involvement, he is unrepentant. The film is doing its job in manipulating Muslims into another Zionist-contrived PR disaster: "Do I have blood on my hands? No. Did I kill this guy? No ... Do I feel guilty that these people were incited? Guess what? I didn't incite them. They're pre-incited, they're pre-programmed to do this."[18]

IN THE SAME MOULD AS THE CARTOONS PROVOCATION

Like the Danish cartoon violence, the same Islamophobic coteries, while distancing themselves from such a crass film and trailer, are quick enough to jump on the bandwagon against Islam, Pipes stating: "The anger is there. But it's more than anger. It is a deliberate effort since 1989 to tell us in the west that we have to play by the rules of Sharia." Pamella Geller writes:

It [the film] was not the cause of these riots and murders.

---

16 Ibid.

17 "Anti-Islam film made by Media for Christ, directed by pornographer," op. cit.

18 M Collier, "Promoters of ' Innocence of Muslim' defend film shift focus on Islam, *Christian Post*, September 14, 2012, http://www.christianpost. com/news/promoters-of-innocence-of-muslim-defend-film-shift-focus-to-islam-81633/

The film was on YouTube for months before the Muslim rage over it began, and that rage was clearly carefully planned and orchestrated. The film is just a pretext to justify the violence and intimidate the West into adopting Sharia restrictions on the freedom of speech, so that jihad can advance unimpeded and unopposed in the West. And you, by focusing on the film and demonizing the filmmakers, are abetting that.[19]

Robert Spencer, casting Nakoula in martyr mode, however, writes that if Nakoula is sent back to jail it will be "not for the meth or the fraud or for the technicality of the probation violation, but for insulting Muhammad. His imprisonment will be a symbol of America's capitulation to the Sharia. If Nakoula Basseley Nakoula is imprisoned, he will be nothing more than the fall guy who became the first offender against the new federal crime of blasphemy against Islam."[20]

---

19   Sheila Musaji, e "Innocence" of the Islamophobes and the Film No One Wants to Be Connected With," *The American Muslim*, September 18, 2012, http://theamericanmuslim.org/tam.php/features/articles/the-distancing-begins/0019363

20   Ibid.

Attack on Syria Planned Nearly Two Decades Ago

Now the world looks on again in confusion and fear as the USA extends its dialectical strategy of "controlled crises" over one of the few remaining redoubts of independence from the "new world order": Syria. Again the lines of opposition are drawn between Russia and the USA in a geopolitical struggle for world conquest. Syria in fact has long been viewed as the major obstacle to globalist ambitions: moreso even than Libya, Iraq or Iran. In 1996 the Study Group for a New Israeli Strategy Toward 2000, established by the Institute for Advanced Strategic Studies, Jerusalem, issued a paper titled A Clean Break. The think tank included people who would become influential in the Bush Administration, such as Richard Perle, Douglas Feith and David Wurmser. The major obstacle was Syria, and the major aim was to "roll back Syria," and to "foil Syria's regional ambitions." Even the recommendation of removing Saddam – "an important Israeli strategic objective in its own right" – was seen as a step towards Syria.[1] The world-conquering ambitions of those misnamed "neo-conservatives" in the Bush Administration were taken on board with gusto by the Obama Administration, with the young paragon of liberal-humanitarian virtues impelled into the White House by a lot of very dubious globalist luminaries who were presumably too obscure for the US electorate to discern when they voted for someone they believed would change America's foreign policy course.[2]

The 1996 paper recommends a propaganda offensive against

---

1   *A Clean Break*, Study Group for a New Israeli Strategy Toward 2000, 1996, http://www.informationclearinghouse.info/article1438.htm

2   K R Bolton, "Obama: Catspaw of International Finance," August 28, 2008, http://rense.com/general83/cats.htm

Syria along the lines of that employed against Saddam, and indeed against everyone who is an obstacle to the "new world order" and/or Israel, suggesting that the "move to contain Syria" be justified by "drawing attention to its weapons of mass destruction."[3] The report suggests "securing tribal alliances with Arab tribes that cross into Syrian territory and are hostile to the Syrian ruling elite." They suggest the weaning of Shia rebels against Syria.[4]

The plan of attack against Syria has been long in the making. Arab regimes have recently fallen like dominoes as a prelude to the elimination of Syria and Iran. The Clean Break recommends the use of Cold War type rhetoric in smearing Syria. We can see the plan unfolding before our eyes. The "weapons of mass destruction" charade used to justify the US bombing of Syria takes the from of alleged chemical attacks on Syrian "civilians," with a compliant news media showing lurid pictures of suffering children, but usually with the comment that the reports are "unconfirmed." The US assurances of "proof" sound as unconvincing to the critical observer as the "evidence" against Saddam. The United Nations supposedly has a report proving that chemical weapons were used, but not who used them. Sure enough, reports have come out that US-backed rebels have committed the chemical attacks as a means of securing a US assault on the Assad government. Two Western veteran journalists, while captives of the Free Syria Army, overheard their captors – including an FSA General - discussing the chemical weapons attack rebels had launched in Damascus as a means of justifying Western intervention.[5]

---

3   *A Clean Break*, op. cit., "Securing the Northern Border."

4   Ibid., "Moving to a Traditional Balance of Power Strategy."

5   "Journalist and writer held hostage for five months in Syria 'overheard captors conversation blaming rebels for chemical attacks,'" *Mail Online*, 12 September 2013, http://www.dailymail.co.uk/news/article-2418378/Syrian-hostage-Domenico-Quirico-overheard-rebels-blame-Damascus-chemical-attacks.html

In an act of statesmanship, Putin pre-empted President Obama's determination to bomb Syria by suggesting that Syria place its chemical weapons stockpiles for disposal with the United Nations; a plan that Syria has accepted. As we have seen in recent days on news conferences, the FSA is livid that the Putin plan has been accepted, as this might have scotched their plans for a Western military assault; although of course there are an infinite number of other ways that the globalists can concoct to justify military action.

Putin sees the offensive against Syria in world historical terms in determining what type of world is being moulded. While Russian ships face US and some French and British ships, he has rebuked Obama's statements – like those of US presidents since the days of Woodrow Wilson and his plans for a "new world order" - that the USA has "an exceptional role." In his appeal to the American people published in the New York Times, Putin questions the USA's strategy stating that, "It is alarming that military intervention in internal conflicts in foreign countries has become commonplace for the United States." Condemning the basis of the "new world order" that is being imposed with US weaponry, Putin writes that having studied Obama's recent address:

> ...I would rather disagree with a case he made on American exceptionalism, stating that the United States' policy is 'what makes America different. It's what makes us exceptional'. It is extremely dangerous to encourage people to see themselves as exceptional, whatever the motivation. There are big countries and small countries, rich and poor, those with long democratic traditions and those still finding their way to democracy. Their policies differ, too. We are all different, but when we ask for the Lord's blessings, we must not forget that God created us equal.[6]

---

6   Vladimir V Putin, "A Plea for Caution from Russia," *New York Times*, 11 September 2013, http://www.nytimes.com/2013/09/12/opinion/putin-plea-

A Syrian man mourns over a dead family member after a poisonous gas attack in Damascus, Syria in August 2013.

"JIHADIST" STRAW MEN

As mentioned in the Clean Break blueprint for regional war, the aim was to create a new "cold war" type global scenario which would continue to uphold the USA as the champion of "freedom," and "western values," even when those values need to been imposed on unwilling peoples with armed force. With the implosion of the USSR a new world bogeyman was required. One was soon created in the form of "Jihadists" who had served US interests well when fighting the Russians in Afghanistan. A scenario had arisen that has all the sings of a dialectical plan: controlled crises, or what the "neo-con" strategist Ralph Peters calls "constant conflict": an "enemy" has been created by the USA and is attacked or supported according to requirements.

Hence, "Jihadists" were created and used against the Russian military. They were at the time portrayed as "freedom fighters." Then when Yugoslavia needed carving up and its component

for-caution-from-russia-on-syria.html?_r=0

parts – especially Kosovo – privatising economically for takeover by predatory international capital, the Kosovo Liberation Army, which had been listed by the US State Department as terrorists and gangsters, became the "freedom fighters" required to overthrow Milosevic. The KLA were suddenly transformed into good Jihadists fighting for freedom. Years of Albanian separatist terrorism against Serbs[7] was suddenly reversed into Serb genocide against Albanian Kosovans, and the "cold war" propaganda machine was turned back on and cranked up to incite war against Serbia. Suddenly it all became a war on behalf of a "new internationalism" and a "new millennium," to quote then British Prime Minister Tony Blair,[8] whose present-day counterpart, David Cameron, is as eager to fight the Syrians. Despite the reduction of Kosovo's economy to ruin, it was opened up to the world for "privatisation," as the war aims of the globalists had demanded,[9] and a state commission exists to busily sell off the old state assets and resources.[10]

When Libya's turn came, the USA supported the "Jihadists" with whom they are supposedly in mortal combat the world over. The strategy was put into operation by Graham Fuller when deputy director of the CIA's National Council of Intelligence, who created the Mujahadeen, to fight the Russians in Afghanistan, and then spawned Al Qaeda. Fuller stated: "The policy of guiding the evolution of Islam and of helping them against our adversaries worked marvellously well in Afghanistan against [the Russians]. The same doctrines can still be used to destabilize what remains of Russian power..."[11] Putin is up against the same strategy

---

7   Chris Bird, "Kosovan Serbs under siege," *The Guardian*, 18 August 1999, http://www.guardian.co.uk/world/1999/aug/18/balkans1

8   Tony Blair, *Newsweek*, April 19, 1999.

9   Rambouillet Agreement: Interim Agreement for Peace and Self-Government in Kosovo, Constitution, Chapter Four, "Economic Issues," Article II (1). http://www.state.gov/www/regions/eur/ksvo_rambouillet_text.html

10   Privatisation Agency of Kosovo, http://www.pak-ks.org/?page=2,4

11   Richard Labeviere, *Dollars for Terror: The Untied States and Islam* (Algora Publishing, 2000), pp. 5-6.

with US support for Muslim separatists in Chechnya, another area of great interest to the globalists and, as one would expect, Freedom House has formed yet another "liberation committee," the American Committee for Peace in Chechnya, Orwellian double-think for "war in Chechnya."

Putin in his recent statement published in *The New York Times* has warned that the same forces are at work in Syria, as they were in Libya and throughout the "Arab Spring" revolts which have created a state of permanent crises in North Africa, which the globalists now aim to extend to Syria and Iran.

Israel's Legacy of Anti-Christian Persecution

While the image of the "mad mullah" and swarming masses of fanatical Muslims poised to rend asunder Western Civilization is one that has been resurrected from prior centuries and is propagated by the apologists for Israel with increasing vigor, the mythic spectre has served to obscure the anti-Christian foundations of the Zionist state. Hence, the spectacle of "Christian Zionist" as among the most fanatical defenders of Israel is an historical travesty as odd as Christian Fundamentalists supporting the League of Militant Atheists in the USSR. Indeed, there is an analogy: The League of Militant Atheists avidly sought the obliteration of Christianity in the Soviet state; Zionists, and Orthodox believers in the Talmud who have a major presence in Israel, are as zealous in obliterating Christianity from the Holy Land as their Bolshevik counterparts of yesteryear. Yet, how widely realized is it that Israel is a state where Christianity is repressed and despised?

A hint of the situation was publicly exposed when it was reported that the Protestant Cemetery of Mount Zion was desecrated in what Christian leaders in Israel state is the latest in "a string of relentless attacks on church properties and religious sites." The smashing to pieces of stone crosses toppled from the gravesites was a particular feature of the vandalism. Unsurprisingly, the news does not seem to have been featured in the manner by which the desecration of a Jewish site would receive from the world's mass media. In particular, there have been no worldwide protests and street parades demonstrating outrage, of the type that takes place when even minor vandalism is inflicted on Jewish sites, when such actions are treated with such gravity as to inspire calls for new laws to stop the "rise of anti-Semitism."

While New Zealand's Dominion Post newspaper, serving the capital region, devoted two sentences to the subject,[1] the most detailed report seems to have been written by Daniel Estrin of the Associated Press. Estrin reports that four Israeli youths were arrested but were released without charge until further questioning. Two of the youths were affiliated with "Hilltop Youth," a group responsible for attacks in recent years on Christian and Muslim sites, and Israeli army property in protest at Israeli government policy; and two youths who were students at a Jewish seminary. There have been many high profile sites vandalized over the past year, including a Trappist monastery in Latrun, outside Jerusalem, where vandals burned a door and spray-painted "Jesus is a monkey" on the century-old building; a Baptist church in Jerusalem, and other monasteries. "Clergymen often speak of being spat at by ultra-Orthodox religious students while walking around Jerusalem's Old City wearing frocks and crosses." "Search for Common Ground," (SCG) an NGO that monitors news reports of attacks on religious sites, states that 17 Christian sites have been reported vandalized over the past three years. However, a police detective in charge of Christian affairs told the "Search for Common Ground" the number of vandalized sites is higher, but Christian leaders did not report many of the attacks to the media. Additionally, SCG does not include vandalism in the Old City of Jerusalem in its survey, because many of the sites are in dispute and the organization wants to be seen as neutral. Hana Bendcowsky of the Jerusalem Center for Jewish-Christian Relations, states that Christian leaders often do not file complaints with police because many are in Israel on special visas and want to maintain good relations with authorities. She states that there is a strong feeling that police are not really interested in the problem, although police spokesmen claim otherwise.[2]

---

1   "Church Target," *Dominion Post*, Wellington, New Zealand, October 10, 2013.

2   Daniel Estrin, "Attack on Jerusalem Graves Unnerves Christians," Associated Press, October 9, 2013, http://bigstory.ap.org/article/attack-jerusalem-graves-unnerves-christians

The Najran Massacre: A Christian Holocaust by Jews

Zionism was created around the fiction that "anti-Semitism" is inherent within the "goyim" psyche, and that Jews must therefore remove themselves from goy society. It was therefore necessary to contrive a history of Gentile-Jewish relations that depicted the Jews as forever facing persecution through the entirety of their history. This also necessitates the portrayal of Jews as at all times sinless victims of that inherent goy psychosis of "anti-Semitism." Another option is the view that the perpetrators of the ages old persecution myth are suffering from paranoid psychosis. Certainly, when it has been Jews with the upper hand they have been none too charitable towards their defeated enemies, as the Torah and other books of the Old Testament quickly show. One of the most famous, recorded in the "Book of Esther," is the slaughter of 75,000 Persians by Jews once they got the upper hand, a slaughter that continues to be celebrated today at the Feast of Purim, where "Haman cakes" are eaten and there is much boisterous rejoicing. In 500AD the Arabs of Najran in southern Arabia converted to Christianity, but in 522 the Jewish Himyarite king of Yemen began the persecution of Christians, who asked for Ethiopian assistance. With the Himyarite defeat of the Ethiopians in 523 the Najran Christians were massacred. Najran had been the first place in South Arabia where Christianity was established, and had a large community with the seat of a Bishopric.

The Jewish King of Yemen, Yusuf As'ar Dhu Nuwas, aimed to create a "Davidic" kingship, but Najran was an important trade route. When the Najran Christians refused to abandon their faith 4,000 were said to have been burned alive. In a document by Bishop Simeon of Beth Arsham, on the Najran holocaust he records that a Najran noblewoman named Ruhm brings her daughter before Dhu Nuwas and defiantly states: "Cut off our heads, so that we may go join our brothers and my daughter's father." The daughter, and a granddaughter are decapitated and Ruhm is forced to drink the blood. King Dhu Nuwas then asks,

"How does your daughter's blood taste to you?," to which Ruhm replies: "Like a pure spotless offering: that is what it tasted like in my mouth and in my soul."[3]

A difference between Islam and Judaism is that whereas the Koran honour Jesus as a prophet and his mother Mary, the Orthodox Jewish Talmud, or religious codex, describes them in what we might call less than flattering terms. Hence, Islam honors the Christian martyrs of Najran, the Koran stating of them:

> "...slain were the men of the pit, the fire abounding in fuel, when they were seated over it, and were themselves witnesses of what they did with the believers. They took revenge on them because they believed in God the All-mighty, the All-laudable..."[4]

As word spread of the Jewish holocaust on the Najran Christians, Najran became a center of pilgrimage that rivalled Mecca. Al-Harith, the leader of the Christian Arabs at Najran, who had been killed, was canonized by the Roman Catholic Church as St. Aretas. The Catholic Church honors the Christian martyrs of the Jewish holocaust on October 24. A Catholic periodical states of the atrocity:

> The leader of these ancient Christians was a certain 'Abd Allah ibn Harith (who became St. Aretas in the Roman

---

3   Joel Thomas Walker, *The legend of Mar Qardagh: narrative and Christian heroism in late antique Iraq* (University of California Press, 2006).

4   Koran, Surah LXXXV, *al-Buruj*
    For a present -day Islamic account see "Dhu Nuwas and the Najan Massacre," Islamic Research Foundation International, http://www.irfi.org/ articles4/articles_5001_6000/dhu%20nuwas%20and%20the%20najran%20 massacrehtml.htm
    It is notable that Zionists cannot even tolerate the mention of Najran on a recent BBC2 documentary about the frank incense trail, and a complaint was made by the Board of Deputies of British Jews to the BBC. Is this, then "Najran Denial"?

Saint Arethas and the Martyrs of al-Najran
from the Menologion of Basil II.

martyrology). He and his soldiers were beheaded. Priests, deacons, nuns and laymen were thrown into a ditch filled with burning fuel. Four thousand men, women, and children were slain, including a boy of five who jumped into the flames to be with his mother.[5]

I cite this example to show that the tales of persecution of Jews by the goyim since ancient times are one-dimensional and have been made into both a religion and a political doctrine that has become central to Jewish thinking and the foundations of the Zionist state; while Jewish persecution of Christians or Muslims, et al, cannot even be acknowledged by Jewish Officialdom on any level. It is the religious zealots of Orthodox Judaism who, however, blow the cover on the pathological hatred some influential sections of both Judaism and Zionism have towards Christianity, while Zionist lobbyists and politicians court self-styled "Christian Zionists."

---

5   William Mulligan, "The Martyrs of Najran," Catholic Near East Magazine, Fall 1977, http://www.cnewa.org/default.aspx?ID=101&pagetypeID=4&sitec ode=us&pageno=1

THE ZIONIST RECORD

When Zionists went blundering over the Holy Land, this broadly termed collection of "Jews" ranged from religious zealots to communistic atheists. Despite those differences what they had in common was an ancient legacy of contempt for the goyim and hatred for Christianity and Islam. From the first arrivals of Zionist terrorists of Stern, Irgun, Palmach and others, therefore, Christians and Muslims were not going to fare well in the "Holy Land."

Monsignor Thomas MacMahon, secretary of the Catholic Near East Association of New York, wrote to the United Nations on August 20, 1948, "there have been constantly some violations and desecrations of Catholic holy places. The associated Press report of August 19, 1948 confirmed that Jewish forces perpetrated criminal acts against 12 Roman Catholic institutions in Northern Palestine... Seven churches, convents and hospitals have been looted by Jews and others seized by force."[6]

Monsignor Vergani, general vicar of the Latin Patriarch of Jerusalem for Galilee reported that, "the chapel was profaned. The altar overturned, the statues of the holy Virgin, Saint Francis and Saint Anthony were broken."[7]

At the Church and Hospice in Tabakam, "the chapel profaned, the door broken open, the statues in pieces, sacred vestments torn and thrown to the floor, the tabernacle opened by force, the chalice stolen, crosses broken."[8]

According to Father Pascal St. Jean, Superior of Our Lady of France Hostel, valuables were stolen, archives plundered, and

---

6   Statement of the Committee of the Christian Union of Palestine, (representing of the Armenian Catholic Patriarchate, Latin Patriarchate, Greek Catholic Patriarchate, and the Latin Parishes of the Holy Land), Jerusalem, May 31, 1948.

7   Ibid.

8   Ibid.

"both chapels, were desecrated, figures of Christ unfastened from crosses and taken away. In the great chapel we came upon Jewish soldiers of both sexes dancing in the sanctuary to the music of the harmonium. Benches were taken outside and used for profane purposes. We have seen mattresses in the great chapel and Jewish soldiers have certainly been sleeping there. I protest against these acts in particular. They are sins committed on the premises of holy worship."[9]

When the Stern Gang went into Jerusalem, breaking a ceasefire in May 1948, the Christian Union of Palestine reported that churches, convents, religious and charitable institutions were destroyed, injuring many women, children, priests and nuns. The Christian union listed the outrages against Christian holy places, including occupation of the convent of St. George of the Greek Orthodox Church, on May 14, 1948; occupation and fortifying of the Hospice Notre Dame de France of the Assumptionist Fathers on May 15, using it as a main base to attack Jerusalem; occupation of the Convent of the Reparatrice Sisters, used as a base, May 15; occupation of the French Hospital run by the Sisters of St. Joseph, under the protection of the Flags of the Red Cross and of France; The Apostolic Delegation under the protection of the Flag of the Holy See, occupied May 18; occupation of the monastery of the German Benedictine fathers, used as one of the main bases against the Holy City; the Convent of St. John of the Greek Orthodox Church.[10]

Holy places damaged by the Zionist forces during this time included: the Hospice Notre Dame de France; Convent of the Reparatrice Sisters, set on fire; church of the Monastery of the Benedictine Fathers; Seiminary of St. Anne hit by two mortar shells, wounding sheltering refugees; Church of St. Constantin and Helena of the Church of the Holy Sepulchre, bomb fragments also damaging the Dome of the Holy Sepulchre; Armenian

---

9   Ibid.

10 Hon. Issa Nakhleh, *Jews Eradicating Christianity from the Holy Land* (New York: Palestine Arab Delegation, ca. 1970).

Orthodox Patriarchate hit by about 100 mortar mobs fired from Zionists occupying the Monastery of the Benedictine Fathers on Mount Sion, the bombs also damaging St. Jacob's Convent, the Archangels convent, and their two elementary schools, library and churches, killing eight and wounding 120 refugees; entrance to the church of St. Mark of the Syrian Orthodox Church shelled, killing the monk Peter Saymy, secretary to the Bishop;, and wounding two others; Convent of St. George of the Greek Orthodox Church, part of the Greek Catholic Cathedral, hit by a mortar shell; Convent of the Archangel of the Coptic Patriarchate, situated over the grotto of the Holy Cross, part of the Basilica of the Holy Sepulchre, shelled May 23; Greek Orthodox Patriarchate shelled wounding many refugees; Latin Patriarchate hit by mortar bombs, damaging the Cathedral; Greek Catholic Patriarchate shelled May 16 and 29.[11]

Among those killed by the Zionist forces, the above named monk Peter Saymy; Father Mammert Vionnet of the Assumptionist fathers and Judge of the Latin Ecclesiastical Court, killed by Zionist forces when they occupied the convent; Father John Salah of the Passionist Fathers, killed when entering his church to celebrate Mass; Brothers Sigismond and Cyrille of the Christian Brothers, wounded inside their school.[12]

On April 16, 1954, Zionists attacked the Greek Catholic Community cemetery in Haifa, and danced on the graves, threw out the human remains of many tombs, and smashed 73 crosses and 50 statues of angels.[13] Several months later in Haifa a procession led by the Carmelite Fathers was attacked near the cave of St. Elijah on Mt. Carmel.[14]

Father Rezk of the Greek Orthodox Church, Jaffa, reported

---

11 Ibid.

12 Ibid.

13 Hon. Issa Nakhleh, *Jews Eradicating Christianity from the Holy Land* (New York: Palestine Arab Delegation, ca. 1970).

14 Ibid.

on August 4, 1956, "armed Jewish soldiers broke through the Church door. Chalices and sacred vases containing the Holy Host were stolen, along with other religious items. "They threw away the icons of Jesus Christ and the holy Virgin in a garden next door."[15]

In January 1963 70 mostly Yeshiva students attacked the Finnish Christian mission School in Jerusalem, and beat the school pastor, Risto Santala. The mob was incited by an editorial in the newspaper Yediot Aharoot, December 23, 1962, which stated that the Christian Mission was converting Jews.[16]

When Zionist forces occupied Jerusalem in 1967, Nancy Nolan, wife of Dr Abu Haydar of the American University Hospital of Beirut, described Israeli soldiers and youths throwing stink bombs at the Church of the Holy Sepulchre. The Church of St. Anne, whose crypt marks the birthplace of Mary, and the Church of the Nativity in Bethlehem, were vandalized. The Warden of the Garden Tomb, Reverend S J Mattar, was shot, and shots were fired randomly into the Tomb in an attempt to kill the Warden's wife. Jews went into the Church of the Nativity and the Church of the Holy Sepulchre, smoking, littering and bringing in dogs.[17]

On the murder of the Warden at the Garden Tomb, Reverend Mattar, Mrs Sigrid W Proft of Switzerland, was an eye-witness, stating that Rev. and Mrs Proft and herself went to the Tomb for shelter from bombing and shooting when the Zionist forces attacked on June 5. The following morning Rev. Mattar went out to go to the house to get some food. Soon afterward the gate was broken down by soldiers. Mattar responded by stating "good morning" "in a kindly and friendly manner." Immediately there were several shots, and shots into the Tomb. When Proft and Mrs

---

15   Statement of the Committee of the Christian Union of Palestine, op. cit.

16   Hon. Issa Nakhleh, *Jews Eradicating Christianity from the Holy Land* (New York: Palestine Arab Delegation, ca. 1970).

17   Hon. Issa Nakhleh, *Jews Eradicating Christianity from the Holy Land* (New York: Palestine Arab Delegation, ca. 1970), 10.

Mattar went up to the house, Rev. Mattar was laying dead with bullets in his head.[18]

In 1968 His Beatitude Maximos V Hakim, Patriarch of Antioch and all the East, stated in New York that he feared Christianity could not survive in the Holy land, and related what he had witnessed, stating that the Melchite Church had lost churches in Damoun, Somata, Kafr-Bur'om and Ikret, a completely Catholic village that the Israelis destroyed on Christmas Day, 1952. He stated that many churches were damaged in the 1967 war, and that many churches were desecrated by male and female soldiers entering the Holy Places "indecently dressed and with their dogs."

When Zionists seized convents and Churches on Mt. Zion in Jerusalem in 1968, they looted gold and silver ornaments. An eyewitness account states that the interior of the Church of St. Saviour had its altar wrecked, and an altar painting destroyed. The valuable collection of church vestments was missing. Armenian and Greek Orthodox cemeteries were desecrated on Mt. Zion, including 14 tombs of Christian patriarchs. Practically every tomb at the Greek Orthodox cemetery was smashed.[19] Likewise with the Catholic cemetery. The Very Reverend Father Andres, Procureua-General in the Holy Land, stated in an article in the Catholic journal, La Terra Sainte, March 1968, that "the Jews actually dragged the corpses out of the tombs and scattered the coffins and remains of the dead all around the cemetery."[20]

In 1970 Archbishop Diodoros of Hierapolis, Greek Orthodox Archdiocese of Amman, Jordan, issued a statement to the United Nations Human Rights Commission, on the desecration of the Holy Land. The Greek Orthodox Church at Ein Kerem, near Jerusalem, had been vandalized and the tombs unearthed, and the corpses of the parish priest and others scattered in the streets

---

18   Ibid., 11.

19   Hon. Issa Nakhleh, "Jews Eradicating Christianity from the Holy Land" (New York: Palestine Arab Delegation, ca. 1970), 8.

20   Ibid.

among garbage, and "the place had been made into a public lavatory." The Saint Michael Church, Jaffa, was set on fire and the remnants were surrounded by cabarets and nightclubs, whose patrons used the courtyard. Bisan Creek Orthodox Church, Beit-Shean had been made into a public lavatory. The Greek Orthodox cemetery on Mt. Zion had been destroyed by Israeli authorities and the bodies unearthed. Many Bishops, clergymen and nuns routinely have their crucifixes spat on in the streets, something that has not abated over the years.[21]

ONGOING

When four Jewish youths desecrated Christian graves and others spray-painted that "Jesus is a monkey," these are not isolated incidences but part of an ongoing process of eradicating Christianity from the Holy Land. They are manifestations of a politicised religious tradition that Orthodox rabbis proudly trace back to the Pharisees of Jesus' time. As Dr Israel Shahak has shown, the fanatical hatred of goyim and Christianity is intrinsic to certain types of Judaism, which have much influence in both Israel and among Diaspora Jewry.[22] A slightly more measured but continual sign of hatred that the influential Orthodox Jews show towards Christians is that of spitting. In 2011 the Israeli newspaper Haaretz reported:

Clergymen in the Armenian Church in Jerusalem say they are victims of harassment, from senior cardinals to priesthood students; when they do complain, the police don't usually find the perpetrators.

Ultra-Orthodox young men curse and spit at Christian clergymen in the streets of Jerusalem's Old City as a matter of routine. In most cases the clergymen ignore the attacks, but sometimes they strike back. Last week the Jerusalem

---

21   Archbishop Diodoros of Hierapolis, April 14, 1970.

22   Israle Shahak, *Jewish History, Jewish religion: The Weight of three Thousand Years* (London: Pluto Press, 1994); Shahak and Norton Mezvinsky, *Jewish Fundamentalism in Israel* (London: Pluto Press, 1999).

Magistrate's Court quashed the indictment against an Armenian priesthood student who had punched the man who spat at him.

Johannes Martarsian was walking in the Old City in May 2008 when an young ultra-Orthodox Jew spat at him. Martarsian punched the spitter in the face, making him bleed, and was charged for assault. But Judge Dov Pollock, who unexpectedly annulled the indictment, wrote in his verdict that "putting the defendant on trial for a single blow at a man who spat at his face, after suffering the degradation of being spat on for years while walking around in his church robes is a fundamental contravention of the principles of justice and decency." When Narek Garabedian came to Israel to study in the Armenian Seminary in Jerusalem half a year ago, he did not expect the insults, curses and spitting he would be subjected to daily by ultra-Orthodox Jews in the streets of the Old City.

...Other clergymen in the Armenian Church in Jerusalem say they are all victims of harassment, from the senior cardinals to the priesthood students. Mostly they ignore these incidents. When they do complain, the police don't usually find the perpetrators. The Greek Patriarchy's clergymen have been cursed and spat on by ultra-Orthodox men in the street for many years. "They walk past me and spit," says Father Gabriel Bador, 78, a senior priest in the Greek Orthodox Patriarchate. "Mostly I ignore it, but it's difficult." ... "It happens a lot," says Archbishop Aristarchos, the chief secretary of the patriarchate. "You walk down the street and suddenly they spit at you for no reason. I admit sometimes it makes me furious, but we have been taught to restrain ourselves, so I do so."

...A few weeks ago four ultra-Orthodox men spat at clergymen in the funeral procession of Father Alberto of the Armenian Church. "They came in a pack, out of nowhere," said Father Goosan. "I know there are fanatical Haredi groups that don't represent the general public but it's still enraging. It all begins with education. It's the responsibility of these men's yeshiva heads to teach them not to behave this way," he says.[23]

Perhaps Father Goosan is being facetious; he surely knows that it is precisely such contempt for Christians that is taught in the yeshiva. The ultra-Orthodox Jews, including the Hassidim who follow the occult teachings of the Kabala, do not recognize goyim as being fully humans. While Reform Jews do not follow such teachings, Orthodoxy, as Shahak showed in his Jewish Fundamentalism in Israel, is a major political force. The Hassidim do not attempt to obscure the true teachings of the Talmud. Although the late Rebbe Schneerson taught that Jews will reign over goyim, he was honoured by American presidents, Senate and Congress as a great humanitarian and educator. In 1991 the Chabad-Lubavitch movement proclaimed "Education Day" in co-operation with President Bush, "to return the world to the moral and ethical values of the Seven Noahide Laws."[24]

---

23 Oz Rosenberg, Haaretz, November 4, 2011 http://www.haaretz.com/news/
    national/ultra-orthodox-spitting-attacks-on-old-city-clergymen-becoming-
    daily-1.393669
24 Public Law 102-14 (H.J. Res. 104) March 20, 1991.

America's Jihad

The Islamic State organization seems to have arisen overnight, well-armed, and swiftly moving through Iraq and Syria, seemingly unstoppable. One might wonder as to how plausible it is to believe the CIA, U.S. National Security Council, and Mossad supposedly hitherto knew little or nothing of the Islamic State jihadists. We are apparently expected to believe that they appeared from nowhere as if by magic.

It is apt to recall the Jihad bogeyman arose from the Mujahideen, which was formed by the CIA as a guerrilla force against the Russians in Afghanistan. The "clash of civilizations," as neocon historians refer to the "war on terrorism," was a contrivance; not the result of an inexorable historical law. By the end of the First World War much goodwill existed between the Entente and the Arabs who had fought together against the Ottoman Empire, with the expectation that the Arab states would achieve independence, thanks to the heroic efforts of T. E. Lawrence and the Arabic fighters. Their guerrilla war against the Turks had been crucial to the war effort, although subsequently besmirched by Zionist propagandists.[1] Thanks to Zionist machinations, the Entente had spoken with a forked tongue to the Arabs while making a contrary promise to the Zionists to back a Jewish state in Palestine in return for Jewish influence supporting the Entente cause, by then in a predicament, in the USA. The result was the Balfour Declaration and the needless prolongation of the war[2] so that the Zionists and the messianists could get their

---

1   T. E. Lawrence, *Seven Pillars of Wisdom* (London: Black House Publishing, 2013).

2   Samuel Landman, *Great Britain, the Jews and Palestine* (London: New Zionist Press, 1936), 2-3. Landman was Honorary Secretary of the Joint Zionist Council of the United Kingdom, 1912; Joint Editor of *The Zionist* 1913-1914; Solicitor and Secretary for the Zionist Organisation 1917-1922; and adviser to the New Zionist Organisation, ca. 1930s.

Al Aqsa Mosque, Jerusalem: Zionists plan to re-build the Temple of Solomon
over its ruins as the centre of a Zionist World Empire.

nose poked into Palestine until such time as being able to dump
themselves en masse after the Second World War.

It is also opportune at this point to recall those who introduced
terrorism into Palestine. The Irgun, Stern and Palmach
underground regarded the British as the "new Nazis," and for
that matter anyone who stood in the way of their messianic
dreams. Hence, United Nations envoy Count Folke Bernadotte,
who had negotiated for thousands of Jews to leave German
occupied territory, was gunned down by the Sternists because
his suggestions for the boundaries of Israel were regarded as
an affront to Jewry.[3] Ultimately, the Zionist dream for Israel
extends the boundaries from the rivers Nile to Euphrates (Genesis
15: 18) and any compromise of captured territory would mean
the surrendering of the deeds of promise from God Himself,[4]

---

3   Bernadotte called on Israel to relinquish the Negev and Jerusalem in return
     for western Galilee. Since the Zionist messianists think they are entitled by
     no less than God to a vast region, this was nothing sort of blasphemy.

4   http://www.globalresearch.ca/greater-israel-the-zionist-plan-for-the-middle-
     east/5324815

unless there is a longer-term motive involved. There cannot be peace in the Middle East until that dream is forgotten, which is not going to happen, any more than the aim of rebuilding the Temple of Solomon upon the ruins of the Al-Aqsa Mosque as the prerequisite for the coming of the Jewish Messiah;[5] the declaration of Jerusalem as the capital of the world, and the elimination of "idolatrous" religions, to be replaced by the Seven Noahide Laws, already promulgated by U.S. Congress.[6] As the Israeli scholar Dr. Israel Shahak documented, such notions are alive and kicking in Israel.[7] Yet we are constantly told of "Muslim fanaticism." We are also told of the hatred Islam possesses for Christianity, despite the recognition of Jesus as a great prophet, and his mother. Meanwhile, *Talmudic* Judaism teaches that Jesus was the son of a whore and a Roman soldier, Pandira, and is in hell boiling in semen. The hatred of Talmudic Jews for Christianity is frequently manifested by the Orthodox custom of spitting on monks and priests, and in many other ways, again documented by Shahak.[8]

In short, the origins of the present Middle East terrorism stem from Franco-British duplicity and Zionist machinations during the First World War, and rampant religious lunacy from Judaism rather than Islam. As the political and judicial theorist Dr. Carl Schmitt pointed out, an outer enemy is often the prerequisite for the formation or maintenance of unity among disparate elements. Hence, Zionism requires "anti-Semitism" to exist. Israel requires the myth of belligerent Arab neighbors ever ready to run them into the Dead Sea. The USA requires a new global bogeyman after the demise of the USSR, to maintain its role as the world's "big brother," albeit one of a particularly vulgar and bullying

---

5   See the plans at: https://www.templeinstitute.org/

6   Promulgation of "U. S. Education Day" honoring Rebbe Schneerson, the Lubavitch Messiah, and the Seven Noahide Laws, Proclamation 5463, April 19, 1986; Public Law 102—14 (H.J. Res. 104) March 20, 1991; Day of International Tribute, June 28, promulgated 2002.

7   Israel Shahak, *Jewish History, Jewish Religion* (London: Pluto Press, 1994).

8   Shahak, *Jewish Fundamentalism in Israel* (Pluto Press, 1999).

type. While Putin's Russia has somewhat served the role once occupied by the USSR, it is difficult to imbed the notion into the world's consciousness that Putinism, like Sovietism, supposedly aims at world conquest, and only the USA can stop this. An added factor is required. Jihadism serves these purposes for both the USA and Israel. Where would the USA have been since the implosion of the Soviet bloc, had it not been for Jihadism? Largely obliged to mind its own business for the first time since before Woodrow Wilson.

MUJAHIDEEN A U.S. CREATION

The ground for Jihadism was sown by the U.S. arming of the Mujahideen against the USSR in Afghanistan. The CIA describes its role in founding Jihadism:

After the Soviet Union invaded Afghanistan in December 1979, President Carter directed CIA to assist the Afghan Mujahideen. CIA came to see that the indigenous Afghan opposition to the Soviets was less an organized movement than widespread opposition by villages and tribes. Through Pakistan, CIA provided the Mujahideen with money, weapons, medical supplies, and communications equipment. Initially the goal was to drain Soviet resources by keeping their forces bogged down. In 1985, CIA shifted from a plan of attrition to one that would help the rebels win. One of the pivotal moments came in September 1986, when the Mujahideen used CIA-provided Stinger missiles to shoot down three Soviet Mi-24D helicopter gunships. As part of this escalation of financial and material support, President Reagan issued new guidance that put the CIA into more direct contact with rebel commanders, beginning an era of CIA interaction with tribal and local leaders that continues through the post-9/11 era.[9]

The CIA then supported the Northern Alliance against the

9   "Afghanistan," Central Intelligence Agency, https://www.cia.gov/library/publications/additional-publications/devotion-to-duty/afghanistan.html

Taliban government. The CIA also claims that it supported the Northern Alliance against Al Qaeda and bin Laden when they moved into Afghanistan from the Sudan. However, an NBC report states of CIA support for bin Laden:

> As his unclassified CIA biography states, bin Laden left Saudi Arabia to fight the Soviet army in Afghanistan after Moscow's invasion in 1979. By 1984, he was running a front organization known as Maktab al-Khidamar – the MAK – which funnelled money, arms and fighters from the outside world into the Afghan war.

What the CIA bio conveniently fails to specify (in its unclassified form, at least) is that the MAK was nurtured by Pakistan's state security services, the Inter-Services Intelligence agency, or ISI, the CIA's primary conduit for conducting the covert war against Moscow's occupation.

The CIA, concerned about the factionalism of Afghanistan found that Arab zealots who flocked to aid the Afghans were easier to "read" than the rivalry-ridden natives. While the Arab volunteers might well prove troublesome later, the agency reasoned, they at least were one-dimensional anti-Soviet for now. So bin Laden, along with a small group of Islamic militants from Egypt, Pakistan, Lebanon, Syria and Palestinian refugee camps all over the Middle East, became the "reliable" partners of the CIA in its war against Moscow.[10] These Afghan veterans became the nucleus for Jihadists further afield.[11]

SERBIA TARGETED

When the U.S. globalists wanted to dismember Yugoslavia and globalize the wealth of Kosovo, again we find the Mujahideen. The USA claims to be fighting Islamic terrorism worldwide. Milosevic's Serbia was on the frontline fighting Islamist

---

10 Michael Moran, "Bin Laden Comes Home to Roost," NBCNews.com, August 24, 1998, http://www.nbcnews.com/id/3340101/#.VD9w2TY5QqR

11 Michael Moran, ibid.

CIA backed Mujahideen, Kunar province. Afghanistan 1985.

terrorism. Rather than U.S. support for the Serbs, the support went to Islamist terrorists and gangsters. Serbs had been the target of Islamists for decades. They aimed to carve out a Greater Albania by annexing Kosovo. The U.S./NATO interest was that of privatizing the vast mineral wealth and other resources of the region run by the State.

In 1998 the Kosovo Liberation Army was described by U.S. special envoy to Bosnia, Robert Gelbard, as "terrorists." The U.S. State Department had previously prepared a report detailing the methods of the KLA to intimidate Kosovan-Albanian ethnics into supporting them. Prior to Milosevic's intervention to restore order, U.S. official sources were reporting that Albanian ethnics were fleeing their villages in their entirety to escape the KLA. Also well-known by American and European police agencies were the drug-trafficking connections the KLA had with organized crime in Europe and Turkey.[12]

---

12   See: Frank Viviano, "Drugs Paying for Conflict in Europe," *San Francisco Chronicle*, June 10, 1994.

The KLA aim was for a Greater Albania including parts of Serbia, Greece, Macedonia, and Montenegro. Chris Hedges, when *New York Times* Balkans Bureau Chief (1995-1998), wrote in *Foreign Affairs* of a map of the Greater Albania found at a KLA compound. Hedges reported: "Between 1966 and 1989 an estimated 130,000 Serbs left the province because of frequent harassment and discrimination by the Kosovar Albanian majority." Hedges mentioned the funding that the KLA was receiving from Islamic states and the presence of Mujahideen in the KLA staging area in northern Albania. In 1981, the *Associated Press* reported that 4000 Serbs fled Kosovo due to anti-Serb riots, and the desecration of Orthodox churches and graves.[13]

When Serb forces attacked Srebrenica, it was to end the armed attacks mounted from the Islamist base on nearby villages. A news report of the time cites "intelligence sources" as stating that it was "harassment which precipitated the Serb attack on the 1,500 Muslim defenders inside the enclave."[14] General Philippe Morillon, commander of the U.N. troops in Bosnia (1992-1993), testified before the International Criminal Tribunal for the Former Yugoslavia that Muslim forces based in Srebrenica had "engaged in attacks during Orthodox holidays and destroyed villages, massacring all the inhabitants. This created a degree of hatred that was quite extraordinary in the region." Between May and December 1992, Muslim forces repeatedly attacked Serb villages around Srebrenica, killing and torturing civilians; some were mutilated and burned alive. Muslim forces in Srebrenica murdered over 1,300 Serbs and had "ethnically cleansed" a vast area.[15]

The *London Spectator* reported that during 1992-1995 the

---

13 13."Minorities Leaving Yugoslav Province Dominated by Albanians," Associated Press, October 17, 1981.

14 Michael Evans, "Muslim soldiers 'failed to defend town from Serbs,'" *Times* London, July 14, 1995.

15 Jan Willem Honig and Norbert Both, *Srebrenica: Record of a War Crime*, (Penguin Books, 1997), p. 79.

Pentagon helped Islamists from Central Asia to reach Bosnia and join the Bosnian Muslims, stating:

> As part of the Dutch government's inquiry into the Srebrenica massacre of July 1995, Professor Cees Wiebes of Amsterdam University compiled a report entitled "Intelligence and the War in Bosnia", published in April 2002. In it he details the secret alliance between the Pentagon and radical Islamic groups from the Middle East, and their efforts to assist Bosnia's Muslims. By 1993, there was a vast amount of weapons-smuggling through Croatia to the Muslims, organised by 'clandestine agencies' of the USA, Turkey and Iran, in association with a range of Islamic groups that included Afghan Mujahideen and the pro-Iranian Hezbollah. Arms bought by Iran and Turkey with the financial backing of Saudi Arabia were airlifted from the Middle East to Bosnia – airlifts with which, Wiebes points out, the USA was "very closely involved."[16]

One of the stated war aims of NATO was that the Yugoslav Federation would become a "free market" economy. The fight for a "free market" economy was not an aim that seems to have been widely publicized by the spokesmen for the U.S. State Department and British Foreign Office at the time. The prize was the Trepca mining complex, which had operated 24 hours a day, having the richest lead, lignite and zinc deposits in Europe, and one of the richest world-wide. Once the moral pontifications of the Rambouillet *diktat* were dispensed with, chapter four makes the aim clear enough: Article I (1): "The economy of Kosovo shall function in accordance with free market principles."[17] A Privatization agency of Kosovo was established, but the economy, including Trepca, remains in a shambles.

16　Brendan O'Neill, "How We Trained al-Qa'eda," *Spectator*, London, September 13, 2003.

17　Rambouillet Agreement: Interim Agreement for Peace and Self-Government in Kosovo.

Russia, Libya, Syria...

Islamists have likewise proven useful within the Russian Federation. The primary pro-Chechnya lobby in the USA was the Freedom House-founded American Committee for Peace in Chechnya. This included some of the most notable neocons and Zionists: Richard Perle; Elliott Abrams; former U.S. Ambassador to the U.N., Kenneth Adelman; Midge Decter of the Heritage Foundation; Frank Gaffney of the Center for Security Policy; Bruce Jackson of the U.S. Committee on NATO; Michael Ledeen of the American Enterprise Institute, and former CIA director R. James Woolsey.[18] It is strange that of these enthusiasts for the rights of Muslims in Russia, all but Abrams and Ledeen were members of the arch-Zionist Project for a New American Century, founded in 1997. A sub-branch was the Study Group on a New Israeli Strategy Toward 2000 headed by Perle, which prepared a blueprint for the reorganization of the Middle East, that calls in particular for "regime change" in Syria and Iran, This seems to be the plan that is be is being followed.[19] While the ACPC changed its name to American Committee for Peace in the Caucasus, it seems to have become largely defunct since 2013. That is the year of the Chechan bombing in Boston. Wayne Madsen, writing for the Strategic Culture Foundation, commented:

> After revelations that an entity called the Caucasus Fund was used by the CIA-linked Jamestown Foundation of Washington, DC to sponsor seminars on the North Caucasus in Tbilisi from January to July 2012, Georgian authorities moved to shut down the fund. The reason given by Georgia was that the organization had "fulfilled its stated mission". Caucasus Fund and Jamestown Foundation events were attended by accused Boston Marathon bomber Tamerlan Tsarnaev, a citizen of Kyrgyzstan born to parents

---

18   "American Committee for Peace in Chechnya," Right Web, http://rightweb. irc-online.org/profile/American_Committee_for_Peace_in_Chechnya

19   Study Group on a New Israeli Strategy Toward 2000, *A Clean Break: A New Strategy for Securing the Realm*, 1996.

from Dagestan. Jamestown had previously held a seminar in Tbilisi on "Hidden Nations" in the Caucasus, which, among other issues, promoted a "Greater Circassia" in the Caucasus.[20]

Madsen remarks of the general strategy:

> U.S. "humanitarian" and "civil society" assistance to radical Islamist groups has, for the past three decades, filtered into the coffers of terrorist groups celebrated as "freedom fighters" in Washington. This was the case with U.S. support for the Afghan Mujahedin through such groups as the Committee for a Free Afghanistan during the Islamist insurgency against the People's Democratic Republic of Afghanistan in the 1980s and the Bosnia Defense Fund in the 1990s. In the case of Afghanistan, U.S. and Saudi money ended up in the hands of insurgents who would later form "Al Qaeda" and in Bosnia U.S. funds were used by Al Qaeda elements fighting against Yugoslavia and the Bosnian Serb Republic and, later, Al Qaeda elements supporting the Kosovo Liberation Army (KLA) in its war against Serbia.[21]

Terrorists supported by the USA to oust Qaddafi were then sent to Syria to continue the American Jihad against stable states. The CIA had been funding a Libyan rebel army since 1988, Khalifa Haftar's Libyan National Army. Haftar had been living for twenty years in Virginia, prior to returning to Libya with CIA and Saudi backing. Patrick Cockburn commented in *The Independent*:

> Even shadier is the background of Abdul Hakeen

---

20   Wayne Madsen, "Washington's 'Civil Society': CIA Financing of Chechen and Caucasus Regional Terrorists," Global Research, May 6, 2013, http://www.globalresearch.ca/washingtons-civil-society-and-cia-financing-of-chechen-and-other-caucasus-regional-terrorists/5333359

21   Wayne Madsen, ibid.

al-Hassadi, a Libyan who fought against the US in Afghanistan, was arrested in Pakistan, imprisoned probably at Bagram, Afghanistan, and then mysteriously released. The US Deputy Secretary of State, James Steinberg, told Congressmen he would speak of Mr Hassadi's career only in a closed session.[22]

MOSSAD DESTABLIZATION

Israel has sought to keep the entire region in a state of destabilization. This serves several factors. A constant state of conflict portrays Israel as the only stable entity in a volatile region. Destabilization ensures that there can be no united front against Israeli's aspirations, which are never-ending. The notion of Jews being surrounded by mad Arabs keeps the Israelis in a state of preparedness and unity. Israel went to the extent of backing the Red Brigades in Italy during the 1970s as part of a destabilization strategy, indicating the extent of the strategy. According to Magistrate Ferdinando Imposimato, who led the investigations into the 1978 kidnapping and murder of former Prime Minister Aldo Moro, "'at least until 1978 Israeli secret services had infiltrated Italian subversive groups. He said that based on confessions of jailed guerrillas who turned police informers there had been an Israeli plan to destabilize Italy. The plan aimed at reducing Italy to a country convulsed by civil war so that the United States would be forced to count more on Israel for the security of the Mediterranean,' the judge said."[23]

The extent of this destabilization strategy has included Mossad backing of Islamists at an early stage. According to a UPI news report on a 2002 Hamas bombing of a Jerusalem city bus, Israeli Prime Minister Ariel Sharon immediately vowed to

---

22 Patrick Cockburn, "The Shady Men Backed by the West to Replace Gaddafi," *The Independent*, April 3, 2011, http://www.independent.co.uk/voices/commentators/patrick-cockburn-the-shady-men-backed-by the-west-to-displace-gaddafi-2260826.html

23 "Arrest Wrecked Brigades' Plan for Massacre," *The Evening Post*, Wellington, New Zealand, January 18, 1982, p. 1.

fight "Palestinian terror" and summoned his cabinet to decide on a military response to the organization that Sharon had once described as "the deadliest terrorist group that we have ever had to face." Active in Gaza and the West Bank, Hamas wants to liberate all of Palestine and establish a radical Islamic state in place of Israel. It has gained notoriety with its assassinations, car bombs and other acts of terrorism. But Sharon left something out.

Israel and Hamas may currently be locked in deadly combat, but, according to several current and former U.S. intelligence officials, beginning in the late 1970s, Tel Aviv gave direct and indirect financial aid to Hamas over a period of years. Israel "aided Hamas directly – the Israelis wanted to use it as a counterbalance to the PLO (Palestinian Liberation Organization)," said Tony Cordesman, Middle East analyst for the Center for Strategic [and International] Studies [CSIS]. Israel's support for Hamas "was a direct attempt to divide and dilute support for a strong, secular PLO by using a competing religious alternative," said a former senior CIA official. ... According to U.S. administration officials, funds for the movement came from the oil-producing states and directly and indirectly from Israel. The PLO was secular and leftist and promoted Palestinian nationalism. Hamas wanted to set up a transnational state under the rule of Islam, much like Khomeini's Iran.[24]

Even when the support for Hamas seemed to be backfiring there were those who continued to see a dialectical advantage: But even then, some in Israel saw some benefits to be had in trying to continue to give Hamas support: "The thinking on the part of some of the right-wing Israeli establishment was that Hamas and the others, if they gained control, would refuse to have any part of the peace process and would torpedo any agreements put in place," said a U.S. government official who asked not to be named. "Israel would still be the only democracy in the region

24   Richard Sale, "Hamas History Tide to Israel," UPI, June 18, 2002; Information Clearing House, http://www.informationclearinghouse.info/article10456.htm

for the United States to deal with," he said. All of which disgusts some former U.S. intelligence officials.[25]

The strategy was confirmed by Mossad defector Victor Ostrovsky, who was told by a prominent Mossad officer that a decision was made to "destabilize Jordan to the point of civil anarchy." The officer explained to Ostrovsky that this would be done by circulating counterfeit money and "arming religious fundamentalist elements, similar to Hamas and the Muslim Brotherhood," assassinating leading figures who are symbols of stability, causing riots in the university to prompt government repression. The plan was also to destabilize Egypt in the same manner, with Mossad running guns to "Egyptian fundamentalists" through Afghanistan.[26]

Ostrovsky further relates that "Mossad had to come up with a new threat to the region, a threat of such magnitude that it would justify whatever action the Mossad might see fit to take." The attitude of many in Mossad and elsewhere in Israeli ruling circles is that in order to maintain "fortress Israel" the "constant threat of war" needs to be maintained.[27]

Supporting the radical elements of Muslim fundamentalism sat well with the Mossad's general plan for the region. An Arab world run by fundamentalists would not be a party to any negotiations in the West, thus leaving Israel once again as the only democratic, rational country in the region. And if the Mossad could arrange for the Hamas to take over the Palestinian streets from the PLO, then the picture would be complete.[28]

This destabilization dialectic is the same as that being enacted on a global scale by the USA to maintain its global ambitions. Since

25   Richard Sale, ibid.

26   Victor Ostrovsky, *The Other Side of Deception* (New York: Harper, 1995), p. 182.

27   Victor Ostrovsky, ibid., p. 251.

28   Victor Ostrovsky, ibid., p. 252.

the Soviet bogeyman no longer exists as justification for U.S. global ambitions, the bogeyman of the "global war on Islamic terrorism" was quickly created as a substitute. While Putin has been demonized to at least keep the semblance of a Russian bogeyman intact, it cannot convincingly be said that Putin aims at "world conquest." However, "Islamism" is a new threat to *world* peace, with a *world* Jihad and the aim of imposing Sharia law over the *world*. This new global threat must be met under U.S. leadership, which generally means U.S. domination, politically, economically and even morally and culturally, or what has been described as the "new *world* order." The Study Group for a New Israeli Strategy stated that Israel's aims must be to:

> Work closely with Turkey and Jordan to contain, destabilize, and roll-back some of its most dangerous threats. This implies clean break from the slogan, "comprehensive peace" to a traditional concept of strategy based on balance of power. Change the nature of its relations with the Palestinians, including upholding the *right of hot pursuit* for self defense into all Palestinian areas and nurturing alternatives to Arafat's exclusive grip on Palestinian society.[29]

Both aims have been fulfilled. As we have seen the backing of Jiahists involves the use of Jordan and Turkey, and the primary target is Syria, now that Saddam has been eliminated from Iraq. While the blueprint was addressed to Israel, one can see the role being played out by the USA in its fulfilment:

> Israel can shape its strategic environment, in cooperation with Turkey and Jordan, by weakening, containing, and even rolling back Syria. This effort can focus on removing Saddam Hussein from power in Iraq — an important Israeli strategic objective in its own right — as a means of foiling Syria's regional ambitions.[30]

---

29   Study Group for a New Israeli Strategy, *A Clean Break*, op. cit.

30   Study Group, ibid.

The Islamic State of Iraq and the Levant (a.k.a The Caliphate)

Suddenly ISIL (or ISIS, the Islamic State of Iraq and Syria) snaps onto the scene to pose the biggest threat to world peace, whose path of terror also happens to be a march through the states that have been marked for destruction by the Zio-neocons; Syria particularly. Like Hafta in Libya, and later Syria, the head of the Islamic State organization, Abu Bakr al-Baghdadi, had links with the USA. He was a "civilian internee" at an U.S. internment center in Umm Qasr, Iraq. He was "unconditionally released" in 2009.

What can be said is that Abu Bakr al-Baghdadi's declaration of himself as Caliph of all Muslims world-wide has spread further factionalism among Muslims. Despite the universal repudiation among even radical Muslims, U.S. foreign policy strategists are building up ISIL as the most potent Islamic force. Assem Barqawi, the spokesperson for the al-Qaeda-affiliated al-Nusra Front – an erstwhile ally of ISIL in the Syrian war – spurned al-Baghdadi's claim to a universal Caliphate, countering: "In short, al-Baghdadi and ISIL have no support whatsoever among Muslims. They are loathed even by their fellow ultra-Salafis, Wahhabis and Takfiris." On the other hand terrorism expert William McCants of the Brookings Institution, said to the *New York Times*: "ISIS is now officially the biggest and baddest global jihadi group on the planet... Nothing says 'hard-core' like being cast out by Al Qaeda." Dr. Kevin Barrett, an Arabist scholar, regards it likely that al-Baghdadi is a mind-control asset from his time at Umm Qasr camp:

> The secrecy surrounding al-Baghdadi's five years in US custody strongly suggests that the self-proclaimed "caliph of Islam" is actually a Muslim version of Jim Jones. His "Islamic State" is a Muslim Jonestown. It is designed to mass-suicide Islam by turning Muslims against each other.[31]

---

31 Kevin Barrett, "Who is Abu Bakr al-Baghdadi?", PressTV, http://www.presstv.ir/detail/2014/07/14/371210/who-is-abu-bakr-albaghdadi/

William Engdahl, a foreign policy specialist, opines:

> Key members of ISIS it now emerges were trained by US
> CIA and Special Forces command at a secret camp in
> Jordan in 2012, according to informed Jordanian officials.
> The US, Turkish and Jordanian intelligence were running a
> training base for the Syrian rebels in the Jordanian town of
> Safawi in the country's northern desert region, conveniently
> near the borders to both Syria and Iraq. Saudi Arabia and
> Qatar, the two Gulf monarchies most involved in funding
> the war against Syria's Assad, financed the Jordan ISIS
> training. Advertised publicly as training of "non-extremist"
> Muslim jihadists to wage war against the Syrian Bashar
> Assad regime, the secret US training camps in Jordan and
> elsewhere have trained perhaps several thousand Muslim
> fighters in techniques of irregular warfare, sabotage and
> general terror. The claims by Washington that they took
> special care not to train 'Salafist' or jihadist extremists, is a
> joke. How do you test if a recruit is not a jihadist? Is there a
> special jihad DNA that the CIA doctors have discovered?[32]

In 2012, Aaron Klein reported that Egyptian officials had talked
of training being given to terrorist forces to be deployed to Syria
by the USA, Turkey, Jordan and Saudi Arabia. The training
camp was at the Jordanian town of Safawi.[33]

Among the tangled intricacies of the Middle East imbroglio a
course was established to bring chaos to the region, formulated
by think tanks where American and Jewish messianists converge.
Their recommendations appear as the ones being enacted, but
these strategists themselves are the heirs to aims of long duration
and a politicized religious fanaticism that is obscured by a
worldwide barrage of propaganda about a new Muslim threat.

---

32   "ISIS in Iraq: A CIA-NATO Dirty war Op?", June 26, 2014, http://www.
      infowars.com/isis-in-iraq-a-cia-nato-dirty-war-op/

33   Aaron Klein, "Mideast War in March?", February 24, 2012, WND, http://
      www.wnd.com/2012/02/mideast-war-in-march/

The ISIS Strategy

What I wrote in October 2014 in regard to the Islamic State organisation was shortly later confirmed by President Obama.[1] His "new" strategy for confronting The Islamic State calls first for the removal of Assad in Syria, in order to allow the "moderate" Muslim militias to assume power. Here we get to the crux of the matter: ISIS was formed as part of a dialectical strategy of "controlled opposition" to create instability in hitherto stable and prosperous states where the U.S.-contrived "Arab Spring" could not work.

CNN breaking the news reports that:

> President Obama has asked his national security team for another review of the U.S. policy toward Syria after realizing that ISIS may not be defeated without a political transition in Syria and the removal of President Bashar al Assad, senior US officials and diplomats tell CNN.

> The review is a tacit admission that the initial strategy of trying to confront ISIS first in Iraq and then take them on in Syria, without also focusing on the removal of Assad, was a miscalculation.

> In just the past week, the White House has convened four meetings of the president's national security team, one of which was chaired by President Obama and others which were attended by principals like the Secretary of State. These meetings, in the words of one senior official, were "driven to a large degree how our Syria strategy fits into our ISIS strategy.

---

1   "America's Jihad," *Foreign Policy Journal*, October 17, 2014.

Related: Obama's "no strategy" comment sparks uproar

"The President has asked us to look again at how this fits together," one senior official said. "The long running Syria problem is now compounded by the reality that to genuinely defeat ISIL, we need not only a defeat in Iraq but a defeat in Syria." The U.S. government refers to ISIS as ISIL.[2]

U.S. presidents, including Obama, do not have brainwaves of strategy. He had received advice on this, and there is no "tacit admission of miscalculation." Indeed Secretary of Defense Chuck Hagel had previously drafted a "highly private" memo to National Security Adviser Susan Rice calling on the USA to strike at Assad first.[3]

Syria, Iraq and Iran were marked for destruction by Zionist, "necon" strategists decades ago. No, there was no 'miscalculation.' The strategy was indeed very calculated and of long duration. Like dialectical strategies in general, they must have much time to work through a process. The aim here was to create chaos to justify further U.S. actions against states that are regarded as the primary obstacles to U.S. and /or Israel aims. Like the destruction of Saddam Hussein, Assad happens to be one of the few popular leaders in the region capable and willing to confront "Islamic terrorism." However, it is not the type of "Islamic terrorism" that American and Zionist hegemonists want eliminating. They are the catspaws of American and Israeli strategies. Like the KLA in Kosovo and the "moderate" Muslim terrorist militias that the USA used to oust and murder Qadaffi in Libya, ISL and their "moderate" counterparts in Syria are part of the same strategy to destroy the Assad regime.

---

2   Elise Labbot, "Sources, Obama seeks new Syria strategy review to deal with ISIS, Assad," November 12, 2014, http://edition.cnn.com/2014/11/12/politics/obama-syria-strategy-review/index.html?hpt=hp_t1

3   Barbara Starr, "Hagel wrote memo to White House criticizing Syria strategy," October 31, 2014, http://edition.cnn.com/2014/10/30/politics/hagel-starr-syria-memo-white-house/

As the State Department now explains, the actions against ISL in Iraq were aimed to allow the USA time to train "moderate" Islamic terrorists to fight both ISL and Assad in Syria:

> In October the U.S. stressed an "Iraq first" strategy with efforts to degrade ISIS in Iraq as the priority and operations in Syria done to shape conditions in Iraq. Washington hoped that would give time for the US to vet, train and arm a moderate Syrian rebels fighting force to combat ISIS, and ultimately the regime of President Bashar al-Assad.[4]

It was part of a package deal: one destroys the dreaded ISIS/ISL while simultaneously destroying the real target of the USA and Israel: Assad's Syria. ISIS/ISL serves as a mere ploy to get to the real target. "The administration has asked Congress for $500 million to train and equip 5,000 vetted rebels within one year."[5]

There is nothing really sudden about the Obama "change in strategy." It has been mooted not only secretly by Hagel, but also in public by Senators John McCain and Lindsay Graham, in The Wall Street Journal:

> How can we arm and train 5,000 Syrians and expect them to succeed against Islamic State without protecting them (and their families) from Assad's airstrikes and barrel bombs? Or expect moderate groups in Syria fighting Islamic State to take advantage of U.S. airstrikes if we do not coordinate or communicate our operations with them? [...]Our efforts to build up a viable Free Syrian Army to liberate Syria from the evils of Islamic State and Mr. Assad will surely fail if the Syrian ruler is not dealt with.[6]

---

4   Elise Labbot, op. cit.

5   Elise Labbot, ibid.

6   John McCain and Lindsay Graham, "To defeat Islamic State remove Assad," October 6, 2014, http://online.wsj.com/articles/john-mccain-and-lindsey-graham-to-defeat-islamic-state-remove-assad-1412636762

McCain stated that the ouster of Assad requires "the U.S. to militarily degrade the Assad regime, upgrade the moderate opposition, change the momentum of the conflict and create conditions for a political solution." McCain states that targeting ISIS with airstrikes provides the USA with the opportunity to also target Syria with air strikes:

> At a minimum, this means a larger role for U.S. military advisers and forward air controllers. It also means declaring safe zones in Syria and telling Mr. Assad that if his forces and aircraft operate there, they will be targeted like Islamic State. Key regional partners realize that we must confront Mr. Assad as well as Islamic State, and they are willing to join America in doing so.[7]

It is a strategy that has been played out before. Dialectically, the power elite creates or sponsors the most extreme of options, which allows it to present a more "moderate" alternative, thereby shifting the center of political gravity.

---

7   McCain, ibid.

U.S. Recognition of Jerusalem as Israel's Capital.

Donald Trump was elected on the wave of a populist backlash. Like his predecessor, Obama, he promised to roll back the USA's global intervention which does, after all, have more in common with Wilsonian Democratic internationalism than traditional Republican, - Robert Taft – "America First" non-intervention. Indeed, Trump's slogan of "America First" got the oligarchic and liberal cabals very nervous, recalling the non-interventionist movement in the USA prior to the Pearl Harbor. Like Obama's promises, Trump's were short-lived. Trump's supposedly "America First" victory was quickly discarded, as the USA retained its position as the standard-bearer of a messianic mission to impose a global "American millennia," and overtly "Amercian millennialists" replaced the first rung of Trump appointees in quick succession.

With Jared Kushner, an arch-Zionist, not only as the President's son-in-law but as a nepotistic-type key adviser, "America First" was not going to be an easy choice, especially when Zionists and pro-Zionist so-called "neocons" have bamboozled many into thinking that the destinies of the USA and Israel are synonymous, and the two are joined at the hip.

Hence, the Israel First lobbies attained a long-held and primary Zionist dream, to have the USA recognize Jerusalem as the capital of Israel. The reaction from Palestinians was of course, predictable, and this is not intended as a critical implication. Why should they, and indeed all Muslims, not be outraged? What should also be asked is, why are Christians also not outraged? The latter can be answered by the generations-old undermining of traditional Christian theology in the conjoining of two normally antithetical words "Judaeo" and "Christian."

There is no "Judaeo-Christian heritage." Even the practises under which Jesus was raised in Galilee were anathema to Judaic orthodoxy. One might discern the seedbed of Christianity and the teachings of Jesus within "Galilee of the Gentiles" and why his teachings were regarded with outrage by the Pharisaic priesthood. One can also discern why there has been such a hatred of Christianity and Jesus in the rabbinical teachings of the *Talmud*[1] and elsewhere. The phenomenon of such an oddity as "Christian-Zionism" is for Zionists and the Orthodox rabbinate (which should not be confounded with Reform Judaism) nothing more than the equivalent of a "shabbez goy," a Gentile hired by Orthodox Jews to undertake menial tasks on the Sabbath. "Judaeo-Christianity" only exists in the minds of craven Gentiles who embrace delusional creeds, or who wish to further their careers by making the correct noises to the right people.

Evelyn Kaye, who wrote of her experiences being raised an Orthodox Jewess, stated of attitudes towards Christians: "We learned nothing of the spread of Christianity, or its development. We heard nothing of Christian suffering in defense of faith. We were kept in ignorance of the times when Christians and Jews and Muslims managed to live peaceably together. I absorbed the idea that as soon as Jesus had arrived and started Christianity, Jews were persecuted for ever after."[2] In common parlance, those who adhere to "Judaeo-Christianity" and "Christian-Zionism" are suckers. There is no such notion among Jews or Zionists. The mere notion is anathema.

Jesus was a Galilean. At the time Galilee encompassed much of Palestine as one of three regions, the others being Judea and Samaria. Jesus spent most of his life in Galilee, and much of his ministry was there. When Israel was conquered by the Assyrians in 733 BC, the Israelites were exiled, and replaced by others, as

---

1   A multi-volume rabbinic commentary on the *Torah* (the first five books of the Old Testament) that forms the basis of Orthodox law and life.

2   Evelyn Kaye, *The Hole in the Sheet: A Modern Woman Looks at Orthodox and Hasidic Judaism* (New Jersey: Lyle Stuart Inc., 1987), 79.

was the Assyrian practise of conquest. When the Hasmoneans[3] conquered Galilee the non-Isrealitish Galileans were forced to convert to Judaism. Thus, in Jesus' time most Galilean "Jews" could only trace the Judaism of their forefathers back a century. A "Galilean" was defined by the rest of Israel as an "outsider." Whatever the ethnicity, the theologian Frederick Bruner, writes:

> Galilee was not just geographically far from Jerusalem; it was considered spiritually and politically far, too. Galilee was the most pagan of the Jewish provinces, located as it was at the northernmost tier of Palestine. This distance from Zion was not only geographic; Galileans were considered by Judaeans to sit rather loosely to the law and to be less biblically pure than those in or near Jerusalem.[4]

Another reputable reference states:

> The population of Galilee was composed of strangely mingled elements-Aramaean, Iturean, Phoenician and Greek. In the circumstances, they could not be expected to prove such sticklers for high orthodoxy as the Judeans. Their mixed origin explains the differences in speech which distinguished them from their brethren in the South, who regarded Galilee and the Galileans with a certain proud contempt.[5]

Whatever else one might say, such a background seems to explain the deadly animosity that existed between Jesus and the Pharisees, the priestly class from which today's Orthodox rabbinate claims descent. It explains why Jesus's teachings were regarded as blasphemy by the Pharisees, and why the

---

3 The ruling dynasty of Judea.

4 Frederick D. Bruner, *Matthew: A Commentary - Volume 2: The Churchbook, Matthew 13-28* (William B. Eerdmans Publishing Company, 2007), 102.

5 *International Standard Bible Encyclopaedia*, 5: Character of the Galileans, Wm. B. Eerdmans Publishing Co., 1939), online: http://www. internationalstandardbible.com/G/galilee.html

early Christians did not practise the strictures of the dietary and other such codes of the Torah for example. In short, there is no "Judaeo-Christian heritage."

This subversive "Judaeo-Christian" theology was victorious over the Catholic Church, under the influence of Jules Isaac, when Vatican II annulled the traditional Catholic doctrines towards Judaism and its traditional prayers for the conversion of the Jews to Christianity.[6] Within Protestantism, the notion of "Judaeo-Christianity" was always there, despite Martin Luther's polemic, the unsubtly titled *On the Jews and Their Lies*. The USA was founded by Puritans, Free-Masons and Deists.[7] Puritanism identified with Old Israel. It did so in Cromwell's England and in the American colonies. The focus was on the Old Testament as it is among Protestant sects today that are most avid in their support of Israel. Oliver Cromwell was regarded in messianic terms by Jewry. He and his Puritan regicides were establishing an "English Zion":

> The first half of the seventeenth century saw a modest change in English attitudes towards Jews thanks to the Puritans' high regard for the Hebrew scriptures and their contempt for Hellenism and paganism. There was a fashion for biblical Hebrew names. Paul, Peter, Anne and Mary were out; Habakkuk, Amos, Enoch, Rebecca and Sarah were in. A Hebrew dictionary (the most complete to date) was produced by the parliamentarian Edward Leigh. The poet and pamphleteer John Milton recommended the teaching of Hebrew in English grammar schools. And in 1653, a radical overhaul of English law was proposed, including the institution of Mosaic Law, with England modelled on biblical Israel. Although nothing ever came of the idea, there was still a drive to create a godly society

---

6   Joseph Roddy, "How the Jews Changed Catholic Thinking," *Look*, Vol. 30, No. 2, January 25, 1966.

7   Nicholas Hagger, *The Secret Founding of America* (London: Watkins Publishing, 2007).

– an English Zion – where pagan holidays and festivities (Christmas, maypole dancing etc.) were abolished.[8]

Dr. Richard Falk, a professor of sociology at Buffalo University, and author of books on Jewish issues, gives a Jewish view on the founding of the American colonies by Puritans on Judaic principles:

> In New England these Pilgrims, as they called themselves, founded the Massachusetts Bay Colony, which they organized according to their understanding of the Five Books of Moses and other Jewish themes. They believed that they were the Children of Israel and therefore sought to live by the commandments of God as found in the Torah. Like the Jews, the Puritans enrolled all their children in school so that they could read the word of God, i.e. the Bible...

> In the end, the King James Bible was printed and distributed in 1611. There are apparently numerous errors in that translation. Yet, it was this Bible which gave Englishmen access to Jewish history and led the Puritans to establish Israel in the New World. They called Massachusetts "the new Zion" and made every effort to follow the commands of the Torah as they understood them. The Pilgrims also used the Hebrew language when naming towns and villages, such as Medina, meaning community, or Salem, meaning peace. The Puritans also used Hebrew names, including Jacob, Israel, Moses, Joshua, etc.

> In 1641 the Puritans adopted a legal code in Massachusetts and in 1650 in Connecticut. These codes were directly taken from the Torah, including Sabbath observance. Puritans believed, like ancient Israel, that they were ruled

---

8   Richard Mather, "'Our English Zion: Oliver Cromwell and the Jews," https://richardmatherblog.wordpress.com/2017/09/18/our-english-zion-oliver-cromwell-and-the-jews/

directly by God and therefore abolished all hierarchies in religion.[9]

Interestingly Dr. Falk regards the "Evangelical Christians" as more avidly pro-Israel than American Jews, and refers to "fifty five million are Christian Zionists." (This might partly explain President Trump's zeal for Israel). Falk continues:

> The Puritan tradition in the United States is by no means dead or abandoned. It lives on in the Evangelical (Ev= good and angel= messenger, hence Evangelic means good message) movement in American Christianity. Today about 55 million American Christians follow the teachings of Jean Calvin (1509-1564) and John Knox (1514-1572) and practice an altered form of Calvinism on which the evangelical tradition rests.

> For that reason these fifty five million are Christian Zionists and, unlike the Jewish community, favor the survival of Israel. The fact is that the most vociferous supporters of Israel in the United States are evangelical Christians and a minority of Jews.[10]

Prior to World War II some in the British ruling classes were heirs to this messianic legacy that identified Britain with Israel. Lord Balfour had been imbued with the Old Testament since his childhood, and he regarded Christianity as owing Jewry a debt of gratitude for its supposed origins.[11] With the destruction of the British Empire by two world wars, neither of which served the British Empire, and shortly caused its collapse under a mountain of debt to the US bankers, and an active program of de-colonialization run by the USA, while attention was turned on

---

9   Gerhardt Falk, "The Puritan States of America," Jewish Buffalo on the Web, http://jbuff.com/c070711.htm

10 Ibid.

11 Douglas Reed citing Balfour's niece, Mrs Dugdale, in *The Controversy of Zion* (Durban: Dolphin press, 1978), 228.

the Soviet world-bogeyman, the USA assumed the role of chief global hegemon in ways unimagined by British imperialism or any other type of old-style European colonialism.[12]

With Britain lumbered with a mandate over Palestine after World War I, its position was that of a caretaker, facing the atrocities of Palmach, Irgun, Stern, and Haganah, as the authorities attempted to control the flood of Jewish refugees from Europe, who were encouraged by the Zionist agencies to settle in Palestine. The USA assumed the messianic role from hapless Britain, and was instrumental in having Israel recognised as a Jewish state in 1948. This was at a time when the Irgun, which became the political party, Likud, as a major political factor in Israel, had as it emblem a raised gun superimposed on a map of a Greater Israel that was depicted as the entirety of Palestine combined into a single Jewish state, with the entirety of the land of Jordan.[13] Ever since, gone is any mention of the (on hindsight) relatively laudable aim of the Balfour Declaration in giving British support for the creation of a Jewish homeland within Palestine, so long as the lives of the Palestinians are not encroached on.[14] It now seems like a sick joke to reflect that this was the supposed intent, for which American lives were sacrificed in World War I. [15]

---

12 F. A. Guimarães, "The United State and Decolonisation of Angola," Lisbon, October 2003, http://www.ipri.pt/artigos/artigo.php?ida=5
Africa-America Institute, http://www.aaionline.org/about-aai/history/1950s/

13 See for example: http://paldocs.net/

14 "The Balfour Declaration," Israel Ministry of Foreign Affairs, http://www.mfa.gov.il/mfa/foreignpolicy/peace/guide/pages/the%20balfour%20declaration.aspx

15 The Balfour Declaration, a letter written by Lord Belfour to Lord Rothschild, was the product of an agreement between the British War Cabinet and the World Zionist Organization, whereby in exchange for British support for a Jewish homeland, Jews would mobilize their influence in the USA to bring America into the war against Germany. The Zionist lobbies had no compunction about sacrificing American lives for their cause, in such vast numbers. The background of the agreement between the British War Cabinet and Zionist organization is disclosed by the Zionist official Samuel Landman in *Great Britain, The Jews and Palestine* (1936). This can be read online: http://folk.ntnu.no/tronda/kk-f/2005/0036.html

Here with Greater Israel we have the basis for understanding what is happening the Middle East, and why Israel can never, in the character of the Zionist ideology and the manner by which Jewish messianism is interpreted, be a harbinger of peace. Moreover, the Greater Israel depicted as the emblem of the Irgun as the entirety of "Trans-Jordan," is a very moderate interpretation of ultimate Zionist ambitions. It is the entirety of the region from the Nile to the Euphrates Rivers, the so-called "Deed of Covenant" said to have been promised by YHWH to Abram that is the real goal of Zionism.[16] Because it is said to be a promise by their God, it is an aim which Zionism can never renounce, and any apparent moves towards "peace settlements" initiated or agreed to by Israel cannot be anything other than deception. Christian-Zionists must undertake theological gymnastics to justify the continuation of a discarded covenant which often seems more important to them than that of the new, at least when it comes to Zionist apologetics.

ZIONIST AND NEOCON PRESSURE

If the Tump Administration accepts Jerusalem as the capital of Israel on the basis of the Jewish religion, and there can be no other justification, *ipso facto* the principle of Greater Israel from the Nile to the Euphrates, must be accepted using the same rationale. Is this the *raison d'etre* for efforts by Trump and prior Administrations in trying to keep the region in a constant state of turmoil, and to finally try to devastate Syria, regarded by Israel as its *primary* enemy? That course was overtly recommended in a document prepared in Jerusalem by prominent U.S. policy-makers associated with The Institute for Advanced Strategic and Political Studies, Study Group on a New Israeli Strategy Toward 2000, entitled *A Clean Break: A New Strategy for Securing the Realm*. This was stated to be a blueprint from which to evolve policy.[17] The formulators were "prominent opinion makers, including Richard Perle, James Colbert, Charles Fairbanks,

---

16 *Genesis* 15: 18-21.

17 *A Clean Break: A New Strategy for Securing the Realm*, http://zfacts.com/metaPage/lib/1996_07_IASPS_Clean_Break.pdf

Jr., Douglas Feith, Robert Loewenberg, David Wurmser, and Meyrav Wurmser."[18]

It should still be asked why prominent U.S. policy-makers were in Jerusalem formulating policies for Israel, as part of a self-described "Study Group on a New Israeli Strategy"? The document identifies Syria and Iran as Israel's primary enemies, stating of Syria "Given the nature of the regime in Damascus, it is both natural and moral that Israel abandon the slogan 'comprehensive peace' and move to contain Syria, drawing attention to its weapons of mass destruction program, and rejecting 'land for peace' deals on the Golan Heights."[19] The document refers to the elimination of Saddam in Iraq as being an important objective, in conjunction with elimination of Syria: "Israel can shape its strategic environment, in cooperation with Turkey and Jordan, by weakening, containing, and even rolling back Syria. This effort can focus on removing Saddam Hussein from power in Iraq — an important Israeli strategic objective in its own right — as a means of foiling Syria's regional ambitions."[20] One strategy is to back rival factions to create destabilization, "supporting the Hashemites in their efforts to redefine Iraq,"[21] and "securing tribal alliances with Arab tribes that cross into Syrian territory and are hostile to the Syrian ruling elite." This includes support for the Shia, who are linked with the Hashemites.[22] These are strategies have been followed to the present day.

In 2016, right after Trump's election, Robbie Martin, editor of *Geopolitics Alert* was pointing out that many "neocons" of the "craziest" type from the Bush era, were jumping aboard the Trump bandwagon. He pointed out that most had favoured

---

18   Ibid, 1.
19   Ibid, 3.
20   Ibid.
21   Ibid.
22   Ibid, 4.

Hilary Clinton's "hawkish" foreign policy which it should be kept in mind included a heavy dose of Russophobia, when Trump was presenting himself as conciliatory towards Russia. The liberal-left "snowflakes" who shed copious tears over the defeat of Clinton, should consider how manic she was in her foreign policy, and would hardly have been more rational than Trump, whose election rhetoric about "America First" foreign policy was fearful to the "neocons." Martin wrote:

> While most Trump supporters had their attention turned to Clinton's brash hawkishness, they failed to notice that some of the craziest of the neoconservative Bush-era war hawks in Washington had split off from the pro-Clinton neocon consensus and favored Trump. Some examples of this include Michael Ledeen, Bill Bennett, Frank Gaffney, John Bolton, and James Woolsey, signatories to the Project for the New American Century, a think tank co-founded by Kagan during the Clinton administration. PNAC is widely known for developing the roadmap for George W. Bush's foreign policy agenda that led to the illegal Iraq War and the invasion of Afghanistan. A total of 17 PNAC signatories assumed official positions in the Bush administration.[23]

The above-named John Bolton, now Trump's new National Security Advisor, stated to NBC News of the Trump Administration's recognition of Jerusalem as the Israeli capital:

> It's a recognition of reality. If you're not prepared to recognize that Jerusalem is the capital of Israel and that's where the American Embassy should be, then you're operating on a completely different wavelength. I think recognizing reality always enhances the chances for peace.[24]

---

23 Robbie Martin , "Trump Promised to 'Drain the Swamp,' but he's Filling it with Bush Era Crazies Instead," MPN News, November 23, 2016; https://www.mintpressnews.com/trump-promised-drain-swamp-hes-filling-bush-era-crazies-instead/222482/

24 Luis Sanchez, "Bolton: Recognizing Jerusalem as Capital of Israel 'Enhances

What John Bolton's rationalization is for this is not known, and it seems likely there is none. There is no apparent sense to it; the mantra of a fanatic. He had stated:

"Whether to move America's embassy in Israel from Tel Aviv to Jerusalem has long been a subject of political debate in the U.S. and abroad. It's time now to resolve the debate by recognizing Jerusalem as Israel's capital city and relocating our embassy there on incontestably Israeli sovereign territory." In this instance he justified the move as one of "diplomatically efficiency."[25]

How seriously is that to be taken? It was a theological question based on a commitment to Jewish messianism; nothing more nor less, and the move followed shortly after the appointment of Bolton as National Security Adviser.

While Trump had alluded in his presidential campaign to moving the U.S. embassy to Jerusalem "as the eternal capital of the Jewish people," in October 2017 he was showing hesitation, stating in an interview that he wanted to secure peace before such a move: "I want to gve that a shot before I even think about moving the embassy to Jerusalem. If we can make peace between the Palestinians and Israel, I think it'll lead to ultimately peace in the Middle East, which has to happen." His attitude was clearly different from that of John Bolton at the time. A report states that four months previously, "In June, Trump signed a waiver on the Jerusalem Embassy Act of 1995, which mandates that the embassy be moved to Jerusalem by 1999. Past presidents have also waived the act out of concern

---

the chances for peace'," *The Hill*, May 13, 2018; http://thehill.com/ homenews/sunday-talk-shows/387477-bolton-recognizing-jerusalem-as-capital-of-israel

25   "Amb. John Bolton: America's Embassy in Israel Should be Moved to Jerusalem – NOW," Christians United for Israel," https://www.cufi.org/ amb-john-bolton-americas-embassy-israel-moved-jerusalem-now/

that it would derail peace talks."[26] Although the report quotes sources as being confident that Trump would move the embassy, his prior stated commitment to "peace" before any such move, would have made recognition of Jerusalem as the Israeli capital as elusive as ever. In May 2017 reports were stating that Trump's lack of enthusiasm was outraging Israelis:

> During his first trip to Israel as president, Donald Trump made no effort toward his campaign promise to move the American embassy from Tel Aviv to Jerusalem. That angered Israeli officials, who said that Trump had gone back on his promise. Michael Oren, a former Israeli ambassador to the U.S. who now serves as deputy minister for diplomacy in the Netanyahu government, told reporters in a May 23 conference call after Trump's visit that he was disappointed that Trump didn't talk about moving the embassy.[27]

It seems that the implementation of the Jerusalem Embassy Act of 1995[28] was not going to happen any time soon under Trump. Did the sudden promotion of John Bolton signal to World Zionism the imminence of a decision? Were the prime movers Trump's daughter Ivanka, and his son-in-law Jared Kushner? Who better placed to apply the decisive pressure? They were among the entourage at Jerusalem celebrating the opening of the U.S. Embassy while Palestinians were being shot by the Israeli army. Here they were blessed by Israel's "chief rabbi," Yitzhak Yosef, whom the BBC stated has compared Blacks to "monkeys," and said that non-Jews should leave Israel if they are unwilling to

26　Alison Colburn, "Trump signals step back from Israeli embassy plan," October 9, 2017; http://www.politifact.com/truth-o-meter/promises/trumpometer/promise/1377/move-us-embassy-tel-aviv-jerusalem/

27　Franco Ordonez, "Israelis angry at Trump's failure to move U.S. embassy to Jerusalem as promised," McClatchy DC Bureau, May 22, 21017; http://www.mcclatchydc.com/news/politics-government/white-house/article152026002.html

28　Senator Robert S. Dole (sponsor) Jerusalem Embassy Act of 1995, https://www.congress.gov/bill/104th-congress/senate-bill/1322/text

subject themselves to Jews. The rabbi's office commented that he was just referring to *Talmudic* edicts.[29] That is the reality of Israel and Zionism, albeit one little understood.[30] These views are the mainstream in Israel, and especially inform the actions of the "settler movement." These are the "religious lunatic fringe" that is not really "fringe," but a major influence, while Zionist apologists, including those of the Trump Administration, refer to the dangers of Islam to "world peace." This is the state that has long had a nuclear arsenal, capable of obliterating European capitals, while the USA feigns outrage at Iran or North Korea having nuclear potential. While there is talk of "mad mullahs" with atomic bombs, should the world be any more comfortable with "mad rabbis" having much greater arsenals. While there is much anguish over an alleged Islamic plot to dominate the world with "Sharia law," nothing is said of rabbis who believe they are ordained by God to determine that non-Jews are to be ruled according to the "Seven Noahide Laws" recognized by U.S. Congress since 1989 as the basis for "civilized society"?[31]

How Did Ivanka Become Jewish?

While any idiot with the right backing might become a president or prime minister how did real estate tycoon Jared Kushner qualify as senior White House adviser? He had no prior political experience. Kushner is an adherent of what is called "Modern Orthodox Judaism," which seeks dialogue with modern secular

---

29 Alina Polianskaya, "Ivanka Trump and Jared Kushner 'blessed' by top Israeli rabbi who compared black people to 'monkeys'," *The Independent*, https://www.independent.co.uk/news/world/middle-east/ivanka-trump-jared-kushner-israel-jewish-rabbi-yitzhak-yosef-racist-us-embassy-jerusalem-latest-a8350536.html

30 See the books of Jewish scholar Israel Shahak, *Jewish Hispory/Jewish Religion* (London: Pluto Press, 1994), *Jewish Fundamentalism in Israel* (London: Pluto Press, 1999). See also: Bolton, "Grave Desecrations, Rabbi's Death Show Rare Glimpses of Israel's Religious Fanaticism," *Foreign Policy Journal*, October 17, 2013; https://www.foreignpolicyjournal.com/2013/10/17/grave-desecrations-rabbis-death-show-rare-glimpses-of-israels-religious-fanaticism/view-all/

31 "Government Leaders Encourage Adherence to the Seven Noahide Laws," Jewish Institute for Global Awareness, http://www.jifga.org/government-leaders-and-the-seven-noahide-laws.html

society, while remaining resolutely Jewish and committed to Zionism and Israel. However, despite the secular interaction, its teachings are influenced by the late Rabbi Abraham Isaac Kook, an adherent Kabbalistic mysticism. Also despite the Modern Orthodox interaction with the outside world, the strictures against marrying outside remain. In 2005 Ivanka and Jared split[32] because the latter's parents were perturbed by their son's intention to marry a non-Jew. Ivanka converted to Judaism in 2010, but conversion is not usually acceptable to Orthodox Judaism. Rabbi Kook, one of the most influential of Orthodox rabbis, and the first Ashkenazi rabbi in Palestine under the British mandate, according to a reputable Jewish source, *Haaretz*, wrote that "the difference between the Israelite soul... and the souls of all non-Jews, no matter what their level, is bigger and deeper than the difference between the human soul and the animal soul."[33]

How then did Ivanka marry Jared, despite the parents' objections? Citing rabbinic opinions there is an indication as to how Ivanka became acceptable:

> since in our generation intermarriage is common in civil courts, we are often forced to convert the non-Jewish partner in order to free the couple from the prohibition of intermarriage. We must also do so in order to spare their children who would otherwise be lost to the Jewish fold. If we are faced with a *de facto* mixed marriage we are permitted to convert the non-Jewish spouse and the children, when applicable. If this is true when a couple is already married, it is obviously true before they have begun a forbidden marriage relationship. The conversion could offset future transgressions and religious difficulties.[34]

---

32 "Jared Kushner once broke up with Ivanka Trump over 'religion issue',"
    Jerusalem Post, August 17, 2016.

33 Yair Sheleg, "A Dark Reminder of the Dark Ages," *Haaretz*, June 28, 2005;
    https://www.haaretz.com/1.4914726

34 Rabbi Marc D. Angel, "Leniency within the Orthodox Movement," My
    Jewish Learning, https://www.myjewishlearning.com/article/leniency-

Further it was considered that,

> It is better to choose the lesser of two evils, even when the choice is not ideal. It is better to stop adding fuel to evil now, rather than risk an increase in transgression. As was stated earlier, if we are permitted to convert one who is already married to a Jewish mate, we may certainly convert one who wishes to marry a Jewish partner in the future. Even if we know that the main and perhaps only reason for the conversion is marriage, yet when all is said and done such a conversion is still *halakhically* valid... [35]

Now through the alchemy of conversion Ivanka becomes a Jew, and would presumably be able to obtain instant citizenship as an Israeli by the "Law of Return," as would her children, assuming rights denied Palestinians including the prohibition of any right of return by Palestinian refugees. So Ivanka could with heartfelt conviction when arriving in Jerusalem for the opening of the U.S. Embassy, state that it was with a "feeling of great joy,"[36] that her people were gaining recognition of their ancient capital. Moreover, Jerusalem's top Israeli football team, "Beitar" renamed themselves in honor of her father, so that he can help make Israeli football great again.

Historical Antecedents of Jerusalem Not Jewish

The Zionist dream for Palestine is based on three primary aims that are of messianic intent: (1) Greater Israel from the Nile to the Euphrates rivers, (2) Rebuilding of the Temple of Solomon on the site of the present al-Aqsa mosque, (3) Jerusalem not only as the capital of Israel, but as the central seat of universal law.

---

within-the-orthodox-movement/

35   Ibid.

36   "Ivanka Trump in Jerusalem for embassy opening as Gaza braces for bloodshed," *The Guardian*, May 14, 2018; https://www.theguardian.com/world/2018/may/13/ivanka-trump-in-jerusalem-for-embassy-opening-as-gaza-braces-for-bloodshed

The first point has already been considered.

The rebuilding of the Temple of Solomon on the third holiest site of Islam is as contentious as the claim over Jerusalem. However it is at the very heart of the messianic Zionist dream. It also remains a constant source of conflict between Israelis and Muslims, with Muslims accusing Israelis of undermining the foundations of the al-Aqsa Mosque in an effort to demolish it.[37] Jewish zealots including members of the Knesset perform rituals at the mosque compound under police protection, in violation of an agreement between Israel and the Muslim custodians of the mosque.[38] The Temple Mount and Land of Israel Faithful Movement exists to agitate and prepare for the expulsion of Muslims from al-Aqsa in order to recreate the Temple of Solomon. Jewish messianic teaching claims that their messiah will not appear until the Temple is built. The Temple Mount movement frankly states what messianic Zionists believe :

- Consecrating the Temple Mount to the Name of G-d so that it can become the moral and spiritual center of Israel, of the Jewish people and of the entire world according to the words of all the Hebrew prophets. It is envisioned that the consecration of the Temple Mount and the Temple itself will focus Israel on:

- fulfilling the vision and mission given at Mt. Sinai for Israel to be a chosen people separate unto G-d, a holy nation, and a nation of priests (Exodus 19:6), and

- becoming a light unto all the nations (Isaiah 42:6) so that the Name of G-d may be revered by all nations and the biblical

---

37 "PA minister accuses Israel of exploiting attack to dig under Temple Mount," *Times of Israel*, July 17, 2017; https://www.timesofisrael.com/pa-minister-accuses-israel-of-exploiting-attack-to-dig-under-temple-mount/

38 "4 Palestinians detained, 2 Israelis evacuated from Aqsa on Jewish holiday, Ma'an News Agency, June 12, 2016; http://www.maannews.com/Content.aspx?id=771850

way of life may be propagated throughout the world.[39]

Regardless of what any Israeli government states, these are the ultimate objectives which messianic Zionists believe are ordained by their God. They will never be relinquished. For example the first prime minister of Israel, David Ben Gurion, a "moderate," and a socialist, asked by *Look* to describe his vision of the future, alluded to this:

> ...In Jerusalem, the United Nations (a truly *United* Nations) will build a shrine of the prophets to serve the federated union of all continents; this will be the seat of the Supreme Court of Mankind, to settle all controversies among the federated continents, as prophesied by Isaiah...[40]

Meanwhile Zionist messianists and Christian-Zionist cattle farmers in the USA keep alert for the miraculous birth of a red cow that can be sacrificed at the "Temple Mount" in Jerusalem and so pave the way for the return of the messiah. *Haaretz* commented:

> According to some Jews, the Messiah cannot come and hail the End of Days without the Third Temple arising in Jerusalem, and since the Temple cannot be built without proper purification, a red heifer must be found. The Temple Institute, an organization dedicated to preparing the groundwork for the construction of the Temple (where the Dome of the Rock is inconveniently standing) has been looking for years. Every few years a red heifer is announced, but is then rejected due to a non-red hair being found.... Some fundamentalist Christians believe that the Second Coming of Christ requires that the Temple be rebuilt, thus they too anticipate the birth of a red heifer as

---

39 "Objectives of the Temple Mount Faithful," http://www.templemountfaithful. org/objectives.php

40 *Look*, January 16, 1962.

a sign of the coming of the end of days.[41]

To inaugurate the coming of the Jewish messiah, according to the messianic tradition, a red cow must be slaughtered at a third Temple of Solomon to be constructed on the site of al-Aqsa mosque. But do Jews have any more historical claim on Jerusalem than Ivanka Trump has to become an Israeli citizen under the Law of Return? When Benjamin Netanyahu said that Jerusalem had been the Jewish capital for 3000, the Israeli prime minister was challenged in *Haaretz* on this claim: "Jews have been unquestionably connected with the city for millennia, yet it functioned as their capital only for short periods in history." The occupation of the site is placed at 7000 years. By 1350 BC "Salem" was a major centre of the Canaanites. The first record of "Israelites" in ancient texts is at 1210 BC. The time assumed to be that of David and Solomon at Jerusalem is not verifiable by empirical evidence. A united Israel was brief, and after Solomon's death the tribes were split again circa 930 BC. While Jerusalem remained the capital of Judah, the capital of the northern tribes was Samaria. Samaria was also the centre of the YHWH cult, not Jerusalem, and there is no certainty that Solomon built the Temple in Jerusalem. [42]

Jerusalem was not founded by any Israelite or Hebrew tribe or ruler, and the occupation of Jerusalem by Israelites has been sporadic in comparison to its relationship with Christians and Muslims. However one interprets the means of the words "Jew," "Hebrew" or "Israelite," those claiming any such descent have lived far longer outside the Biblical boundaries of "Israel" than within. From the expulsion

---

41 The Temple Mount Red Heifer Saga: Engineering the Apocalypse? *Haaretz*, July 19, 2015; https://www.haaretz.com/jewish/.premium-the-red-heifer-wrong-all-along-1.5376396

42 Philippe Bohstrom, "Jerusalem: The Not-so-eternal Capital of the Jewish People," *Haaretz*, May 17, 2018; https://webcache.googleusercontent.com/sear ch?q=cache:UBeCwGEYDlEJ:https://www.haaretz.com/archaeology/

of Jews by Rome in 135 A.D. until the early 20th century, few Jews existed there, and the Jewish scholar Moses Maimonides wrote of his travelling to Jerusalem circa 1165AD where he could find only two Jewish families. By 1492 there were about 5,000 Jews in Jerusalem after their expulsion from Spain. By 1900 there were approximately 35,000 Jews throughout Palestine.[43]

Around 3000 BC the centre was called Roshlamem and was occupied by the Jebusites until conquered by David circa 1000 BC. The city was captured by the Babylonians ca. 586 BC, and the Temple built by Solomon was destroyed. In 538 BC King Cyrus of Persia permitted the Jews to reoccupy the city, and rebuild the Temple. Rulership passed to the Macedonians, to the Ptolemic dynasty, and then the Seleucids (Macedonian led Persian empire), who Hellenised it. After the success of the Maccabean revolt the Hasmonean Kingdom was established in 152 BC with Jerusalem as the capital. Rome established Herod as a puppet ruler, under whom the Temple was expanded. In 96 AD Hadrian Romanized Jerusalem and renamed it Aelia Capitolina, and Jews were prohibited from entering until the 4th century AD. Hadrian renamed the whole province Syria Palaestina after the Philistines. Up to the 7th century Jerusalem came under the Roman, Byzantium and Sassanid (last pre-Islamic Persians) empires. The Jews were permitted to return when the Islamic Caliphate extended its rule over the city in 638. Jerusalem was captured in 1099 by the Christian crusaders, becoming the Kingdom of Jerusalem, fell to Kurdish Sunni Muslims under Saladin in 1187, was regained for Christendom in 1229, and recaptured by Islam in 1244. It then came under Mamluk rule, until the rise of the Ottomans and their capture of Egypt in 1517. Under Mamluk rule both Jews and Christians were permitted to worship. The Ramban Synagogue, the oldest in Jerusalem, was permitted to be built in Old Jerusalem in 1267.

---

43   George W. Robnett, *Conquest Through Immigration: How Zionism Turned Palestine into a Jewish State* (Pasadena: Institute for Special Research, 1968), 41.

It seems that through the many successions of rulers and inhabitants in "Jerusalem" since the Bronze Age, the Jews were the more minor and transient, and lived there when permitted by conquerors. Their fortunes in the city seemed to have been respected by Muslims; a tradition which Zionism has not reciprocated. The foundations of Jerusalem seem to have been built by non-Israelites, and it is questionable whether the famous Temple of Solomon was built by Judaeans. No such mighty nation of Israel under David or Solomon is recorded by Egyptian or Assyrian texts. There is no archaeological evidence for the Kingdom of Israel. B.S.J. Isserlin, Head of the Department of Semitic studies at Leeds University, wrote that *"Solomon ... in the eyes of Israelite historians, marked the apex of Israelite achievement. Curiously,* no reference to him or his father David, or their empire in a non-Israelite source is known ..."* [44] *"... in Jerusalem nothing has as yet been brought to light which can be ascribed to Solomon with certainty."* [45] *Among academics there is no agreement that there ever was an ancient Israelite state under Solomon and David.* Philip Davies, professor emeritus of biblical studies at Sheffield University, states:

> If we did not have bible stories about a "United Monarchy," would any archaeologist ever suggest such a thing existed? Why are possible Iron Age structures in Jerusalem assigned to David and not Saul? It's because the history of Judah is not solely in the hands of academic archaeologists but religious believers and Zionists, who have their own history - one that the rest of us do not believe in.[46]

It is also suggested by archaeologists that what is assumed be Jewish constructions in Jerusalem were built by the Jebusites.

44   B. S. J. Isserlin, *The Israelites* (London: Thames & Hudson, 1998), 72.

45   Ibid., 81.

46   Philippe Bohstrom, "Did David and Solomon's United Monarchy Exist?," *Haaretz,* November 21, 2017; https://www.haaretz.com/archaeology/MAGAZINE-timna-mines-support-biblical-tale-of-king-david-s-united-kingdom-1.5466612

Professor Israel Finkelstein of Tel Aviv University, states, according to the *Haaretz* report, "if anything, David and Solomon ruled over little more than a village located on the Temple Mount."[47]

---

47   Ibid.

Postscript from the Right

I write unapologetically from the 'Right' of politics. Yet in recent years there has been an odd situation. The Nationalist Right, hitherto in conflict with Zionism because of the inherent character of the doctrines, often now has not only an anti-Muslim position motivated by opposition to Third World immigration, but also combines this with a growing sympathy for Israel. It is said that politics makes strange bedfellows. Well, this situation is downright perverse. It seems that often the swarthy and even black faces of many Muslims and the fair complexions of many Israelis are sufficient for Rightists to define their positions on the Middle East, Islam and Zionism. That many are being so easily befuddled by banalities is a symptom that some on the Nationalist Right do not know their ideological foundations. A dose of Francis Parker Yockey is required three times daily until cured, and the Nationalist Right can again understand that the USA, so far from being the 'leader of the Western world', is the bulwark of the West's cultural decay.

Is our Western cultural heritage really that which excretes from Hollywood, MTV, Maddison Avenue; that which Yockey called 'ethical syphilis'? And who is it that stands behind, and in front, of much of this social and cultural pathology? It is not Islam. Do Muslims run the banks, publishing houses, newspapers, Television networks, movie industry? Is it Muslims who provide the scriptwiters, song-writers, producers, directors, and financiers for the putrescence that is today called 'Western Civilisation'? Our Civilisation has been terminally sick for decades yet there are those on the Right, whose outrage is directed at the wearing of the Burqa, or even the head-scarf or the building of a Mosque. Demonstrating against the building of a globalised fast-food outlet would be of more relevance in defending Western culture and racial health. If Islam has been in decay for centuries, from

263

its position as a High Culture, which introduced much of value into Western Civilisation, then so too has the West. Those on the Nationalist Right who claim to stand for Western resurgence are not going to succeed by aligning themselves with the main architects of the West's cultural and social decay.

Until recently this was understood. The Arabs, with the inspiration of T. E. Lawrence, fought with heroism some crucial battles for the Entente during World War I, albeit betrayed, as we have seen. World War II saw the forces of Western renewal and Islam fighting common foes. As we have seen also, the Arabs were not inclined towards Marxism, which was being infiltrated into the lands like a virus by Jewish Marxists and Marxist-Zionists.

When General Francisco Franco and the military rose against the Marxists and Communists in Spain, at their side were Arab warriors. When a Republican plane bombed the Arab quarters in Tetuán, Morocco, and the Arabs turned on the Spanish troops in the mistaken belief that they had been responsible, the situation was resolved by Grand Vizier Sidi Ahmed el Ganmia. The first action of Franco on returning there was to confer the Grand Vizier with the Cross of San Fernando with Laurels. 'A Moor was thus the first recipient during the Civil War of Spain's highest decoration,' wrote historian Brian Crozier.[1] Moorish troops were important in helping to liberate Oviedo in 1936.[2] In 1937 a mixed force of Spaniards, Moors, and Fascist Italians took Malaga. In 1939 Moors marched into Barcelona.[3] Arab friendship with Franquist Spain remained during the time when the state was being ostracised. Moroccan and Egyptian dignitaries visited Spain at the time of the U.N. boycott. In 1952 Spanish Foreign Minister Martin Artajo toured Amman, Cairo

---

1   Brian Crozier, *Franco: A Biographical History* (London: Eyre and Spottiswood, 1967), pp. 186-187.

2   Brian Crozier, ibid., p. 221.

3   Brian Crozier, ibid., p. 288.

and Baghdad.[4] Just as the Entente owed the Arabs a debt for their assistance during World War I that was never repaid; so all of Western Christendom owes the Arabs a debt for their help in defeating Bolshevism in Spain, in a struggle that saw Churches burned and nuns and priests killed.

The Muslims and Fascist Italy were able to work in accord in developing Italy's African colonies. Mussolini was looked upon as the protector of Islam. In Tripoli, Libya, in 1937 Mussolini received the 'Sword of Islam', with a sense of deep honour. In East Africa the Italian administration officially recognised Muslim holidays, and encouraged the building of schools and mosques.[5] The Muslim courts were recognised. Louise Diel, a journalist touring East Africa, was told that Muslims there were deeply loyal to Mussolini, and said they owed him much. 'Our fellow-believers throughout the world know that too. As Mussolini has had regard for us, so may he count on us too'.[6] The historian Denis Mack Smith, an anti-Fascist, wrote that 'Fascist administrators in Libya, Somalia and Eritrea did much that was good, they did much to control slavery, epidemics and inter-tribal fighting'.[7]

Inspired by the social-nationalist doctrine of Italy, similar movements were formed by Arabs: white, grey and steel shirt movements in Syria; blue shirts and green shirts in Egypt; tan shirts in Lebanon and Syria, and white shirts in Iraq.[8] The Syrian Social Nationalist party remains a major factor in Lebanon, and in the Arab struggle against Zionism.

---

4   Brian Crozier, ibid., p. 475.

5   Louise Diel, *Behold Our New Empire – Mussolini* (London: Hurst and Blackett, 1939), pp 29-30.

6   Louise Diel, ibid., p. 194.

7   Denis Mack Smith, *Mussolini* (London: Wiedenfield and Nicholson, 1981), p. 99.

8   Stanley G. Payne, *A History of Fascism 1914-1945* (London: UCL Press, 1995), p. 352.

Benito Mussolini waving to resident Muslims in Tripoli, Libya. 1937.

After World War II Arab and European nationalists collaborated in opposing Zionism. The German war hero Otto Skorzeny, who had led the rescue of Mussolini from Communist partisans, taught Palestinian refugees guerrilla warfare and remained a close friend of Palestinian leader Yasser Arafat. Major General Otto Remer, harassed by the German state, served as a political adviser in Egypt and Syria for decades. Johannes von Leers, an expert on Zionism and the Middle East at the German propaganda ministry, converted to Islam, which he had long admired, and advised the Egyptian Ministry of Information, through arrangements with the Grand Mufti of Jerusalem. There were many other veterans who received sanctuary from the Arabs and in turn assisted them after World War II in their conflicts with Zionist aggression.

The French Nationalist Dr. Christian Bouchet, who has served with the supposedly anti-Muslim Front National and other movements of the Nationalist Right for many years, has commented:

Whoever browses the catalogues of nationalist bookstores, whoever reads nationalist newspapers and magazines, whoever visits Internet forums where young and not-so-young activists of the nationalist right express opinions will immediately notice that rabid anti-Islamism reigns. The cause would seem clear: Islam is the enemy of the French nation and of European civilization, and therefore of the nationalist movement. But beyond 'the obvious,' and beyond appearances, is it reality? An objective approach to the facts calls for a reply in the negative: Islam was not always looked upon negatively by nationalists, and at present, hostility toward it is not absolute in the ranks of committed rightists.[9]

Bouchet states that the French Right had been sympathetic towards the Arabs since the late 19th century. Gustav Le Bon, a leading influence on Rightist doctrine (especially with his socio-psychological study of mass behaviour and social revolt, The Crowd, 1895) wrote in his Civilisation of the Arabs of the great cultural legacy that Islam had given Europe.

We must bear in mind that the Arabs - and the Arabs alone - are the ones who guided us to the ancient world of the Greeks and Romans. European universities, including the University of Paris, based their curricula on translations of their books for six hundred years and used their methods of research. The Islamic civilization was one of the most amazing that history has ever known. ... If the Arabs had taken over France, then Paris would have become like Cordova in Spain, a centre of civilisation and knowledge, where the man in the street was able to read and write, and even compose poetry, at a time when the kings of Europe did not even know how to write their names![10]

---

9   C. Bouchet, 'The Nationalist Right and Islam', *Voxnr*, 2 June 2011, http://www.voxnr.com/cc/d_france/EFpZppEpukNhQxrIIY.shtml

10   Gustave le Bon, *The Civilization of the Arabs* ([1884] Tudor Publications, 1974).

Friedrich Nietzsche had commented on this also, writing of the 'wonderful culture of the Moors in Spain', of its origins in 'noble and manly instincts'.[11]

Arab chemists discovered: Sulphuric acid, Aqua regia, Nitric, Potassium, Sal ammoniac, Silver nitrate, Corrosive sublimate; and the chemical processes: Distillation, Sublimation, Crystallization, Coagulation, Cupellation. They invented the processes for manufacturing paper from cotton, linen and rags. The word Algebra is derived from the Arabic word Al Gabr. The word Algorithm is a variant taken from the name of Al Khwarizimi, father of Algebra. The 'zero' was invented by bin Ahmad in 976. Al Razi wrote *Al Hawi,* one of the nine volumes constituting the whole library of the Paris Faculty of Medicine in 1935. This contained the first description of eruptive fevers such as smallpox and measles. Ibn Sina's five volume *Qanun fi-l-Tibb* ('Precepts of Medicine') on physiology, hygiene, pathology, and therapeutics was the basis of medical studies in French and Italian universities for six centuries. Ibn al-Haytham, author of the *Book of Optics* is regarded as the father of optics who explained and proved the theory of vision, and was the first to give an exact description of the eye, lenses and binocular vision.[12] And so we might continue. It ill-behooves Westerners to regard Arabs and Muslims as 'towel-heads'. To these we owe much that has helped to shape our own great Western High Culture, which has itself been brought to decay by those who run the banks, entertainment industry, and media.

Maurice Bardèche, a leading French 'Fascist' intellectual in post-war France, wrote that, 'In the Koran there is something virile, something one can call Roman'.

The 1985 issue 53 of the journal of the French 'New Right', *Elements,* wrote favourably of Islam. Bouchet writes that 'it was

11 F. Nietzsche, *The Antichrist*: Section 60.

12 'Contributions to Civilisation,' http://www.canadianarabcommunity.com/contributionstocivilization.php

in this issue of *Elements* that Guillaume Faye, future harbinger of Islamophobia, wrote: "no matter what feeling is inspired by the vision of the world conveyed by Islam, the awakening of Arabo-Islamism constitutes an objectively favourable fact for the destiny of Europe.""[13]

Of particular interest is that Jean-Marie Le Pen, founder of the Front National, so far from embracing the Islamophobia of some of the Euro-Right, pointed out that the globalists are seeking a compliant Islamic world that will not resist globalisation. We have seen how American diplomacy in France in particular is manipulating Islamic youth. Le Pen stated in an interview with *Arabies*, issue 98:

> They're provoking French fears of what is commonly called 'Islamism' or 'Moslem religious activism.' The ones who provoke or manipulate these fears, not hesitating to grossly distort Islam's message to make it better fit their conceptions, do it from a very precise standpoint: that of the globalist utopia and the ideology of Human Rights which assumes the destruction of cultural identities and the rejection of transcendence. Their dream is of a sterilized Islam rendered harmless.[14]

Le Pen further explained to the journal of the youth wing of Front National:

> It's this [American] hegemony which is in large part hostile to the national idea in general and nations in particular. Among themselves nationalists share a body of values common to civilizations whether Christian or even Moslem. These values go from patriotism to respect for the past, from attachment to the soil to love of family, and to all values that flow from them: fellowship, charity, honour, devotion, sacrifice, etc.[15]

---

13 C. Bouchet, ibid.

14 Cited by Bouchet, idid.

15 Cited by Bouchet, idid.

In Italy in 2003 the media reported that Hassan Bendoudouh, professor of Islam and an official of the 'post-Fascist' National Alliance led by Giofranco Fini, stated: 'I am a partisan of Fini and Allah. Islam is a religion of the Right, in that it honors family values and respect for parents and the ancestors'.[16] Likewise France's Front National has included Islamic officials, such as Le Pen's adviser on Islamic affairs, Sid-Ahmed Yahiaoui, and electoral candidates who see no complication in being French and Muslim, unlike the problematic character in claiming to be a Zionist and a Frenchman, Englishman or German.

Dr. Bouchet, explains the rise of Islamophobia among the Nationalist Right as the result of the propaganda of 'the Evil Empire, the pro-American and Zionist networks'. Further:

> As is known, it's favorably viewed in certain nationalist and French nationalist circles to refer, in a manner reminiscent of 'the clash of civilizations, to the confrontation between Islam and the free world. That helps sell newspapers and has the enormous advantage of furnishing a simple explanation of the world's complexity, one easily accepted by a movement looking more for conspiracy theories than political or geopolitical thought.

> Now, ideas must be put back in their historical context. The source of the 'clash of civilizations' theory goes back to 1990. The Soviet Bloc's collapse took away the U.S.'s role of defender of the free world; there was danger for the U.S. in the multipolar world which they saw replacing the bipolar one. Therefore a replacement adversary was needed so that America could continue in its role as world policeman. The office of U.S. Secretary of State switched therefore from its 'red' theme, namely, Moscow is orchestrating a worldwide terror network consisting of Third-World revolutionary Marxist groups, to its 'green' theme, namely, there is a worldwide terror network consisting of revolutionary

16   Cited by Bouchet, idid.

Islamist groups. At the same time, the U.S. Secretary of State adopted the Lake doctrine of 'rogue nations,'[17] the majority of which, as if by some strange coincidence, are Moslem.

... As for these intellectuals who have theorized about the 'clash of civilizations,' you know them both: it's Bernard Lewis and Samuel Huntington. Both insist on the importance of the Zionist Entity to the West's resistance. And that introduces a second level of understanding of the anti-Islamist phenomenon, i.e. supporters of the Zionist Entity have grafted their struggle onto that of the American party. By developing a gigantic amalgam of Islam / Islamism/ violence-in-North-African-neighorhoods / obscurantism / attacks-on-women, etc., they try to make ordinary Frenchmen believe that in Paris as in Tel Aviv the troublemaker, the killer, the terrorist, the one favouring a return to the Middle Ages is the same: the Arab and the Moslem.[18]

Hence, factions of the Right, having moulded a career out of following the U.S. pied piper of anti-Sovietism, supposedly in defence of Western Civilisation, have exchanged this mantle for that of anti-Islamism. Bouchet explains: 'They were militant anti-communists when the U.S.A. had to justify its occupation of our continent by citing the "danger of the Red Army," now they're militant anti-Islamists when the U.S.A. has to justify its worldwide ambitions'.[19]

Certain paradoxes appear, such as the anti-Islamism that was spawned by homosexuals such as Holland's Pim Fortuyn, or the radical feminism that is implied in attacks on Muslim traditions.

---

17 See: Alex Miles, *U. S. Foreign Policy and the Rogue State Doctrine* (New York: Routledge, 2013), p. 142. Anthony Lake was President Clinton's National Security Adviser.

18 C. Bouchet, op. cit..

19 C. Bouchet, ibid.

There is the spectacle of the so-called 'extreme Right' English Defence League demonstrating against the building of Mosques in Britain, parading with the Israeli flag and the rainbow flag of homosexual activism; or Holland's Geert Wilders (who worked on a Kibbutz in his youth) calling Jerusalem 'the cradle of our Judaeo-Christian civilisation'.

Yet Zionism will never support the Nationalist Right in its struggle for a resurgent Europe and Western Culture. Zionism demands that the Jew wherever he resides in 'Diaspora' throughout the world places his loyalty to Israel first. In 1975 Nahum Goldmann, a longtime World Zionist leader, declared unequivocally before the World Jewish Congress at Jerusalem:

> At the time of crisis for Israel when its policies are rejected by many countries in which Jews live, conflict is bound to occur. The only solution is to acknowledge the existence and fight for the recognition of double loyalties. The real test of our solidarity with Israel will come when we support it against the views of the States in which we live.

Hence, any form of nationalism other than that of the Jewish is anathema to Zionism, and the Zionists have fought tooth and nail to destroy any Nationalist resurgence as inimical to Jewish interests. When Senator Joseph McCarthy started to campaign against Communist subversion, although he did not address the Jewish issue at all, Zionists saw 'McCarthyism' as the basis for an emerging American Nationalism. They were foremost among those who sought his destruction. The response of the Anti-Defamation League of B'nai B'rith, a pervasive intelligence gathering and smear-mongering agency, was to embark 'on one of the earliest campaigns to thwart right-wing extremism by fighting the terrifying plague of McCarthyism'.[20] The Jewish media commented: 'almost 100% of the names turned up by Senator McCarthy's committee on subversive activities happened to be Jewish'.[21]

---

20 'Anti-Defmataion League 1950-1960 The Early Post War Years, ADL, http://63.146.172.78/ADLHistory/1950_1960.asp

21 *B'nai B'rith Messenger*, 26 March, 1954.

When Rabbi Benjamin Schultz founded the American Jewish League Against Communism, he was universally condemned by the primary Jewish organisations, which issued a joint statement in 1954 under the name of the National Community Relations Advisory Council, representing the American Jewish Committee, American Jewish Congress, Anti-Defamation League, Jewish Labor Committee, Jewish War Veterans, and Union of American Hebrew Congregations.[22]

When the USSR turned against Zionism, Jewish Communists became among the staunchest partisans of U.S. Cold War policies, as we have seen. From this communistic background emerged the misnamed 'neo-conservative' movement, which presents loyalty to Zionism as synonymous with loyalty to the USA. The 'neocons' however have nothing in common with traditional American conservatism, which eschews American global adventures, including opposing uncritical support for Israel. In order to distinguish genuine American conservatism from the neocons, the Jewish academic Dr. Paul Gottfried, a critic of Israel and Zionism, coined the word 'palaeoconservative'. Palaeoconservatives are bitterly condemned by the neocons and their Zionist backers.

When Patrick Buchanan, former aide to Presidents Nixon and Reagan, sought the Republican nomination for presidency in 1992 and 1996 and ran for the Reform Party in 2000 he stood on a genuinely conservative platform of opposition to free trade, economic protectionism, opposition to globalisation, and support for traditional Christian values. He was vehemently attacked by the Zionists. In 1992 Rabbi Avi Weiss formed the Coalition for Jewish Concerns to disrupt Buchanan's campaign meetings. Buchanan was condemned by both the American Jewish Committee and the American Jewish Congress for stating that his meetings were 'for Americans, by Americans', in response to Rabbi Weiss' activities. In 1999 Abraham Foxman, head of

---

22 'Rabbi Schultz Assailed by National Body's Memorandum', *The Jewish National Post*, 31 December 1954.

the Anti-Defamation League, stated that Buchanan should be 'flushed out' as 'dangerous. The American Jewish Congress took out anti-Buchanan newspaper advertisements. Buchanan opined on television interviews that he was being attacked for defending 'traditional Catholic values.' Rabbi Nachum Shifren, who supported Buchanan, was excommunicated by the Supreme Rabbinical Court of America, calling him a 'Jewish traitor'. This meant that under their siruv law a good Jew must not walk within 12 feet of the excommunicated individual, count him for religious activities, accord him any honours within the Jewish community, or transact business with him.[23]

When Australian politician Pauline Hanson, a naïve woman who knew nothing of Jews or Zionism, formed her mildly conservative One Nation Party even this received the damnation of Zionism. The *Australian/Israel Review* published the names of 2,000 members of Hanson's party which they had acquired illegally.[24]

The core doctrines of the Right, based on what are held to be timeless values and traditions, transcend differences in religion, nationality, and ethnie. That is why a German National Socialist such as Johannes von Leers could convert to Islam, or a French traditionalist such as René Guénon. That is how the Italian philosopher Julius Evola[25] could introduce Eastern religions and philosophies to the West, while being among the foremost heralds of a resurgent West. How the Fascist American poet Ezra Pound, could also be an admirer of Confucianism and translator

---

23 'Rabbi Nachum Shifren: Jewish Traitor: Writ of Excommunication', Supreme Rabbinical Council of America, 2000.

24 'Gotcha! One Nation's Secret Membership List', *Australasia/Israel Review*, July 1992.

25 Evola wrote on Tantra, Hinduism, Shinto and Islam.

of Chinese texts,[26] or the British author D. H. Lawrence[27] could see the atavism of the Aztec-Mexicans as having something to teach the West in its epoch of decay. The real 'clash of civilisations' is not between the West and Islam, but between traditionalists – the 'Right'- of all nations, races, and religions, against the social and moral pathology of the USA and the latter-day Pharisees.

---

26 Ezra Pound, *Canto XIII, Cantos LII-LXI, Cathay, Chinese Written Characters as a Medium for Poetry, The Great Digest* (Ta Hsio), *The Unwobbling Pivot* (Chung Yung), *The Analects* (Lun-yu).

27 D. H. Lawrence, *The Plumed Serpent* (London: Secker, 1926).

About the Author

Kerry Bolton has diplomas and doctorates in psychology, social work studies, theology and divinity. He has been a contributing writer for *Foreign Policy Journal,* and *New Dawn.* Widely published in scholarly journals, including: *Journal of Social, Political, and Economic Studies*; Arktos Journal; *The Occidental Quarterly, International Journal of Social Economics; India Quarterly; World Affairs; Irish Journal of Gothic & Horror Studies;* etc., with around 300 papers and articles published over the course of ten years. Winner of a 2018 university Literary Award, he has served on a peer review panel; co-edited a scholarly journal; and is a fellow of several academic societies.

His books include: *Geopolitics of the Indo-Pacific; Stalin- An Enduring Legacy; Artists of the Right (two volumes); Russia & the Fight Against Globalisation; Peron & Peronism; The Parihaka Cult; Babel Inc.; Yockey - a Fascist Odyssey; The Psychotic Left; Opposing the Money Lenders; The Banking Swindle; Revolution from Above; The Decline & Fall of Civilisations; The Occult & Subversive Movements,* and has annotated a collection of Oswald Spengler's articles: *Prussian Socialism & Other Essays.*

9 781912 759187